# THE EVERYTHING
## PARENT'S GUIDE TO
# THE STRONG-WILLED CHILD
### 2ND EDITION

Dear Reader,

Raising a strong-willed child can seem like corralling a team of wild horses or trying to herd cats, both seemingly impossible tasks. If you are blessed with a strong-willed child, you may find yourself taxed to the max, wondering what you have done to deserve such a difficult job.

You may find that conventional child development and parenting books do not help you, as your child has a tenacity that seems unusual, and, at times, alarming, and the usual, sweet, gentle parenting techniques don't seem to apply. I want to invite you to think of your child and all those inborn qualities as positive, even if they are challenging. Together, we want to dive into the depths of creative parenting so that you are able to genuinely view the kernels of greatness and uniqueness within your child. He or she may not be typical, but your child is truly wonderful. Don't forget it!

We can work out some ways for you to develop a cooperative relationship with your son or daughter, preserving your dignity and energy along the way. The techniques you learn may not be fodder for conversation with other parents of more docile children, but you can forge an unforgettable, rewarding relationship that will launch your child into a happy, fulfilling adult life.

Ellen Bowers, PhD

# WELCOME TO THE

# EVERYTHING®

## PARENT'S GUIDES

Everything® Parent's Guides are a part of the bestselling Everything® series and cover common parenting issues like childhood illnesses and tantrums, as well as medical conditions like asthma and juvenile diabetes. These family-friendly books are designed to be a one-stop guide for parents. If you want authoritative information on specific topics not fully covered in other books, Everything® Parent's Guides are your perfect solution.

**Alerts**
Urgent warnings

**Facts**
Important snippets of information

**Essentials**
Quick handy tips

**Questions**
Answers to common questions

When you're done reading, you can finally say you know **EVERYTHING**®!

**PUBLISHER** Karen Cooper

**DIRECTOR OF ACQUISITIONS AND INNOVATION** Paula Munier

**MANAGING EDITOR, EVERYTHING® SERIES** Lisa Laing

**COPY CHIEF** Casey Ebert

**ASSISTANT PRODUCTION EDITOR** Melanie Cordova

**ACQUISITIONS EDITOR** Brett Palana-Shanahan

**SENIOR DEVELOPMENT EDITOR** Brett Palana-Shanahan

**EDITORIAL ASSISTANT** Matt Kane

**EVERYTHING® SERIES COVER DESIGNER** Erin Alexander

**LAYOUT DESIGNERS** Erin Dawson, Michelle Roy Kelly, Elisabeth Lariviere

Visit the entire Everything® series at *www.everything.com*

# THE EVERYTHING

## PARENT'S GUIDE TO

# THE STRONG-WILLED CHILD

## 2ND EDITION

A positive approach to increase self-control,
improve communication, and reduce conflict

Ellen Bowers, PhD

Avon, Massachusetts

An Everything® Series Book.
Everything® and everything.com® are registered trademarks of F+W Media, Inc.

Published by Adams Media, a division of F+W Media, Inc.
57 Littlefield Street, Avon, MA 02322 U.S.A.
*www.adamsmedia.com*

ISBN 10: 1-4405-3342-3
ISBN 13: 978-1-4405-3342-6
eISBN 10: 1-4405-3848-4
eISBN 13: 978-1-4405-3848-3

Printed in the United States of America.

10 9 8 7 6 5 4 3 2 1

**Library of Congress Cataloging-in-Publication Data**

Bowers, Ellen.
  The everything parent's guide to the strong-willed child / Ellen Bowers.—2nd ed.
    p. cm.
  Rev. ed. of: The everything parent's guide to the strong-willed child / Carl E. Pickhardt.
c2005.
  Includes bibliographical references and index.
  ISBN 978-1-4405-3342-6 (pbk. : alk. paper)—ISBN 1-4405-3342-3 (pbk. : alk. paper)—
ISBN 978-1-4405-3848-3 (ebook : alk. paper)—ISBN 1-4405-3848-4 (ebook : alk. paper)
  1. Child rearing. 2. Discipline of children. 3. Child psychology. I. Pickhardt, Carl E.
everything parent's guide to the strong-willed child. II. Title.
HQ772.P493 2012
649'.64—dc23
                                    2012004286

**All the examples and dialogues used in this book are fictional, and
have been created by the author to illustrate disciplinary situations.**

# Dedication

*To you, the reader, who has embarked upon the rewarding
and challenging journey of raising a strong-willed child.*

# Acknowledgments

I want to acknowledge Adams Media editor Brett Shanahan,
for entrusting this project to me; my family and friends,
for encouraging me in this work and putting up with my
disappearing into the computer for weeks at a time; and certain
special people who give me steady, continuing support—Fay,
Orchid, Jeanine, and Harriet Kaiser. I appreciate you.

**will·ful·ness** (wĭl´-fəl-nəs)

▶ *n.* A person's power of self-determination to direct, to persist, to resist, and to prevail.

# Contents

# Introduction

What is a strong-willed child? How did he or she come to be that way? How can parents nurture the positive aspects of their child's strong will, moderate the negative aspects, and not act and react in ways that make a challenging situation worse? These are some of the questions this book answers.

Strong-willed children can be perplexing creatures. The child may feel injured, scared, or otherwise upset by something that has happened and go on strike against parental instruction. "I can't! I won't! Leave me alone!" screams the child, who becomes lost in the emotion of the moment. Because the child's feelings have overwhelmed his thinking, parents have to help him calm down and get past the emotions before they can expect him to follow directions.

Although all children can be strong-willed on some occasions, some children are much more intensely so than others. Strong-willed children are not different in kind from other children; they differ only in the degree to which need for self-determination rules their lives. But that degree makes an enormous difference in what is required of you as a parent.

It helps to think of the concept of volition—human choice. Parents have volition and so do children. The big surprise is that willful children are quite aware of how much choice they have in their behavior. It's the parents' task to temper that a bit.

For most parents, occasional willfulness is tolerable, but continual willfulness can create a negative tone in the family as it quickly gathers shaping power of its own. The more often a willful act achieves its objective, the more powerful willfulness becomes.

If a child repeatedly acts strong-willed now and gets what he wants, then through habit he learns to be even more strong-willed later on. What this child must be taught is how to manage a strong will growing up so that it works for—and not against—him in adult life.

CHAPTER 1

# *Strong Will* Means *Willfulness*

What does it mean to say your child is strong-willed? The strongest indicator of the willful child is anger when she doesn't get what she wants. Her intense desire then turns her aspiration into an imperative, and an imperative into a condition. "I want to have" turns into "I must have" turns into "I am entitled to have," and the result is anger when the willful child is denied what she now feels entitled to. How does this happen?

## What Is *Willfulness*?

For the purposes of this book, a *strong-willed child* is defined as one who often expresses a high degree of willfulness—the power of self-determination to direct, to persist, to resist, and to prevail. At certain moments or most of the time, this child can be determined to:

- Direct his actions or the actions of others
- Persist in the face of discouragement or of refusal to be given what is desired
- Resist conforming to social rules or giving in to social pressure
- Prevail in a challenge, confrontation, conflict, or competition

On occasion or what may seem like all the time to you, such children are determined to get their way. Parents often describe how their strong-willed child demands, insists, complains, corrects, takes charge, pursues, refuses, controls, dominates, has the last word, won't give up, won't quit, won't let go, won't give in, won't back down, won't shut up, won't settle for less, won't let the matter drop, and won't admit defeat.

## The *Will* in *Willfulness*

For any person of any age, having power of will is important. Will is a strong motivator. It drives people to take control of personal choice and act effectively on their own behalf, rise to challenges, achieve goals, recover from setbacks, and cope with adversity.

Helping children harness their power of will in order to accomplish, to achieve, to try again, to persevere is one important responsibility of being parents. It is part of the parental coaching role to encourage and inspire flagging effort in a tired or discouraged child. Athletic coaches often say that the mental side of coaching —figuring out how to assess their team's level of collective will and how to mobilize that will in order to maximize performance on the playing field—is the hardest part of their job. Try to keep a positive mental image in your mind as you go along. Envision your child cooperating and yourself as calmly leading the way.

 **Essential**

With a willful child, parents will win some, lose some, and compromise a lot. In the immortal words of the defiant adolescent, "Get used to it!" That's how parenting is.

## When Will Is Lost

To appreciate the importance of will, consider what happens to people when that power is lost. Consider unfortunate individuals in mental institutions or confined to nursing homes. Boredom, help-lessness, and depression sometimes result from the lack of will-power: "There is nothing to do, there is nothing to be done, there is nothing I can do." The danger of these dark emotional states is that self-defeating thoughts can lead a child in a self-destructive direc-tion. This is the opposite of what you want.

### Boredom, Helplessness, and Depression

The bored child, lacking the will to direct himself, engages in foolish risk taking with friends because, he figures, at least he has something to do, and inactivity feels intolerable. The helpless child takes cruel mistreatment from teasing at school without objection. Lacking the will to defend or assert himself, the boy feels he has no other choice but to accept the torment, learning to be the vic-tim. And the depressed twelve-year-old, mourning how childhood comfort must be given up to enter the scary world of early adoles-cence, copes with loss by scratching and cutting himself, creating pain to manage pain instead of seeking help to talk it out.

### 🛑 Alert

Loss of willpower to engage in healthy growth—to keep active, to keep trying, to keep caring—is a significant event in the life of a child, and parents should pay attention if it persists. Significant loss of will-power can result in serious harm.

### "Can Do" and "Can't Do" Children

As parents, you should always monitor your child's strength of will. Children with a "can't do" attitude are expressing a lack of will. In that state of mind, they are at risk of giving up, giving in, going along with outside influences, often prone to dependency on peer pressure for deciding what to do. Lack of effort, lack of resourcefulness, lack of confidence, lack of effectiveness are all some of the consequences that result when willpower is lost.

Four common statements that reflect "can't do" thinking are:

- "I can't do that," and so they don't make the effort.
- "I couldn't do that," and so they rule it out as a possibility.
- "I can't do anything about that," and so they submit to helplessness.
- "I couldn't say no to that," and so they surrender.

As parents, you want your child to have a "can do" attitude. You want your child to have enough willpower to try to solve life's problems. You want your child to be resourceful in the face of obstacles, to believe that there is always something she can try—if not to change an undesirable situation, at least to adjust to it in a positive way. One characteristic of strong-willed children is the "can do" way they take charge of their lives. This is a trait to be grateful for, if you possibly can remember that during the difficult times.

### Essential

Whatever reservations you may sometimes have about your strong-willed child, recognize the good side—that he is a "can do" child most of the time, motivated to make choices to act on his own behalf. If there is one motto a willful child seems to live by, it is this: "Where there's a will, there's a way."

## The Conditional Shift

What separates willful children from those who are not is how they manage not getting what they want. When children who are not generally willful don't get what they want, they may feel sad, shrug off the disappointment, and then go on to something else. Willful children, however, tend to have a different response.

## Telltale Anger

When a strong-willed child doesn't get what she wants, she gets angry and won't relinquish going after whatever she has been denied, or if she does let go, she will carry hard feelings or resentment away from the situation. Why does the willful child feel angry? The answer is because willful children often make a conditional shift by turning what they want into what they believe they should have.

- "If I want it, then I should get it."
- "If I'm refused it, I should be given a good reason why."
- "If I don't want to do it, I shouldn't have to."
- "If I argue, then I should win."

Then, when any of these beliefs are violated, that seems unjust, and so they get angry. A condition of assumed entitlement has not been met.

## A Conditional Shift in Action

Imagine this scene. At the park, a willful four-year-old wants to swing so much that she feels entitled to swing as long as she wants, despite the fact that other children are waiting for a turn. Told at last to get off the swing by a parent so other children can get on, the willful child gets angrily upset. "That's not fair! I'm not done swinging!"

In this situation, it is the parent's job to help the willful child learn to disconnect "should" from "want," to let go of the conditional view through which she sees the situation. So the parent says something like this: "I know when you want something very much it feels like you should be allowed to get it, but life isn't like that. Wanting something very much doesn't mean we should get it. Wanting just means there's something we'd like to have or do, and maybe we'll get some of it, and maybe we won't. And if we don't, we'll still be okay."

# One-Step Thinking

To be an effective parent, it is important to understand how willfulness can be grounded in a child's tendency to resort to one-step thinking when he becomes impatient or frustrated. Children are born one-step thinkers. That is, at birth, they are ruled by want, impulse, and instant gratification. This is how they are equipped to identify what they need and to let you know what they desire. So when an infant fusses or cries or calls or grabs, these are all one-step attempts to cope with whatever the child would like to start or stop happening.

As parents learn to read these nonverbal signals, figure out and respond to what the child wants, the child develops a sense of effectiveness. When crying repeatedly results in being held, then the child learns that one possible outcome of crying is getting picked up. So one-step thinking works. For the time being, the child's actions are rewarded.

However, parents can't just let a child grow up managing his likes and dislikes with one-step thinking. Eventually everyone, children included, has to learn delayed gratification. It is simply a requirement to get along in civilized society. Without the skill of delayed gratification the child painfully learns that other people will often resist the child's demands for accommodation.

 **Fact**

Teach your strong-willed child some delayed gratification—delaying action long enough to consult judgment, reason, and values before acting on impulse, on feelings, and for immediate gratification. It is the capacity for this more mature type of thinking that allows the child to discipline his willful nature so that it serves him well and not badly.

## Two-Step Thinking

As the child grows up, parents begin to encourage two-step thinking. They do this by teaching the child to delay action until he has taken the time to think about past and possible future consequences of an action before making a decision. "Before you spend all your money on a treat right now, you might want to think about what saving this money could allow you to buy later." Following this advice, the child takes the time to think twice, asking himself if what he wants is really worth having right now. The second step of two-step thinking is assessing past and possible consequences and consulting judgment, reason, and values before deciding how to act. Your child will need help with this process.

## One-Step Thinking Affects Willfulness

Full of themselves and insisting on what they want, strong-willed children's tendency to be impulsive works to their detriment.

"I don't care if it's yours, I want it!" (The child will get into trouble at school for taking what doesn't belong to him.) "Nobody can tell me what to do!" (The child defies adult authority only to get hurt by ignoring a safety rule.) "It's my way or no way!" (The child's friend is discouraged from coming over to play again, since all play has to be on the host's terms.) These types of statements reflect strong will and shortsightedness, and they lead to unhappy outcomes. Your child will be unable to have and keep friends.

Teach your willful child to think twice. Having already claimed the power of personal choice at a young age, every child must be taught to delay, think, consider past and possible consequences, and use some judgment to moderate a tendency to indulge impulsive choice. "I know what you want to do, but stop and think and ask yourself what is wise and right to do."

## Parents and One-Step Thinking

A large part of what any child learns about how to behave is through imitation. The parents are the most powerful role models in a child's life. Thus, if parents act on impulse, emotion, and make demands, children learn this is the way to get their needs met. Yelling at a child to stop yelling only encourages him to yell some more. Hitting a child to stop him from hitting a younger sibling only teaches him that, if you're bigger, hitting is okay.

Although growing up is hard for children, acting maturely can be equally challenging for adults. An immature outburst, such as, "I'll show you who's boss!" isn't helpful as an example. The most powerful way to teach a child to become a calm, modulated person is to be one yourself. Constantly envision yourself in that way, and it's easier to realize.

### Essential

One measure of adult maturity is a parent's capacity to maintain two-step thinking in the face of a child's one-step provocation. There has to be a grownup present in the family dynamic, even if the child is horribly acting out.

## How Children Learn Willfulness

Some willfulness seems naturally endowed. After all, children do not enter this world as a blank slate. They are endowed with genes they inherit from their parents, which determine certain physical characteristics, personality, temperament, and aptitudes. Although some infants emerge complacent and compliant from the outset, others seem to be born strong-willed. These children are born unusually committed to satisfaction of their needs and desires, with a tenacious personality and intolerance for frustration that is easily aroused when what they want is not immediately forthcoming. Even children who are by nature willful usually increase that willfulness as a function of the parental nurturing they receive.

This is where the parent's place as role model is of paramount importance. You must realize that your example is very important.

## ⓔ Alert

Parents who grow up intimidated by their own critical, angry, or even violent parents are often fearful of offending their own children. Their children may then become extremely dominant as a result of their submissiveness; these children may also become extremely willful because healthy social, emotional, and economic boundaries have not been clearly defined.

## When Parents Are Their Own Worst Enemies

There are many direct parental behaviors that encourage strong will in children. Consider just a few. There are the adoring parents who indulge their child so much she comes to feel entitled to be indulged. There are the permissive parents who give so much freedom the child becomes accustomed to making all of her own choices. There are the insecure parents who can't say "no," who don't want to displease their child. There are the guilty parents who allow their child to exploit their feelings of remorse. There are the neglectful parents who are too preoccupied with their own lives to adequately supervise their child. There are the argumentative parents who by example and interaction teach their child to stubbornly argue back. This creates a negative role model. There are the enabling parents who continually rescue their child from the consequences of ill-advised decisions. There are ambitious parents who by insistence and example instill a will to win and excel at all costs because anything less is deemed not good enough. There are the inconsistent parents who don't stand by or follow through with what they say. There are demanding parents who give grown-up responsibility to a child, expecting her to contribute to the family and take charge of her own life while very young. In all these ways, and in many others, parents can be their own worst enemies, actually creating willfulness in their child.

There are also overindulgent parents who can spoil a child by giving emotionally and materially in such abundance that no want seems to go unmet. This is an unrealistic way to live. Parental overindulgence is one major contributor to the willfulness of a strong-willed child. Let's hope that none of these types of parenting describe you. If you see yourself, the awareness is a good beginning to the process of change.

It's at the parenting extremes that willfulness is most powerfully nurtured—by strong-willed parents and by weak-willed parents, by overindulgent parents and by neglectful parents, by oppressive parents and by permissive parents.

## Assessing Parental Responsibility

Therefore, if parents have a continually willful child or have a child who is going through a willful phase, it is important that they do not get so preoccupied with their child's determined behavior that they ignore their own. The critical question for parents of willful children to ask is, "Are we, through our actions or inaction, inadvertently encouraging more inappropriate willfulness in our child?" Parents must continually assess their own behaviors so they are not acting to make a child's willfulness worse. Go through a simple exercise. List ten things you could do or not do to make the child's willful behavior worse. Then ask yourselves, "To what degree are we doing any of these things now?" This will help you see areas where you can start making changes immediately. Grab hold of the focus on your child and shift it back to yourself. Mentally think of a mirror and adjust what you see.

## CHAPTER 2

# Hallmarks of a Strong-Willed Child

To begin to appreciate how willful children can be a handful for parents, consider the six Ws of willfulness—want, won't, why, win, when, and whose. Around each of these issues, parents of a willful child frequently find themselves hard-pressed.

## Where There's a Will, There's a *Want*

Although most parents know the basics of what their baby requires—food, rest, cleanliness, comfort, play, exercise, soothing words, affectionate touch, for example—only the infant knows exactly when he wants those needs met. Some infants are easily scheduled and soon satisfied, quickly coming to adjust to the timing, kind, and amount of attention they receive. Living on parental terms seems to work okay for the child because, by and large, the child goes with the parent's ways without complaining.

Other infants, however, are less content with this compliant arrangement. Operating on their own schedules, they loudly let it be known when wants are unsatisfied, and they signal intense and protracted distress until they are met. This is a signal to parents that a strong-willed child has arrived into their care. "He just keeps fussing and crying until we give her what she wants. He won't give up!" In willful children, where there's a will, there's a want.

Now parents wonder, "Maybe we shouldn't respond to every cry if the more often he complains, the more often we give him what he wants. After all, we don't want to spoil him. Besides, he's supposed to live on our terms. We're not supposed to live on his." So the parents decide to let the infant cry himself to sleep after they have already settled him in bed several times, and after half an hour of wailing, the exhausted child finally does give in to sleep. "Now he's learned who's in charge," conclude the parents, "although it sure is hard to hear him cry that long."

But this is a mistake. For the baby to feel firmly bonded to parents, to feel empowered to express a want and know that it will be met, and to predict that parental care is there when needed, parents need to meet the baby's need any time the infant has the will to express it. During the first year of life, rewarding a willful want with the desired response is *not* spoiling the infant; it is helping that hungry, lonely, hurting, or frightened little child to feel attached, secure, trustful, confident, and effective. This isn't spoiling.

## Where There's a Will, There's a *Won't*

By age two, most children begin opposing parental rules and requests by delaying or refusing to do what they are told to do or not to do. This obstinacy is an act of courage—the child's daring to resist the most powerful people in her world. Appearing to test adult authority, the child is really testing her growing power of personal choice.

In most cases, if parents continue to be firm in their request, don't overreact and fuel the child's refusal by getting upset, the child learns to go along with what parents want most of the time. The willful child, however, is more intense and more dedicated to refusal, often surprising parents with the way she digs in his heels and makes a scene when she decides not to do what they ask. In willful children, where there's a will, there's a won't.

Beware similarity conflicts between stubborn parent and stubborn child, each refusing to give in to the other or back down. The harder the parent refuses, the harder the child learns to refuse in return. Better for the parent to disengage and think of another, less confrontational approach to take—like talking out and working out the conflict instead of stubbornly going toe to toe. In a power play there's rarely a winner. This is a time to be creative. Realize you're the more experienced person and come up with a way around the battleground.

## "Won't" Can Wear a Parent Down

It is the intensity and persistence of the willful child's "won't" that wears parents down, sometimes causing them to relent. And when they relent, the child feels more empowered. Parents may get too tired to keep after the request they made after the child delays or refuses, or they may feel uncomfortable in conflict, and so they back off. And when they do, the child learns that delay and refusal work. For parents, it is important to remember that your influence is much greater than you imagine. You may not be able to control the child, but you can greatly influence the child.

A willful "won't" can also take other common forms. The willful child often won't admit making a mistake, won't admit having done something wrong, won't apologize for doing wrong, and won't accept constructive criticism for mistakes or correction for misbehavior. "Leave me alone! I don't want to listen to you! I don't want to talk about it!" But parents must be steadfast: "You can put off the discussion, but you cannot make it go away. Before you get to do anything else you want to do, we will need to have our talk." Concentrate on being calm and firm.

## Four Propositions for Independence

At a very young age, a willful child can come to four very significant understandings about parental influence: the four propositions for independence.

- "My parents won't always stick to what they say."
- "My parents can't make me."

- "My parents can't stop me."
- "My choices are up to me."

Each successful "won't" only encourages the child to feel more confident in her power of resistance. Of course, understanding these four propositions for independence is empowering at any age, but the willful child tends to learn them very young. Then, when parents punish refusal, the willful child loses the skirmish, but wins the battle. Punishment just certifies the child's power to disobey. It is better for parents to let the child know that disobedience is a choice the child is free to make, but not a choice parents are willing to live with. "You can choose to delay what we want, but you can't get out of doing what we want, because we will keep after you until it gets done. And before you get anything else you want from us, we will get what we want from you." Don't forget for a moment that you are in charge. You may have a lot to deal with, but you're still in charge.

## Distract-and-Return

So how are parents to deal with a willful "won't" at the tender ages of one to three? Distract-and-return is best. Instead of arguing with your child or insisting that she do what you want when she refuses, distract the child to something positive. "Come look at this." "Come play with me for a minute." Then, having restored a positive context to the relationship, return to your original request in a few minutes and see if your child is not more inclined to cooperate. If so, reward her compliance with approval, appreciation, affection, or praise. If she is not yet in a mood to comply, distract the child again and draw her attention to something else positive and then return to your request again. In general, parents have more power to be consistent with what they want than the child has power to resist. Remember that the child's attention span is shorter than yours. She may be bright, persistent, and clever, but you are more mature and experienced.

27

But suppose your willful child has caught you in a time crunch. She refuses to put on her shoes so you can leave to pick her brother up on time when the school bus arrives. Now you have to weigh which is more important—a timely pick up of your older child or an obediently shod younger child before you leave. In order not to penalize the older for the younger, you take the younger child out barefoot.

You win some, and you lose some. However, what you lose on today you resolve to start working on earlier tomorrow. And you're even prepared to bargain her "want" for your "will." "If you want to have your usual snack with your brother when he gets home from school tomorrow, you will need to have your shoes on when we leave to pick him up."

## ⊛ Essential

When a child under the age of three refuses what you ask with a "won't," use distraction and then return to pursue what you are after. Distract the child from the negative situation into doing something positive with you, thus breaking the child's negative mindset, and then, after a few minutes of pleasure or play, return to your original request. Repeat this procedure as often as necessary to gain the child's consent.

## Where There's a Will, There's a *Why*

Now consider the preadolescent eight-year-old, feeling grown up enough in childhood to question parental rules and restraints, to want an explanation. "Why should I? I want to know why," the child asks. So parents take the child seriously and take the time to explain, and the curious child, feeling satisfied, complies.

With a willful child, however, "Why?" is not simply a request for information, it is a challenge to parental authority. Roughly translated, it complains, "I shouldn't have to!" At issue is what right parents have to tell the willful child what to do or not to do. It's not information the child is after; it's justification. In willful children, where there's a will,

#630 01-08-2018 3:10PM
Item(s) checked out to p1434340x.

TITLE: Alternative cars
BARCODE: 37653018474729
DUE DATE: 02-03-18

TITLE: Cool cars and trucks
BARCODE: 37653018493562
DUE DATE: 02-03-18

TITLE: Wheels on the truck go 'round and
BARCODE: 37653021679975
DUE DATE: 02-03-18

TITLE: Building emotional intelligence :
BARCODE: 37653015361089
DUE DATE: 02-03-18

TITLE: The everything parent's guide to
BARCODE: 37653018818776
DUE DATE: 02-03-18

```
      #630   01-06-2018 3:10PM
   Item(s) checked out to p1434340x.


TITLE: Alternative cars
BARCODE: 37653018474729
DUE DATE: 02-03-18


TITLE: Cool cars and trucks
BARCODE: 37653018493562
DUE DATE: 02-03-18


TITLE: Wheels on the truck go 'round and
BARCODE: 37653021679975
DUE DATE: 02-03-18


TITLE: Building emotional intelligence :
BARCODE: 37653015361069
DUE DATE: 02-03-18


TITLE: The everything parent's guide to
BARCODE: 37653018818776
DUE DATE: 02-03-18
```

there's a why. Sometimes you can simply say, "because I said so," or "because I'm your parent and that's that." You can even add, "When you're a grownup, you can make all your own decisions, but not yet."

## The Meaning of Why

The problem is, when parents give an explanation for their demand or limit, the willful child protests, "That's not a good reason!" And with such a child, there never is a reason good enough to justify being asked to do something he doesn't want to do or being denied something he wants. Resist the temptation to engage in fruitless debates.

Willful children also frequently ask "why?" because they feel entitled to know more than parents may want to tell. "Why we won't buy what you want is because we're trying to spend less right now as a family," explain the parents, not wanting to go into details about one partner's possibility of being laid off at work. But with willful children, one "why?" just seems to beget another. "Why do we need to spend less now?"

## The Parent Rules

To the "Why?" requesting an explanation that parents either cannot or do not want to give, it is best to stop the endless questioning by simply saying and repeating if necessary, "This is what we can tell you; we cannot tell you anymore."

 **Fact**

Parenting is not a popularity contest. A strong-willed child may often see your rules as simply there to frustrate his wants. You must explain that it is not for pleasure or power that you take these stands, but for a purpose—to protect and promote his best interests. The parent has to have a loving, authoritative stance.

To the "Why?" that challenges their right to authority, parents can repeatedly explain something else: how they are obliged to follow "the parent rules" of responsible parenting, even when that obedience is hard to do. "The reason why we have the right to tell you what you can and cannot do is because your welfare is our responsibility. As long as you depend on us, the parent rules say that we must set rules and limits for you. The hardest part of our job is doing what we feel is right when you feel we are wrong. But because we love you, we will do the best job for you we can, even when you don't agree with what we are doing. Just remember: we are never against you." Sometimes the less said, the more power you have. If you deeply *believe* in what you're doing, the child will comply.

## Where There's a Will, There's a *Win*

During early adolescence, between ages nine and thirteen, the child typically begins the separation from childhood and no longer wants to be defined and treated as "just a child" anymore.

Now there is more opposition to parents from a young person who increasingly doesn't like being told what she can and cannot do. Pushing against and away from parental authority for more independence, the early adolescent wants to create more social freedom and to assert more individuality.

On both counts she is more willful to live with and more determined to get her way. In willful children, where there's a will, there's a win.

### The Stakes

During adolescence, parents, for the sake of safety and responsibility, take more unpopular stands for the young person's best interests against new freedom she may want. This means there is more frequent disagreement between them. And after some complaining and argument, the adolescent usually consents to live within the limits that parents firmly set.

With a willful early adolescent, however, there are two issues at stake, not one. First is the specific disagreement, about freedom to go bike riding after dark, for example. But second, and equally important, is the principle of winning for its own sake. Losing an argument with parents feels like giving in to their terms and losing face. That's why having the last word feels so important to a strong-willed child.

## Arguing to Win

Willful children, particularly in adolescence, are often determined to debate until they win the argument or gain the freedom they want. They may exert tremendous effort to wear you down. Arguing to win is the order of the day. So what are parents supposed to do? Should they be equally willful back and refuse to declare defeat? Again, resist the impulse to participate in a power play.

 **Question**

**What is the most common willpower that willful children lack?**
Patience with delayed gratification. Strong-willed children often lack the ability to wait for what they want without complaining or somehow hurrying time along. Willful children believe they "can't wait" for what they want. A parent's job is to teach them that they can. Speak and act calmly, reassuring the child that waiting is possible.

Arguing to win at all costs only encourages the child to do the same. Better to declare "no contest" and take the issue of winning off the table by declaring something like this to your willful adolescent: "After explaining why I want something, I am not going to argue with you about it. After all, whether or not to cooperate with me is always up to you. Of course, if you choose not to cooperate with me, then I have choices about what I want to do in response." To which declaration the willful child may ask, "Well, what will you do if I go bike riding after dark anyway?" This is when you clarify with your child that the issue is not who wins, but how her choices can influence your own. "That's for me to decide," you explain.

# Where There's a Will, There's a *When*

"When can I have it? Why can't I have it now?" Willful children are often ruled by a desire for immediate gratification. They are inclined to go fast through life, to hurry up rather than to slow down when one of their wants is concerned. Urgently the six-year-old pleads, "I know my birthday is tomorrow, but can't I open one present now? I hate having to wait!" Any delay can seem like torture because every want feels so intense. Where there's a will, there's a when.

## Enduring Impatience

For the willful child, anything worth waiting for is worth having now. When should a want be satisfied? Immediately, if possible. Many willful children lack an important kind of willpower that they will need in life—patience, the capacity to endure delay for what they want or even do without. Willful children who are ruled by impatience are easily frustrated and soon end up angry, using anger when they can to get what they desire.

Parents can teach patience by teaching planning. "Let's think out the steps that need to be taken for you to get that to happen." Parents can teach patience by teaching consequences. "When you have completed all your chores, then you get to do what you want." A child who understands consequence is a happier child. You, as the parent, can help the child predict logical consequences. Lead him along in a confident way.

## Savers and Spenders

Here's a telling question to consider. When it comes to managing money, is your willful child a spender or a saver? At issue is the management of "when"—when will money be spent, now or later?

**Fact**

Desire for immediate satisfaction ("I can't wait") and attraction to temptation ("I can't resist") often rule the decisions willful children make, sometimes resulting in feelings of regret later. "I wish I had taken the time to think first." "I wish I hadn't let myself be persuaded." These children actually need more willpower—the willpower to be patient and the discipline of self-denial.

Spenders are ruled by pleasure in the moment. If money burns a hole in your child's pocket, then you may have some patience to teach. To help the child delay spending now, see if you can get him to begin saving for something later. Saving requires patience with slow accumulation, regular deposits, and interest growing over time. Saving has material value, but more importantly, it has psychological value. Willpower is used to restrain immediate want in favor of pursuing a long-term objective. Savers demonstrate impulse control and the ability to delay gratification.

## Where There's a Will, There's a *Whose*

Strong-willed children can be proprietary over what they have—be it position, privileges, or possessions. What they want, they want to own. The question "Whose is it?" asks to whom something of value belongs. If it belongs to someone, then that person controls who gets to use it. And willful children usually like to be in control not just of what they do, but also of what they have. Where there's a will, there's a whose.

### The Firstborn Child

Consider the oldest child, first born and firmly established in the center of the family, used to having a monopoly on what parents have to give, having to adjust to another child in the home. At first the oldest was excited by the fantasy of having company, a playmate, someone to take care of. But fantasy soon degenerates into reality when it becomes clear that this younger sibling is a rival for parental attention, approval, time, and family resources. If the youngest is particularly cute and winning, the oldest can become more willful in response. "Whose is the place on the bed between my parents? Mine!" So the oldest starts acting very territorial and possessive and tries to push the young intruder out.

## Sharing

Sharing can be hard to learn for an oldest child who is used to having uncontested access to everything the parents provide. But to get along in the world, everyone must learn to share. To that end, parents teach the child to take turns, to let the other person go first, to compromise, to sacrifice for others, and to sometimes do without. Most important, the willful child needs to be taught that contentment does not depend on having it "all," but on understanding that when it comes to satisfying wants, "some" has to be enough.

 **Fact**

A willful child can be very possessive of whose way is the right way to get things done. Intolerant of opposing beliefs, the child will insist on "doing it my way!" Parents need to help the willful child accept the legitimacy of other people's lifestyles, value sets, and points of view. This will require time and thoughtful conversation.

In willful children, where there's a will, there's a want, so they can act very intense. Where there's a will, there's a won't, so they can act very stubborn. Where there's a will, there's a why, so they can act very challenging. Where there's a will, there's a win, so they can act very combative. Where there's a will, there's a when, so they can act very impatient. And where there's a will, there's a whose, so they can act very possessive. Willfulness takes a variety of common forms, and parents must be alert in order to contend with them all.

Mentally keep your compass clear. In spite of all the loud objections, you don't have to go every way the wind blows. Take a deep breath and remember that you signed up for parenthood for the long haul. You're the leader in the situation.

CHAPTER 3

# In Praise of the
# Strong-Willed Child

Willfulness is a person's power of self-determination to direct, to persist, to resist, and to prevail. Often adults, using this definition, will go on to describe a strong-willed child by equating "directing" with being domineering, "persisting" with being stubborn, "resisting" with being argumentative, and "prevailing" with being combative. Why would you have this negative way of thinking?

## Negative Connotations

Being called *strong-willed* by adults is usually not complimentary to a child. Like it or not, we still live in a rather hierarchical society where those on top are in charge, and in general, children traditionally are best seen and not heard. Of course, there are dramatic exceptions to these ideas, but in many ways, they prevail. A generally negative perception of willfulness in children still prevails, so when friends or family or teachers complain to parents about the child's willful nature and behavior, or when parents continually encounter it at home, it can be challenging to keep a positive perception of their strong-willed child.

Then there is a related question: "Who wants to be known as a strong-willed child?" When a child's reputation precedes him, slanderous preconceptions can await his arrival in a new social situation. Imagine the second-grade teacher saying to the third-grade teacher, "Watch out for him, he's a troublemaker" or "Good luck with him, he can really be a handful."

Getting a reputation as a strong-willed child can create negative perception, reception, and treatment. This last possibility is particularly important because how a child is treated contributes a lot to how the child learns to treat himself. Be alert to labels that can harm your child and do everything you can to keep the focus positive.

## Alert

The great social vulnerability of strong-willed children is the frequent negative response they can receive from the world. They may internalize the criticism and correction that they often receive, becoming painfully self-blaming in response: "I'm nothing but trouble." They need your loving contradiction at home.

## The Positive Side of Willfulness

What is extremely important for both parents and child to understand is that willfulness also has a powerful positive side. "To direct" can be equated with being outspoken; "to persist" can be equated with being dedicated; "to resist" can be equated with being principled; and "to prevail" can be equated with being successful. Just think of all the jobs that require strong will. To name a few—executives and salespeople, lawyers and doctors, inventors and artists, professional athletes and coaches, police and military officers, politicians and managers, and leaders of all kinds. Society needs people who are willing to be willful. Remember former President Truman's truisms? "If you can't take the heat, stay out of the kitchen," and "The buck stops here."

Being strong-willed has a strong positive side, and parents need to see that, appreciate that, and nurture that so their willful child learns to do the same. Always remember that it takes a strong will for your child to develop many traits you prize. Consider the following, all of which require strength of will:

- To speak up for what's right
- To practice and improve a skill
- To achieve excellence
- To overcome adversity
- To maintain consistency of effort
- To oppose what's wrong
- To defend or protect self-interest
- To express one's personal opinions
- To be patient
- To be loyal
- To be hardworking
- To set and pursue goals
- To satisfy curiosity
- To resist temptation
- To stand up for self or others
- To stick to principles
- To recover from setbacks
- To finish what one starts
- To keep agreements and commitments
- To speak the truth
- To stick to a healthy regimen
- To keep trying
- To dare to risk
- To face fear
- To create and invent
- To compete
- To lead

In a host of positive ways, you will benefit from encouraging the development of a strong will in your child. But remember that willful self-determination, like any character trait, can be a double-edged sword. The child who refuses to quit when the going gets tough can also refuse to give up when parents are tired of arguing. With a strong-willed child, the role of parents is to encourage the positive, moderate the negative, and not act in ways that make the difficult side worse.

 **Essential**

> Willfulness is power, and like any power, it can be abused. It is a good servant, but a bad master. It is the parents' job to help the strong-willed child learn to channel willfulness so that it serves the growing child well and not badly.

## Stereotypes of the Strong-Willed Child

Stereotypes are usually grounded in ignorance and distrust. "She's probably just like the rest of them." Stereotypes are prejudicial. "All teenagers are troublemakers." Stereotypes are often used to justify mistreatment. "I wouldn't trust her if I were you."

**Alert**

> List all the stereotypes you have ever heard about what a typical strong-willed child is like. Then ask yourself, "Do we ever think about our child, talk to or about our child, in these negative terms?" If so, stop. It's difficult to raise a child you don't like. Work to alter your perception of the child. Concentrate on keeping a positive image in your mind.

Among adults, there is a stereotype of the strong-willed child, and the disparaging description goes something like this: A typical strong-willed child can be difficult in a host of ways. She can be intractable, argumentative, unmindful, oppositional, self-centered, inconsiderate, insensitive, oversensitive, and domineering; is never wrong; and is a bad loser.

## The Willful Spirit

Parents need to cherish their child's willful spirit and not try to crush it for the sake of compliance. Crushing the negative side will diminish the positive side, and what influence parents gain from this does not compensate for what esteem the child has lost.

What makes parenting a strong-willed child so challenging is having to act as guardian of the child's willful spirit and at the same time provide guidance to channel how that determined spirit is expressed. Remember, the world tends to give more negative than positive responses to a strong-willed child, so, at least at home, your strong-willed daughter needs to know that even though you may often disagree with her choices, you always genuinely think well of her. Let her know she is loved.

Remember the connection between willpower and want in a willful child. *Willpower* identifies what is wanted. *Willpower* pursues what is wanted. And *willpower* doesn't stop until it gets what is wanted. Even arguing and resisting, the willful child can earn a parent's grudging admiration: "That kid just won't quit."

 **Essential**

A child's strong-willed spirit needs to be cherished by parents, not censored. This means that, no matter how often you are at odds with your child, you should always maintain and communicate your larger positive perception of her.

# Contrasts with a Weak-Willed Child

One way to appreciate a strong-willed child is to contrast him with another child—one who is weak-willed. Some characteristics of weak-willed children include the following:

- **Depends on others for direction:** "Whatever you decide is what we'll do."
- **Gives in to group pressure:** "I can't refuse what others want."
- **Gets easily discouraged:** "It got too hard, so I gave it up."
- **Is defeated by failure:** "When I couldn't do it the first time, I stopped trying."
- **Is intimidated by authority:** "I wouldn't dare refuse what a grownup asked."
- **Doesn't think for self:** "I believe what I'm told."
- **Avoids conflict:** "I'd rather go along than disagree."
- **Won't speak up:** "I'd rather other people did the talking."
- **Lacks initiative:** "I'm no good at getting started."
- **Is timid:** "I'd rather people approach me rather than have to approach them first."
- **Is indecisive:** "I hate having to make hard decisions."
- **Is passive:** "Whatever happens is okay with me."
- **Backs down:** "When people push, I let them have their way."
- **Holds few firm opinions:** "What I think depends on the situation."

## 🅴❗ Alert

Many a weak-willed child who learned to automatically submit to a domineering, threatening, or critical parent grows up to marry a strong-willed partner, reenacting the familiar submissive role. And when he becomes a parent, this person can also be in danger of acting out the old pattern of submissiveness with a strong-willed adolescent.

Sometimes it's useful for parents to appreciate the problems of disinterest, inertia, passivity, dependence, and extreme compliance that they do not often confront in their willful child.

Where strong-willed children require channeling and restraint by parents, weak-willed children need help developing assertiveness to advance and defend themselves.

Parents are influence brokers. The most valuable personal resource parents have to give children is attention. Willful children can exercise a lot of personal power in the family when parents allow it. Power is the ability to get one's way. And because they can push and resist so hard, they can monopolize a lot of your attention. You must be careful not to feel pressured or obligated to cater to the willful child at the expense of other children in the family who are less demanding but still have equally legitimate attention needs.

 **Essential**

Having the power to get one's way and to get attention are strengths of the willful child, filling him with a sense of effectiveness and esteem. However, parents must limit that power so the equally important needs of other children in the family are not overlooked or neglected.

## Being Self-Defined

Willful children are strongly self-defined, and there is strength in this. Their interests, wants, likes and dislikes, temperament, and personality are pronounced because willfulness brings out these characteristics. In words and actions, the strong-willed child seems to say to parents, "I know what I believe; I know what I want; I know who I am!" Willful children usually have a definite opinion and a definite identity. They are not wishy-washy. They are not ambivalent. They are not uncertain. They are not hard to figure out. Coupled with this strong self-definition is a corollary characteristic, a demand for the child's definition to be accepted: "Take me on my terms!"

## Taking Symbolic Stands

With definition, ownership often follows. Children take a stand for something they want. "Since the age of four, our daughter has let it be known that the only person allowed to brush her hair is herself. We don't know why, but that's just how it is."

"Why" is often because the child is using a specific definitional act to take a symbolic stand. In this case, the young child is laying claim to control over her body. "It's my hair, and I will take care of it however I like!" If parents can live with these proprietary definitions, it is generally best to let the willful child have her way. After all, she is assuming responsibility for self-definition and self-care in the process.

More complicated for parents, however, is when a child takes a symbolic stand to create a new definition that they may not like. That's the problem with strengths; they are always double-edged. What works to one's benefit can also work to one's detriment. For example, a willful early adolescent (ages nine to thirteen) may want to show parents that she does not want to be considered just a "child" anymore. To that end, she may redefine behavior to make this symbolic point. Instead of doing what is asked of her without complaining, as she has done in the past, she may argue with every single parental request, no matter how large or small. Her capacity for argument with parental authority comes to symbolize new independence.

To parents who disapprove of this new behavior, punishment may seem to be the answer, but it is not. What really matters to your child is not the specific issue at disagreement, but the symbolic issue that she is communicating—new growth has taken place, and she will not be as easy to convince as she was before.

Better for parents to understand that it takes two to argue. You can simply refuse to respond. Instead, repeat your request until it is finally met: "This is what we need to have you do, and this is why." The explanation acknowledges that, as a more independent person now, she is entitled to a reason for your request. If she keeps trying to argue, simply repeat what you said before: "This is what we need to have you do, and this is why." Say it calmly. Use insistence to wear down resistance. Accept the compromise of the early adolescent age. Your more independent child gets to have her say in order to save face.

 **Fact**

> Self-absorption in a high-interest activity is a common strength in willful children. Being choosy, they tend to choose different activities until they find what calls to them, and significant interests become central to their self-definition and are a major source of self-esteem. Intolerance with interruption is the downside of the self-absorption: "Not now, I'm not done yet!" This is common in gifted children.

### Problems with Being Self-Defined

Two problems come attached to this strength. First, willful children don't like being interrupted or stopped in a beloved pursuit before they are ready. And second, like many gifted children, they can become so preoccupied with a high-interest activity that they are not inclined to invest energy in less interesting skills that would enhance their development.

In general, parents are well advised to clearly contract over the time allowed and allotted to pursue that interest on any given day, keeping it in context with what else needs to be done. When your child protests, "Just five more minutes, I promise!" you can reply with, "That is not what we agreed. I want to support your doing what you love, but I need your agreement to stop when something else needs to be done."

By restricting themselves to only working on things they love, willful children may have problems at school. "What's the point of studying what doesn't interest me?" the child wants to know. "I do great in math but I hate language arts. So why should I have to work on vocabulary? It's boring!" In response, parents have to take a dual stand, supporting what is loved and insisting on what is boring. But don't make doing a fun activity a reward for finishing a boring one. If you do, a power struggle is likely to ensue because the willful child will be in the position of defending and fighting for the right to do what is loved, and become further antagonized toward what is not. Instead, just keep repeating and insisting that boring work must be completed, too. It's a fact of life.

## Making Declarations

Willful children speak their mind. They describe their feelings. They express their needs and wants. They state their opinions. They ask questions. They confront differences. And they protect their "rights," willing to object to treatment that they consider unfair. They speak up and declare what matters to them.

 **Fact**

Children who will speak up to a parent about what they dislike or want changed are more likely to be able to speak up to peers and resist peer pressure than children who always stay quiet and act compliant at home, no questions asked and no objections raised.

### Teaching Appropriate Declarative Language

When speaking up does not accomplish what they intensely want, it is tempting for willful children to amplify their communication with yelling or to use harsh language to get their way: "You're being dumb not to let me go! You're acting stupid! I hate you!" At this point, parents must set aside discussion of what the child wants and address the tone and content of language being used. The child is declaring himself, but doing so in a destructive way.

Old-fashioned good manners go a long way at any age. Children may need to be taught particular phrases and gracious tones of voice. Model them in your home, and they will copy you.

So when your willful child, having declared a want and been denied, resorts to name-calling ("dumb," "stupid") and then uses the word "hate," immediately set the issue at difference aside and declare that language unacceptable and not allowed. "If you are disappointed or frustrated because of my decision, you can say so, and I will listen. You can say you are very angry with me, but you cannot say you hate me. We don't allow that kind of language in the family. And I will not be called hurtful names just because you are not getting your way. I don't call you bad names and I don't want you doing that to me." Because willful children tend to speak up so strongly to a parent, they must be taught to do so in acceptable ways.

## The Willful Refusal to Declare

Although as a rule willful children are strongly declarative, there can come a time when they are strongly not. For example, the rebellious twelve-year-old may go on strike against telling parents about anything that is going on his life in order to keep them away from what he doesn't want them to know. He may think, "Freedom comes from keeping my parents in the dark."

In frustration at being shut out of their child's life, and whatever is going on, the parents complain, "He won't talk to us and there's nothing we can do!" Wrong! Parents can hold their son accountable for refusing to communicate with them. They can confront him with the consequences of refusing to be his usual declarative self.

They can say, "Of course, whether you talk to us or not is entirely up to you. You have the right not to communicate. However, we need to let you know the consequences of that choice. First, in our ignorance, we will come to our own understandings of what may be going on, understandings that may be false and that you may not agree with. And second, based on those understandings, we may make decisions about what you must and cannot do that you do not like. For example, if we conclude that your sullen attitude is due to taking drugs, we may decide to restrict your social life and increase your work around the house to help you get straightened out. If, however, you want to tell us what is going on and influence our decisions with helpful discussion, then you can choose to communicate with us. As we said, it's up to you."

# Determination

Willful children are committed to pursuing what they want. They are not easily discouraged. They are goal-directed. They are not prone to giving in or giving up. If they really want something, they develop the discipline to keep after it, even sacrificing other enjoyment to work for what feels most important. They are highly motivated. Setbacks only increase dedication. Adversity is just a challenge to overcome.

 Alert

Even if otherwise cooperative and compliant, willful children can be resolutely independent when it comes to pursuing what they love. Protecting an area of ultimate concern, they often brook no parental interference in that part of their life. "Don't tell me how to do my music. It's not up to you. It's up to me!" Sometimes it's okay for parents to back off.

Determination takes many forms. The willful two-year-old is determined to figure out how to take the puzzle block apart and refuses to quit until the problem's solved. The willful eight-year-old begins a drawing of a meadow, carefully penciling in hundreds of blades of grass until the picture is complete. The willful twelve-year-old keeps practicing ball handling until dribbling becomes second nature. All three children become committed to doing what it takes to do what they want. When, in all three cases, parents support this power of self-determination, they are empowering their child.

When a willful child is determined to choose a certain path despite parental cautions or objections ("I want to take all honors classes no matter what you say!"), you may want to let the child have her way when you believe only experience can teach what your explanation cannot. In this case, there may be valuable lessons to be learned from how much accelerated schoolwork the child has the energy to accomplish.

You can make the following agreement: "Since you feel so strongly about it, we will support your choice in this matter if you will do two things for us. First, take the time to think through possible hard consequences of this choice. And second, should any problems occur, be willing to take responsibility for working these problems out as best you can."

Holding her accountable allows her to learn whatever lessons are there to be taught from the consequences of willful choice. Maybe she will pull it off. If so, you as parents have something to learn. You underestimated your child. If not, and if your predictions come true and the amount of work proved to be too much, don't say, "We told you so!" Your daughter already knows that. Say instead, "Good try. Now you need to think about what is best to do next." Be willing to help work through the consequences, but don't coddle.

### Fact

Power of choice is important to the willful child—so important that, once gained, she will not gladly give it up. Power of choice becomes both a matter of pride ("Look at what I decided to do!") and a matter of principle ("I should be allowed to decide for myself!"). This is why, when the power of choice is denied, willful children can get so upset and angry. Their pride has been hurt and a principle has been violated. "That's not fair; you've always let me decide who my friends can be before!"

Consequences are a fact of life at any age. Part of your job as a parent is to assist the child in working through the results, especially when they are embarrassing or disappointing. Approach this side of parenting with empathy and tenderness. Your bruised little one may not act appreciative at the moment, but gratitude will be stored away in some corner of her heart.

## CHAPTER 4

# Problems with Being a Strong-Willed Child

Without question, being a strong-willed child can create problems for the individual. Parents can help their child reverse or reduce these problems. None of what follows means that your child will develop these problems, only that the potential is there.

## Powerful to a Fault

Power is the capacity to get one's way. Willful children have a lot of power—to direct, to persist, to resist, and to prevail. To the degree that family and friends keep giving in to this power, the child becomes increasingly willful.

Willful children are good at getting their way—going after what they want, refusing what they don't want, and getting others to do for them what they don't want to do for themselves.

Supporting healthy power, like ambition, is what parents want to do; supporting unhealthy power, like coercion, they want to avoid. To enable the growth of unhealthy power only makes a difficult situation worse and does the child a disservice by encouraging the growth of traits that will cause the child trouble in adult life.

For example, imagine parents who feel like their eight-year-old is running the family. He gets furious when they refuse him what he wants, and he gets so upset that they feel they must finally give in to stop things from getting out of hand. They have to tiptoe around, always walking on eggshells. But how has he gotten this way? The parents have allowed it. They have given their power to him and are blaming him for what they've done. When a willful child is powerful to a fault, it is usually because of parents who have given up sticking to normal demands and setting healthy limits. It takes courage, clarity, and consistency to effectively parent a strong-willed child who will respect nothing less than parental firmness.

### Willful Threats

For some parents, there are times when their willful child can be scary. Consider willful threats such as "If you don't let me have what I want . . . :

- "I'll hurt myself!" (at age five)
- "I'll run away!" (at age eight)
- "I'll hate you forever!" (at age ten)

It can feel daunting to face down an intensely upset willful child and hold to the demand or limit that you have imposed, particularly if you have a fearful childhood history of being domineered yourself. But growth is just a gathering of power, from dependence to independence, and it is your responsibility as a parent to help your child gather power in appropriate ways. It is inappropriate to give in to a willful child's emotional extortion. You don't have to respond to the little dictator.

 **Essential**

Giving in to a tantrum rewards emotional extortion. Better to say, "When you are through acting so sad and mad and are willing to talk about how you feel, I am willing to listen. But what I asked you to do (or said you cannot do) still stands."

### Getting Away with What Isn't Wise

Sometimes a willful child can lose by winning. Backing parents off a healthy stand, the child gets to do something that is against the parents' better judgment, and their judgment proves correct. The child lands in trouble from being given freedom unwisely gained. So after his tireless pleading and promising, parents relent and let him go spend the night with a friend who they know has little adult supervision. And then the two friends sneak out and get picked up by the police at a party that the parents would not have approved of.

"It's your fault for letting me go, so you should get me out of this!" protests the child. At this point, parents need to make a clear separation of responsibility. "Yes, letting you go over to your friend's was our responsibility. But what you chose to do there was up to you, and so the consequences are yours to pay." For parents, it may feel easier to give in to their child's willful want now, but if they know it is not wise, they are only borrowing trouble from later on.

## Controlling to a Fault

Like any power, willpower can be hard to limit. The more a child has, the more she becomes accustomed to, and the more she wants. There never seems to be enough, because the older the child grows, the larger the world becomes, and the more there is to try to control.

### ❶ Alert

Beware the extremely charming child. The child can use charm for willful effect, being so disarmingly hard to resist, cleverly getting what she wants. But the more often charm works, the more willful the child becomes. Very young children who are very cute often learn to use acting cute to get their way. Parents find her darling ways irresistible.

That's what willpower is really about: exercising the ability to control oneself, external events, and others. Control of self can take the form of perfectionism and the drive to perform error-free. Control of events can take the form of managing every situation, imposing and satisfying a personal agenda. Control of others can take the form of insisting on how others are supposed to act and dictating their behavior. The secret here is for the parents to exert more self-control. Adult self-possession will ease the tension in the relationships in the home. Your child will soften as you ease up on being controlling yourself.

 **Fact**

Parents find themselves getting angry when their willful child is exercising too much control at home, but they are really angry with themselves. They are angry for conceding authority and putting the child—instead of themselves—in charge of what happens in the family.

## Control of Self

Willful children can be susceptible to perfectionism. They may set personal performance standards that are extremely demanding, tolerate no mistakes, and forgive no failure. Consequently, willful children can be unduly hard on themselves when they don't manage to live up to their very high standards. They can fly into a rage for not performing up to their ideal: "I'm so stupid!" Remind the child that name-calling isn't allowed, even toward oneself.

Parents need to intervene at this sign of intense personal pressure to help their child understand the control she should be taking. "When you fail to meet your standard of performance, instead of pressuring yourself to push harder or punishing yourself for not meeting it, we want you to consider a third choice: ask yourself if that standard was realistic. Consider lowering it to one that you are more likely to meet. Personal standards are not fixed. They are not genetic. They are chosen. And your responsibility is to set reachable standards that you can meet with reasonable effort. Excessive and unreasonable standards that you set will only cause you stress."

 **Essential**

One reason why willful children can get so upset after losing a competition is that they never considered the possibility of defeat. Wanting to win so badly, they believe that they should win all the time. Parents need to help them modify this unrealistic expectation: "No one wins all the time."

### Control of Events

When any disagreement, game competition, or athletic event routinely becomes a "must win" situation, the child's self-esteem may depend on winning. And she can push herself and others very hard and become extremely unhappy when she does not prevail. Losing an argument, getting beaten at a game, being defeated in a sport can cause the child to feel deeply sad or very angry. In tears or in a rage after losing, she literally seems unable to accept defeat. She may be called a poor sport by other children. "She needs to learn to lose," advises the coach.

And as parents, you need to help the highly controlling, highly competitive willful child learn to make a separation between effort and outcome. "It is good to try your best," you can tell her. "So take pride in your effort, but accept that you cannot control how chance and circumstance will unexpectedly influence everybody's play. Understand that the effort you make is no guarantee of the outcome you want."

### Control of Others

Parents can feel tyrannized by a willful child when "King Boy" or "Queen Girl" becomes enthroned in the family: "All we can think about is what she's going to want or not want us to do next, and what she'll do if she can't have her way!" Driven by this preoccupation, they direct all their attention to the child, giving up even more control, focusing on what the child is going to want at the expense of considering their own wants. Meanwhile, the child enjoys the dominance she exerts.

Social dominance at home is based on two kinds of control: what the child can "make" parents do and what parents can't "make" the child do (defiance). Both giving orders and refusing to obey feel empowering. To counter these types of control, parents need to let the child know that she can make requests but she cannot give orders, and that her requests will not automatically or immediately be met. "You can ask what you'd like us to do, but you cannot tell us what to do." As for defiance, parents need to let the child know that, when they have made a request, they will keep after its fulfillment until it is met: "You may try to delay doing what we ask, but you cannot get out of doing what we ask, because we will keep after you until you get it done." Keep after the child in the manners department, as well. Do not permit bad speech or behavior toward you or siblings.

Watch for control-taking behaviors—particularly bullying and bossiness—with her friends or siblings. To the willful child, it can feel like the end justifies the means (coercing other people). Your child acts so bossy with her friends that they refuse to come over. Bossiness is offensive and bullying is abusive. In both cases, parents need to call the child's attention to the social damage being done. Teach her specific things she can say and not say.

That's a common problem for willful children—in going for control with other people, they can focus on their objective at the expense of the relationship. Parents have to keep weighing in on the side of the relationship: "To win your way and lose a friend is not a good bargain." Sometimes the question, "Do you want to be right, or have a relationship?" can help the child sort things out. She may decide she values the friend.

# Independent to a Fault

Used to getting his own way, the willful child can become accustomed to going his own way, independent of what others say or want. "Don't tell me what to do! Don't tell me how to do it! I'll decide!" The willful child can resent being directed and can resist directions. Willful children are firmly wed to their personal agendas.

## Going It Alone

Intent on going his own way, the willful child can be impatient with people getting in his way, which is why many such children shy away from operating in groups and prefer to go it alone, participating in individual sports, not team sports, for example. "I don't like playing on a team because they don't play the way I want to play."

Once he has made up her mind about what he wants, he wants it without any interference. For this reason, many willful children in elementary and middle school find working in groups to be an aggravation. "I hate having to do this project with other people. They just slow me down and what we end up with isn't everything I want. I'd rather just work alone." He really dislikes having his individual achievement depend on the performance of others. But if the group project is unavoidable, the willful child will often take charge of the group, dictating and doing most of the work just to have the project suit his vision and meet his standards. He does what he can to turn "our way" into "my way."

## Alert

Sometimes the willful child is acting like a puppet on a string, and parents fail to see or fault the puppeteer. Because a willful child can be so easily excited, incited, and upset, another sibling may take advantage of this vulnerability, secretly provoking his strong-willed sibling to get this attention-grabbing rival in trouble with parents. Beware a secret aggravator in your family.

As parents, you don't want to deny or depreciate the strength of individuality and independence that your willful child possesses, but you can still talk to him about the importance of learning to cooperate and collaborate as well. Learning to compromise is an essential cooperative and collaborative skill. Remind him of the saying "None of you is as smart as all of you." Tell him, "The more ways you have of looking at a problem, the broader your understanding becomes. The more different ideas you can include, the richer your project becomes."

This does not discount the individual creativity of your child. It is simply encouraging him to learn the skills of group creativity as well. The willful child who prefers individual sports should also be given a chance to appreciate the possibilities of a team sport. Remind him, "In many situations, people working together can accomplish more than a single person working alone."

## Being Difficult to Coach

One common by-product of being independent to a fault is being uncoachable. "I know! I know! I know!" protests the willful child when given explanation or offered instruction. "I can figure it out! Let me do it by myself! I don't need your help!" But after a frustrated or failed experience, the child may belatedly accept your assistance. The child can learn after the fact that accepting help before the fact could have saved some difficulty and distress. Sometimes, the child learns that following parental instructions is the easier way.

## Willing to Try Anything

Often associated with the independent streak that accompanies willfulness is a tendency to be driven by curiosity and challenge. The strong-willed child may try anything, to engage in risk taking to see what many experiences are like, without considering the consequences. The willful child always seems up for an adventure. "Our son never met a dare he didn't like."

When willfulness carries with it this devil-may-care sense of independence, parents absolutely must allow the child to learn from the consequences of risk taking, even if unpleasant. You must give practical cautions when you know your child is going to take risks. The independent child is determined to learn from experience, which often means learning the hard way—from his mistakes.

## Exceptional to a Fault

Parents naturally believe their children are special. In appearance, in precocity, in talent, in charm, in personality, or in some characteristic, they believe their child is above the norm or otherwise remarkable. Treating the unique as exceptional, however, can cause the child to believe her own rave reviews. "I know I am special because my parents treat me so." She begins to view herself in the mirror of her parents' exaggerated perceptions.

 **Fact**

Sometimes a child is so forceful, winning, talented, or precocious that parents encourage her to get away with anything, granting her immunity from rules and responsibilities that other children must abide by. Boasted one such child, "I can do no wrong in my parents' eyes." Parents must be on guard against this special treatment.

When the child in question is also a strong-willed child, this exceptional treatment can often increase willfulness to harmful effect. Consider two common examples: the overindulged child and the star child.

### The Overindulged Child

"All we want to do is make her happy; we adore her so!" And so the smitten parents work to please the child any way they can, satisfying her wants and celebrating her outstanding qualities, until continued indulgence causes her to feel not only very special, but entitled to very special treatment—from attention given to desires gratified to resources provided. When she already happens to be a strong-willed only child, this cultivated sense of entitlement increases existing willfulness. The parents are unwilling to set healthy social, emotional, or financial boundaries, setting the child too free for her own good. "I don't have to play by other people's rules! My own are all that matter."

The problem here is not really so much with the child's demands as it is with the parents' enjoyment of overindulging their child. Wanting to give to their child is a natural part of loving their child, giving being an expression of that love. They want to do what they can to make their child happy, and they do not want to do anything to make their child unhappy. Parents need to moderate indulgence with a willful child, or that child will start expecting overindulgence as her due. To this end:

- Give the child the gift of not getting everything desired.
- Give the child the gift of having to work for what is wanted.
- Give the child the gift of enjoying giving to others.
- Give the child the gift of knowing that getting some of what one wants, not everything, is good enough.

## Essential

Overindulgence by parents can create a sense of entitlement in the child: "Since I am treated specially, I deserve to be." In turn, entitlement empowers willfulness: "I expect to be given whatever I want."

Preschool and school experiences can be helpful here. Thus, the only child at home has the experience of being treated as one of many at school, learning to delay or do without all the attention that is desired, learning to share with other children, and generally learning to operate on less self-indulgent and entitled terms. Doing service in the community also moderates being so special.

## The Star Child

Some willful children perform very well for themselves, developing outstanding athletic, academic, appearance, artistic, leadership, and other capacities that bring a great deal of social approval and attention in response—adults basking in the glory of the high-achieving child. Treated as stars in their small social world, part of the special treatment they receive may be exceptions to normal rules and expectations for celebrity's sake.

Thus, some teachers, basking in the child's reflected glory, may be willing to let a star child's neglected homework assignments be made up late with full credit given instead of the zero that is normally given for missed work. They don't want poor academic performance to jeopardize her outstanding athletic performance on the field of play. Sometimes star students are allowed to break normal social rules, to get special exceptions made, acting outlaw and getting away with it, adults excusing the problem behavior to protect and preserve the prominent child.

Parents also can get caught in the star trap. For example, their straight-A student is doing so well academically that they choose to overlook increasing infractions of rules at home that mask a substance problem they do not suspect. It never occurs to them that a good kid who earns such good grades could get into trouble with drugs. But it can happen.

### Alert

Willful children who star in some area of performance in their lives should be held to the same responsible account as any ordinarily performing child.

# Self-Focused to a Fault

Preoccupation with what one wants or doesn't want can cause a strong-willed child to spend a lot of attention and energy on himself. This is why strong-willed children are commonly criticized by parents for being extremely self-centered or selfish. "All he ever thinks about is what he wants. It's always 'Me! Me! Me!' What about what other people want? What about us?"

This accusation is often true. Personal wants can feel so urgent and intense that the willful child cannot see beyond them, cannot see that other people have needs and wants as legitimate and important as his. This is why parents have ongoing issues to address with their willful child: thinking beyond oneself and mutuality.

 **Fact**

> One way to moderate a willful child's excessive self-centeredness is to regularly involve him in community service. Learning from the plight of people less fortunate can lessen the willful child's self-preoccupation, while volunteering can become an object lesson in placing the needs of others before the needs of oneself.

### Thinking Beyond Oneself

Parents of a strong-willed child may sometimes feel that only one person's needs matter, and that person is not either of the parents. The mother who has been playing for over an hour with her strong-willed five-year-old declares an end to the game in order to pick up household tasks put aside for play. "Play with me! I want you to play with me! You never play with me!" objects the child, who sees only his own interrupted wants and has no perception of what else his mother needs to do.

Parents may be disturbed by this insensitivity and unresponsiveness to others that the willful child is demonstrating. "He acts so greedy, as if he's the only one in the relationship that counts, the only one who is even there! Is he blind? Doesn't he care about the welfare of other people?" The answer to these questions is partly "yes," and partly "no."

Yes, the willful child can be so caught up in the demands of self that the reality of other people's needs is overlooked. No, the child is capable of caring, but he needs to be reminded about what else to care about. For this reason, when a willful child acts self-focused to a fault, parents have to help the child see beyond himself, to understand and appreciate the needs and wants of other people, too. "I know you're disappointed that I am ending our play. Why am I stopping the game now? Think about it. Pretend you are me and tell me what else I might be wanting or needing to do."

## Mutuality

When willful children enter adolescence around ages nine to thirteen, they tend to become more willful still, because early adolescence, with its social separation from family and push for more independence, is a very self-centering period of growth. At this time, if parents let growth tendencies prevail, their relationship with their child may be increasingly on one-way terms; that is, the child's way.

"It's all for him and nothing for us! It's all giving on our side and nothing but taking on his!" If parents allow this condition to continue, they will end up resenting their child. Instead, they should insist on living in a two-way relationship. They should insist on mutuality.

*Mutuality* in a relationship means that the needs of both parties are recognized and respected in these ways:

1. There is *reciprocity*, which means that each person acts in the relationship to contribute to the other's good.
2. There is *compromise*, which means that when a difference in wants arises, each party is willing to go beyond his immediate self-interest to create a solution that both can support.

3. There is *consideration*, which means that both parties, knowing each other's sensitivities so well, do not purposefully attack each other's vulnerabilities.

In a family where a willful adolescent has come to rule:

- When it comes to reciprocity, he appears to believe, "My needs are the only ones that count."
- When it comes to compromise, he appears to believe, "My way is the only way I will accept."
- When it comes to sensitivity, he appears to believe, "My feelings matter and yours are of no concern."

When parents find themselves in a one-way relationship with their ruling child, they have helped to create a spoiled child. In his ignorance, the child may feel that getting parents to live entirely on his terms is good, but it is not. It will spoil him for later caring relationships with people who, unlike parents who are committed to stick around out of love and obligation, will refuse to live in a relationship where a healthy exchange of mutuality is not observed.

A primary responsibility of parents with a willful child is to foster the child's ability to participate in loving relationships by insisting that he live with them in reciprocal, mutual terms. With their ruling willful child, parents must take a stand for mutuality for their own sake and for the long-term interest of the child. If parents don't want to live with a terminally self-serving child or adolescent who is all take and no give, then they must take strong stands to bring mutuality back into the relationship.

- To reestablish reciprocity, let the child know that for parents to give, they must first receive. "We're happy to do for you, but only after you've done for us."
- To reestablish compromise, let the child know that agreements have to work in the interests of both parties to the

agreement. "For us to give some to you on this, you are going to have to give some to us."

- To reestablish sensitivity in the relationship, let the child know that any inconsiderate or hurtful words or acts will stop the flow of resources, services, and permissions until amends are made. "We don't treat you that way, and we expect that you will not treat us that way, either."

# Intolerant to a Fault

Used to wanting her own way, used to pushing for her own way, used to believing that her way is the right way, a willful child can be intolerant of other people's ways and of changes that occur, when either conflicts with her own way. "That's not how you're supposed to do it!" "This is not what's supposed to happen!" "My way is the right way!"

Inclined to be dictatorial when it comes to knowing the proper approach or desired outcome, the willful child can be intolerant to a fault, that intolerance expressed in inflexibility.

## Inflexibility

When it comes to change, most willful children like to dictate how the process unfolds and what outcome is reached. "When we start getting ready to move, I want to be the one to put my things in boxes, and when we get in the new apartment, I want to choose how to decorate my room." And parents may agree with these requests because they serve the larger purpose of moving and getting settled in.

Lots of life changes, however, are less susceptible to the child's power of control, which is why change causes her to feel out of control, anxious, and angry on that account. "The new school is completely different from the one I was used to. I hate it! I won't go back!" But going on strike against unwanted change does not make change go away. Rigidity, refusing to change to adjust to change, is not the answer. Flexibility and adaptability are what the willful child needs to learn. To that end, parents must encourage the child to make the best of a hard situation, mourning what has been lost leaving the old school, then looking for the unexpected benefits that are waiting to be found in the new one. "There are gifts in every adversity," you can explain, "and we will help you take advantage of new possibilities and discover new friends."

For every strength that parents nurture in their child, some degree of liability is created. Hence, the child who feels secure in knowing exactly what her parents expect of her, enjoying consistent family routines, being able to rely on his parents' commitments, and having a sense of personal control, can come to count on this vital support in a rigid way and have trouble adapting to change.

- "But you never told me this might happen; this isn't fair!" (And there are violated expectations.)
- "But we've always done it this way; I don't want to change!" (And there are violated household routines.)
- "But you promised; you can't go back on your word!" (And there are violated parental commitments.)
- "But I don't like not being in charge; it isn't fun!" (And there are violated personal controls.)

### Teaching Flexibility

In their desire to create security at home, parents may inadvertently reduce their child's capacity to deal with the normal chaos of life—unanticipated events, changed plans, broken agreements, and unpredictable circumstances. Hence the parents' dilemma: how to give the child security and teach flexibility at the same time?

Within the sheltered social reality of family, parents can teach flexibility by approaching some events expectation-free.

CHILD: "What will it be like when we get there? What will we do?"
PARENT: "I don't know exactly. We'll just have to see what it's like and then figure out what we want to do."

Parents can treat routines themselves as partly flexible.
CHILD: "Why aren't you going to read me a bedtime story tonight?"
PARENT: "Because I'm tired and really need to get to bed myself. Maybe there's a way for you to do a bedtime story for yourself instead."

Parents can treat their commitments as what they intend to do, but cannot always guarantee.
CHILD: "But you said we could, you did!"
PARENT: "I meant the promise when I made it, but that was before everyone got sick. I still plan to keep that promise, but now we'll have to do it another time."

Parents can moderate their only child's desire for personal control, particularly in play relationships with other children.
CHILD: "I didn't have any fun because they wouldn't play by my rules."
PARENT: "Getting friends to play by your rules is one way to have fun, but there are other ways—playing by rules everyone agrees to, and playing by other people's rules."

Protection is no preparation. Sheltering that focuses only on security sets the child up for some unexpected adjustments in the outside world, where adjusting is necessary for healthy survival. Change is actually the only constant in life.

Overindulging the self-willed child doesn't create happy adults. Therapists' offices are filled with adults who are unhappy, not because their parents abused them but because they were so catered to that they do not know how to navigate their way through the treacherous waters of real life. This isn't what you want for your child.

## CHAPTER 5

# Working for Willingness

The more willful the child, the more preoccupied with control parents tend to become. "How can we get him to start doing what we want?" "How can we get him to stop doing what we don't want?" "How can we make clear that we are in charge?" Getting your strong-willed child to cooperate with what you want can feel like it's taking a monumental effort on your part. You must teach your child the willingness to work with you, not against you.

## The Illusion of Parental Control

Since raising a child is such an important undertaking, parents want power commensurate with this serious responsibility. Responsibility without control can cause parents to feel helpless, frustrated, afraid, embarrassed, and even ashamed. "Can't you make your child behave?" asks an indignant stranger in the store, irritated by the four-year-old who won't stop excitedly running around. And most parents take this as a personal criticism.

Not being able to control your child is not a problem. It is a reality that parents accept early on if they are wise and honest enough to admit it. For example, arriving home from the hospital with his parents, the little child starts wailing. Alarmed, new parents wonder what is wrong and what is right to do. Believing they must do something to stop the crying, one of them gently picks up the little child and rocks him, all the while mumbling sweet assurances. When, after a couple of minutes, the baby ceases to cry, the triumphant parent congratulates himself: "I stopped his crying!"

 **Fact**

It is only in recent decades that parenting has been viewed as a separate activity from childrearing. It is helpful to keep in mind that all the advice given by the experts is from an adult point of view. For centuries children were reared without such pondering.

On second thought, however, he admits that, for whatever internal cause, the baby chose to stop crying. Now he acknowledges the fundamental law of parenting: the child's behavior is always going to be up to the child. At most, as a parent, he can choose to try to influence choices the child makes.

The parent who believes in influence rather than control will have an easier time with a willful child. Essentially, you are powerless over the child's behavior, but you do have a tremendous amount of influence.

It helps to recognize other influences on your child that make total parental control an impossibility:

- The culture into which the child is born and its media messages
- The temperament of the child and genetic influences
- The child's choices
- Exposure of outside circumstances when the child is not at home
- The child's companions and peer pressure
- Chance events and luck

## Fact

> Parental discipline is not a matter of always getting your way; it is a matter of continually trying to find ways to persuade the child to live within your rules and according to your family values. In this process, you will win some, lose some, compromise a lot, and let a lot of small stuff go.

## What Parents Do Control

Certainly parents control some important elements in their child's life. Demonstrating control of these elements can definitely have influential effect.

- **Positive and negative treatment given:** "Without my parents' encouragement, I wouldn't have tried again."
- **Services and resources provided:** "Unless I pick up my dirty clothes, my parents say I'll have to wash them myself."
- **Freedoms and privileges allowed:** "If I do all of my chores this week without having to be reminded, I'll get to take a friend out for a treat this weekend."
- **Expectations and rules to live by:** "The only reason I keep doing homework, even though I hate it, is because I'm supposed to do my best."

## Question

> **If parents can't control their child, what can they do?**
> They can control themselves. Parenting is the ongoing process of making choices to influence decisions children make. To change their child's behavior, parents must be willing to examine and change their own.

Of course, what parents are really controlling in each of these situations are their own choices, hoping to influence the choices their child makes.

## Loss of Self-Consciousness

When parents feel they have lost control of their child, what has really happened is that they have lost something in themselves. They have suffered a loss of self-consciousness. For example, they have become totally preoccupied with their willful fifteen-year-old's free-spending ways. The problem as they see it is that he is totally irresponsible, constitutionally unable to make his allowance last the week for which it was intended.

No matter how often they explain and explain, by Thursday or Friday, he is back asking for money again. "What's the matter with him?" they ask. What they don't ask is "What's the matter with us?" The problem isn't that their impulsive son keeps running out of money. The problem is their own impulsive behavior—refusing to let him suffer the consequences of his decisions.

### Essential

If, despite correction, your child continues to misbehave, then you know you are doing something wrong. Your negative attitude may be arousing a resistant response, your ineffective choices may lack influential power, or you may be enabling conduct you wish to stop. Don't focus on your child's actions, focus on your own: "How can I alter my own behavior to encourage my child to change?"

The first commandment of effective parenting is "Parent, know thyself." The parents who yell at the child to stop yelling are only teaching the child to yell. Always ask yourself, "Am I modeling the behavior I want my child to stop?" "Am I enabling behavior I wish to stop?"

## What Parents Don't Control

It helps for parents to recognize areas of influence they don't control that contribute to how their child develops or turns out. Parenting is only one of many significant factors that impact the course of a child's life. Placing excessive faith in parenting causes parents to presume too much control. Treat parenting as important, but not all-important. It is not all-powerful; it is simply one source of influence among many.

Consider just a few more factors parents don't control:

- The impulses the child has or choices the child makes
- The child's physical vulnerabilities and strengths, innate capacities, and personality
- The child's rate or course of developmental growth
- The child's social experiences away from home
- The popular culture of the time
- The local and larger history that unfolds over the course of the child's growing up

# Willingness Is Cooperation

When parenting a strong-willed child, be aware of the risk of crushing the child's spirit. Instead, the task for parents is to continually work for the child's willingness to go along with what parents want and don't want.

Parents who set a positive, cooperative tone in the home will be rewarded with more cooperation from the child. Is cooperation modeled in the parents' relationship? The child will copy that.

### Rewarding Willingness

Willingness comes in two forms: going along with what parents want and refraining from doing what parents don't want. Your job is to reward acts of willingness with appreciation, approval, affection, and praise, which are more powerful than rewards such as particular freedoms, privileges, objects, or money. While your relationship carries on, concrete rewards will soon be spent or will lose the child's interest. Thus, your child may really want that new accessory for her computer, but she does not want it nearly as much as she wants your approval—to shine in your eyes.

Unfortunately, many parents seem most aware of willingness when they don't get it, taking it for granted when they do. By not rewarding acts of willingness that are given, parents end up losing a chance to encourage their continuation.

Even though your nine-year-old has delayed, disputed, and dragged out your three-minute housekeeping request for over an hour before finally getting it taken care of, that doesn't justify your treating completion with impatience: "Well, it's about time!" Always express appreciation when willingness is given: "Thank you for getting it done."

### Keeping the Larger View in Mind

Sometimes desperate parents of a willful child, who seems to oppose them at every turn and to run totally free of their restraint, come to mistakenly believe that he never gives them any willingness at all: "He's a wild child; he never does what we want!" This statement is emotionally true at that moment, but it is factually false because almost no child is 100 percent unwilling.

### ⊛ Essential

When you take for granted or ignore a child's act of willingness, you reduce the likelihood that it will be repeated. The child does not feel that his effort is valued. "Why should I keep doing what you ask if you never appreciate what I do?" thinks the child.

At this juncture, parents need to take a time-out to let emotion subside enough for a realistic perspective to take hold. Think about it. If a child acted unwilling all the time, then parents would be without any influence. No behavior they wanted would occur, and no behavior they did not want to occur would go undone. How frightening!

The parents of this wild child are exhausted, believing their parenting is bankrupt. "We're fighting a losing battle morning, noon, and night. Trying to get him up and ready for school each day takes everything both of us have to give. We have to argue and chase him around the house just to get him dressed, fed, homework packed for school, and in the car." But do they thank him for getting dressed, eating breakfast, getting ready for school, and for getting in the car? No, because they feel those are things that he is supposed to do, and in fact, they may even get angry that he doesn't do them on time. But these parents are not taking advantage of all those opportunities to reinforce the willingness they get and so encourage more of the willingness they want. And getting angry simply gives him power to arouse their emotions, power that he should not have but is probably glad to take.

In most cases, parents do not see and fully appreciate all the willingness they are being given. Take the parents in the above example. Their child behaves appropriately as a passenger in the car—not yelling, hitting, refusing to sit still, or throwing things. But why does he not behave badly? "Because we've taught him those kinds of behaviors make our driving unsafe," the parents say. The parents were extremely firm and clear and consistent about what they wanted and got the desired response.

 **Fact**

> Delay is not unwillingness. It is willingness, but at the child's pace. It is a compromise, as though the willful child were saying, "You can tell me what, but I will tell you when. And when I get enough 'when,' I'll do what you want."

And with this description, the parents have located, within all their frustrated efforts, a successful example of, and formula for, effective parenting with this strong-willed child. The next time they feel like their wild child is unmanageable, they must ask themselves, "With the current problem, are we being as firm, clear, and consistent as we need to be?"

 **Essential**

No willful child is completely unwilling to go along with everything parents want and do not want done. If parents will take the time to calm down and rationally inventory all the kinds of willingness—given on time or after a while—that they are still being shown, they will usually find their child's unwillingness is the exception, not the rule.

## Motivating Cooperation

As soon as parents discern that their child is extremely self-determined to direct, persist, resist, and to prevail, they need to begin training the headstrong girl in the basics of family cooperation. Cooperation is the willingness they want, and it can and must be taught.

### Encouraging the Practice of Cooperation

On a daily basis, parents are well advised to consistently initiate seven kinds of cooperative demands. On each occasion, they then need to follow through with insistence until those demands are met, and they need to reward the willful child with some combination of appreciation, approval, and praise for cooperation given.

Consider these basic training demands, which require the child's cooperation in order to be fulfilled:

- **Share what you have:** "Take turns with that so each of you has a chance to play with it."
- **Tell me the truth:** "Give me adequate and accurate information about what is going on."
- **Listen to me:** "When I am talking to you, give me your attention."
- **Keep your agreements:** "Do what you promised me."
- **Be of assistance:** "Give me your help."
- **Follow directions:** "Do it the way I have described."
- **Obey the rules:** "Remember how you're supposed to act."

### Essential

If by the age of two your child reveals herself to be willful, you must on a daily basis initiate demands to cooperate in order to convince the child through practice that cooperation with parents is a normal part of family life. Practice is the foundation of habits, and you want your willful child to learn the habit of cooperating with you.

As a parent, you have the right to make and enforce family rules. Some rules will be nonnegotiable—not stealing, hitting others, and not calling others bad names. Other rules are somewhat flexible—finish homework before watching TV, finish chores before going out with friends, save money for a special purchase. Exceptions can be made under some circumstances. Family rules are articulated as facts and firmly carried out, but not with threats or force.

### Contracting

Because willful children are often so preoccupied with what they want, they can decide to act without being mindful of what you want from them. After a while, parents can feel they are coming out on the losing end of this competition of wants more often than not. Sometimes contracting can encourage cooperation.

Each morning you can take the time with your child to list a lot of the things that she is going to want you to do for her—services and resources you will provide. Then you list the things you want from her—acts of help she can provide. Then turn this into a contract. "I will be happy to do these things for you, and I will expect you to do these things for me? Agreed?" In most cases, the child will agree to be finished with the matter. But to show you are serious, and if you have cause to believe she will "forget" the morning conversation tonight, write it down and both sign it. This way, when evening resistance arises—"I never said I'd help you fold the laundry!"—you have a written document to back up your request.

## Cooperation and Making Choices

The simplest way to train a child to cooperate is to establish basic systems of instruction through experience. Children must learn that there is a connection between choice and consequence. They must learn through experience that, for every choice the child makes about cooperating or not cooperating with you, a consequence from you will follow. In general, the choice of willingness to go along with what you want will yield a positive response from you. A choice of unwillingness will not yield a positive consequence from you.

There are common choice/consequence connections parents frequently use to encourage willingness in their child; some are positive and some are negative.

### Positive Systems
In general, when it comes to encouraging willingness, positive consequences work better than negative ones because of their long-term impact on the child's desire to work with you. Over time, receiving mostly positive responses increases the value of the relationship for the child, whereas receiving mostly negative responses tends to reduce it: "Why should I do what you want when all you ever do is punish me?"

Positive systems for using the choice/consequence connection to encourage willingness include:

- Using recognition systems, parents positively respond with appreciation, approval, affection, or praise to every act of willingness that they are aware of receiving from the child. "Thanks for remembering to bring in the trash."
- Using exchange systems, parents agree to do something positively valued for the child after the child has done something that the parents value positively. "Since you helped me bring in the groceries, you can have the snack you wanted."
- Using permission systems, parents predicate a freedom on a condition being met. "You can go to the party if you give me the information about arrangements I require."
- Using earning systems, parents attach points to performing desirable behavior, with a certain number of points entitling the child to an agreed-upon reward. "For feeding and cleaning up after the dog each day all week, you earned enough points to get another action figure for your collection."

## ✅ Fact

In early adolescence unwillingness increases as children become more actively and passively resistant to authority and parents tend to become more negative in the face of this rising resistance. In fact, to get willingness during adolescence, parents need to be more positive, not less.

### Negative Systems

Negative systems influence willingness by allowing or applying unwelcome consequences. Used only occasionally, these systems can persuade a willful child to cooperate. Parents have to watch out, however, that they are not too heavy-handed. If you act extremely negative, a power struggle may ensue. The willful child may be willing, all right, but not the way parents want—willing to go down in flames to prove they can't make him or they can't stop him. Generally, positive responses have far more power to influence willingness. Too much punishment creates a fearful child.

**❗ Alert**

Don't use too negative a consequence to threaten a child. When parents use a fearful consequence such as dire threat or physical hurt to motivate willingness, the child may go along with what they want, but at considerable expense to the relationship. The cost of coercion is loss of trust, loss of honesty, loss of closeness, and, in extreme situations, loss of love.

Negative choice/consequence connections include the following:

- Using accountability systems, parents hold the child responsible for coping with unhappy consequences of poor decisions. "You have to clean up what you spilled."
- Using warning systems, parents promise the child what consequence will happen if timely compliance is not given. "I'm going to count to three, and if by three you have not started to get ready, I will follow through with what I promised."
- Using penalty systems, parents attach a negative consequence of their choosing to discourage repetition of misbehavior. "For lying to me, there is going to be some more work for you to do around here in addition to your normal chores."

## Subverting Cooperation

When a child is in a position of unwillingness, ignoring or resisting your demands, first remind yourself that you have no control over the child's behavior. This is not a problem to try to change. It is a very important reality to accept.

The loss of control for parents to be concerned about is not over their child, but over themselves. They can subvert cooperation they want by losing control of their own behavior in two common ways. First, they may emotionally load a situation by overreacting to a child's resistance and end up intensifying an encounter better handled by a cooler head and a more reasoned approach. Or, they can repeat unproductive choices because they cannot think of what else to do. In both cases, they have lost control over their own effective decision making, reducing the likelihood that they will be given the willingness they want.

### 🔔 Alert

When parents believe they can control their willful child's decision making, they are in danger of losing control by trying to force control, at which point the child ends up in control by demonstrating how powerless the parents actually are. "I don't care how mean you act or angry you get, the more you punish, the more I'll fail!"

### Emotional Loading

Emotional loading occurs when parents choose to apply inflammatory labels or inflammatory interpretations to their child's behavior, offending the child and upsetting the parents in the process.

How can parents emotionally load a child's problem? "All I did was not turn in some homework and fail a test and my mom got really scared, my dad got really angry, and we had this big fight. 'Do you want to be a failure in life?' they yelled. I never knew I could get them so upset just by making a few bad grades!" And then the willful child, injured by their label and incited by their upset, decides to get back at parents for the insult by deliberately failing again.

The lesson is, if you want cooperation in resolving a significant issue with your willful child, do not complicate the issue with wild emotions. Exploding at your child to go to bed on time, to stay in bed, to go to sleep, will not get you the cooperation you desire. It will increase the unwillingness you do not want by emotionally inflaming an ordinary disagreement. So get a grip on yourself. The less emotional parents remain when working a problem through with their willful child, the more likely they are to get the cooperation they desire. "Here's a clock. I want you to try staying in bed for an hour, and if you still can't get to sleep by then, I want you to come in and tell me so we can try again."

## Repeating Unproductive Choices

"Nothing works!" protest the parents. "There's nothing left to do!" Parents may give up exploring new ways of behaving with the child to encourage a more timely bedtime, for example. And instead, they keep repeating unproductive choices that recent history has shown have failed. They cajole, they plead, they bargain, they get angry, they make threats, and night after night the war over bedtime is reenacted to predictable, dispiriting, and exhausting effect. Repeating choices that have proven ineffective will not get parents the cooperation they desire.

"But we've tried everything!" they argue. This is the wrong attitude. Parents have never "tried everything," because there an infinite number of experimental approaches and responses for them to try. What parents have run out of is the will to try, to keep thinking up new choices for influencing their child. Three techniques for breaking out of this inability to come up with new ideas are violating the child's prediction, enlisting the child in the problem solving, and brainstorming with a friend.

### Violate the Child's Prediction

Ask yourself, "How does my child predict I will act when this problem comes up again?" Perhaps you answer, "When she delays going to bed on time, she probably predicts that I will disagree with her excuse and begin an argument." So surprise her. Agree with her excuse. Compliment her excuse. Tell her you'd like to hear other good excuses, and you'll be lying down on her bed when she wants to come in and tell you some more. Who knows, it might work.

 **Essential**

Just because a child is strong-willed does not mean that all refusals to cooperate are deliberate acts of willful opposition. Sometimes parents have unrealistic expectations of the child's capacity to perform. Sometimes parents demand faster change than the child can manage. The child perhaps can do no more and resists in order to save face.

### Enlist the Child in the Problem Solving

Instead of treating bedtime resistance as just your problem, understand that the nightly fights are probably also a problem for your child. So, during a relaxed morning time, ask your child what she thinks might work to make bedtime go more smoothly. She may have some ideas of her own. "Well, I'd like us to have a friendly way of going to bed. I'd like to have some fun together before I go to sleep."

### Brainstorm with a Friend

Ask a friend to work with you to come up with twenty crazy ideas for getting your child to bed on time. No objections to any of the ideas allowed. Try reversing things. Take bedtime away from her. Treat it as a privilege, not an obligation. Tell her, "Tonight you can't go to bed until we think you have earned it. We have three jobs you have to do before you can lie down and read yourself to sleep."

With a willful child, parents must keep generating new and different choices for influencing her behavior. Gaining cooperation depends on parents never running out of new options to try.

## CHAPTER 6

# The Problem with Being a Strong-Willed Parent

T hrough inheritance, imitation, and interaction, strong-willed parents often have strong-willed children. If you were born strong-willed, there is some likelihood that one or more of your children will also have that self-determined characteristic. If you model strong-willed behavior, there is some likelihood that one or more of your children may identify with your willful ways and react similarly. The way you are has a more powerful influence on them than the parenting you provide. Your way of being with yourself, with other people, and with the world all set the example that the child follows. The interesting thing is that neither of you are fully aware of the traits being modeled and learned.

## Characteristics of a Strong-Willed Parent

Know thyself. This is probably the most important requirement for being an effective communicator and disciplinarian, because then you understand the human nature you have to work with (what you can actually control) when parenting your child.

There is nothing especially wrong with being a strong-willed parent, any more than there is anything wrong with being a strong-willed child. In fact, as you have seen, there is much to be valued in self-determination.

What is wrong, however, is for parents not to recognize their own strong-willed characteristics, because then ignorance may lead them to create and increase problems with their own willful child. "I don't understand why my son argues with me all the time and feels he has to have the last word! I've argued with him about it for as long as I can remember, but for some reason, he just won't change. But neither will I!" In this situation the parent doesn't understand his part in the problem. Like father, like son, but because the father is unaware of his willful nature and behavior, he can't see how he has created the problem with his son.

## Fact

A strong-willed parent who believes he can defeat a strong-willed child is sadly mistaken. A parent who rules by making threats and issuing ultimatums will continually collide with a headstrong child who proudly refuses to be bossed around. To avoid this costly conflict, the adult must be flexible, not rigid, request cooperation and not just command obedience.

### Are You Strong-Willed?

Here's a chance to see if perhaps you are a strong-willed parent. How many of these statements apply to you?

- I don't take no for an answer.
- I don't back down to anyone.
- I hate losing an argument.
- I don't like changing my routine for other people.
- Once I make up my mind, I stick with it.
- Once I start something, I finish it.
- When I make a commitment, I keep it.
- When in disagreement, I tend to listen with my mind made up.
- I like to take the time to do things right.

- I get upset when I make mistakes.
- I don't like admitting mistakes.
- I don't like to apologize.
- I like other people to do things my way.
- I try to be perfect.
- I expect other people to live up to my standards.
- I don't give up.
- I will win at all costs.
- I need to know everything that is going on.
- I don't trust other people to take care of my business.
- I never admit defeat.
- I don't like being told I'm wrong.

Obviously, this is not an exhaustive list of strong-willed characteristics. However, if you checked off a majority of them, you might consider that you could be a strong-willed parent.

## Becoming Less Strong-Willed

Look back at any of the characteristics you checked off. Most of them are within your power to change. And you might choose to change in those instances where your willful behavior is triggering a similar willful response in your child. For example, you find yourself in an ongoing similarity conflict with your child. You won't admit defeat or back down, and neither will he. You are both extremely stubborn. Aware of this, you have a choice. Either you can keep doing this dance of stubbornness with him every time a disagreement arises, or you can change your own behavior and introduce a different step. "We certainly do view what your friend did in different ways. I'd like to hear more about your take on his behavior; then I'd like to tell more about mine." So you introduce the alternative of discussion instead of the old step of arguing to win. It helps to truly envision a warm cooperation occurring with your son. The mental picture somehow brings about the reality.

**Alert**

Strong-willed parents and a willful child must work out a compromise between what parents want to have happen and what the child is willing to do. Parents who are rigidly uncompromising often raise a child who learns to be the same.

## You Teach What You Are

On the plus side, a strong-willed parent communicates a well-defined presence to respond to, so a child knows where that parent stands and what behavior to expect from that parent. On the negative side, a strong-willed parent often encourages, by imitation and interaction, a strong-willed response from a child who, if not born willful, can learn to become that way.

 **Fact**

It is helpful to look at your own family background in terms of power and control. What were your parents' ways of governing the family? How did they discipline you? Take an objective look at the willful behaviors in your family.

### The Power of Imitation

Many parents believe they provide a single model of behavior that their child is influenced, by example, to follow. This belief is not true. Actually, each parent provides two models to follow, not one—how to be and how not to be. So your child may pick up your sense of humor and the enjoyment of getting people to laugh, but may elect not to incorporate your use of sarcasm, which can sometimes humiliate and hurt. "I like my mom's way of clowning around and being silly, but I don't like when she uses it to put people down."

Strong-willed parents can be unaware how imitation of their ways is at the root of their problems with the willful child. For example, consider parents who believe their rules should be obeyed who have a daughter who, according to them, has no respect for rules at all. They complain, "She doesn't believe in following rules—ours or anybody else's!" But they have underestimated the power of imitation. Just because their daughter opposes the parents' rules doesn't mean she doesn't believe in rules. In fact, the opposite is the case—she has learned from her parents that following rules is extremely important. So important that she has made up her own rules and, like her parents, will stick to them no matter what. The real difficulty is her rules are different from their rules. The challenge is to discuss and create a set of rules they can all live with, at the same time consenting to go along with some of her rules if she will consent to go along with some of theirs.

Conflict can create resemblance. As parents change their model, the child often changes in response. Parents who are alcoholic or otherwise addicted, for example, often become strong-willed —self-centered and controlling to a fault. Identifying with these personal characteristics, although not using the substance, a child can become willful in similar ways—thoughtless and demanding of others. When, however, the alcoholic parent enters recovery and begins to live differently within himself and with others, becoming more sensitive and considerate to live with, the child has a different model of behavior to imitate, and often does.

## The Power of Interaction

It is a peculiar irony about nurturing a strong-willed child that the same willful outcome can be achieved from opposing kinds of parenting. A strong-willed child can emerge as easily from oppressive parenting as from parenting of the permissive kind. With an oppressive parent bent on dictatorial control, a child can strengthen willpower by regularly opposing overbearing parental authority. Excessive parental restriction can make freedom extremely desirable.

With a permissive, neglectful, or overindulgent parent, a child can be given so much power of choice that self-determination becomes the only authority she will obey. Excessive personal choice can create intolerance for parental limits and restraints.

When parents complain that their willful child is a fussy eater, they usually have only themselves to blame. By turning up her nose at what's for dinner and being offered something else, the child learns to eat only what she likes and to refuse what she does not.

### Question

**What is a good example of the power of interaction?**
"Because my parents were never satisfied with how I did, I ended up becoming very critical of myself."

In general, it is best that parents don't turn mealtime into a battle of wills: "You will sit at this table for however long it takes you to eat what has been put in front of you!" Better to eliminate any alternative eating choice. When parents consistently withdraw the option of something else to eat, food fussiness usually disappears. "This is what has been prepared. You can choose to eat it or not. However, if you choose not to, then you may find yourself having to go hungry until the next meal."

## The Tyranny of Now

For strong-willed parents, time can be a problem. Part of their agenda, in addition to determining the rules, priorities, and schedule that the child is expected to observe, is demanding the child do what the parents want when asked, which means "Now!" In service of this need for immediacy, strong-willed parents can face difficulty in two ways: with intolerance for delay and with incapacity to create delay.

## Intolerance for Delay

Strong-willed parents don't like having their requests and demands put off by a child who is more interested in continuing to do something else. "I will in a minute!" objects the child. "You'll do it when I ask," replies the parent, growing impatient, "and that means now!" Such power plays on both sides can lead to temper tantrums, a likely sign that the child has been overly indulged.

Impatience is a form of frustration that can soon lead to irritation. It causes parents to be vulnerable to emotional reactions, when rational responses would serve them better. An impatient parent with an impatient child usually leads to an angry outcome, and the issue between parent and child becomes more emotionally inflamed. It helps, also, to keep in mind that that the more people involved in a decision or action, the longer it's going to take. If one of those people is a child, it's going to take even longer.

When a child, discovers that delaying compliance is a button he can push to get an impatient, irritable, or angry parental response, the young person will use power of delay to manipulate you to his benefit. "It's easy to get my dad upset. All I have to do is put off what he wants, when he wants it done." Don't be trapped by this tactic. Just coolly keep after what you want until you get it.

## Incapacity to Create Delay

One operating principle for some strong-willed parents is to tackle a problem with their child as soon as it arises. So, when an infraction occurs, parents believe they must make an immediate decision about a consequence: "You didn't stay off the phone and do your homework as I asked and you agreed, therefore you are grounded from the phone for the next week!" But by responding so quickly, the parent didn't take time to fully investigate the offense as the child explains and complains: "I was just using the phone to get some of the assignment I forgot to write down. You're not being fair!"

Some strong-willed parents have a tendency to react too quickly. They decide impulsively instead of giving themselves time to think, and then they end up with a decision that is ill-advised. They don't delay long enough to consider what really happened and what is best to do, because they feel delay is a sign of uncertainty, when in fact it shows judgment. "So what are you going to do, not let me go out?" asks the child, impatient to be told. "Why won't you tell me now?" "Because," answers the parent, "I don't have to decide now. I'll take my own good time. You will just have to wait to find out my decision. That's part of your consequence for doing what you shouldn't."

 **Essential**

> When you impulsively make an inappropriately severe disciplinary response, give yourself freedom to retract and modify the decision. It's a lesson not lost on the child: parents can make, admit, and correct mistakes, too. "I was tired from work and overreacted to what you did and I would like to change what I said. Just cleaning up the mess you made is consequence enough."

If you believe that any parenting problem must be resolved right now, or any response to your child's demand must be made right now, then you are in danger of becoming trapped in the moment without sufficient time and space for reflective choice. Whenever you feel jammed into making a parenting decision right now, resolve to grant yourself a delay for time to think. The purpose of delay is deliberation.

## Power Struggles

Strong-willed parents want to be in charge, and they can resort to extreme measures to establish their control. "I will do whatever it takes to prove that I am the boss in this family and not my child!" Typically, strong-willed parents enjoy unquestioned authority during their daughter's life up to about age nine or ten. This is the age of command, when the parents believe they should be able to do the telling, and the child believes she must do what she is told. The compliant child does not question parental authority. Both parents and child agree that the parent is in charge.

### 🔔 Alert

Strong-willed parents who insist on always being "right" can end up doing wrong by ignoring relevant information and discounting constructive suggestions from the child because they are so busy defending their authority. Instead of treating the child as an opponent when it comes to resolving a difference, treat the child as a collaborator with whom to solve a common problem.

The onset of adolescence, however, between ages nine and thirteen, brings some degree of change. The child leaves the age of command and enters the age of consent, going from believing "you can tell me" to believing "you can't make me or stop me." Now willing to challenge parental authority, the child now understands that parents are powerless to make him do anything without his cooperation or consent.

For strong-willed parents, this change demands an unwelcome adjustment. They do not like their loss of control, and they often resent the early adolescent for taking away their power. In response, they can overreact with all sorts of power plays. For authoritarian parents a more useful skill is to become in control of one's responses. Make a deal with yourself, that no matter what the infraction or what degree of defiance you observe, you will remain cool, calm, and collected.

### Isometric Encounters

"I'll show you who's boss! You don't leave the supper table until I say!" and the angry parent physically forces the child to stay seated while the child struggles to stand up, at last giving up resistance because the parent is larger and stronger. So the strong-willed parent has won, right? Wrong. This can create all kinds of results, including eating disorders.

 **Essential**

Never get trapped in an isometric encounter with your strong-willed child. You don't need a more powerful opponent than you already have. Instead, declare your stand, recognize your child's disagreement, put a delay on discussion until you have cooled down, and then return to work out the differences.

The parent has prevailed at the moment; but to his detriment in the long term. He allowed an isometric encounter to occur. Isometrics are strength-building exercises. Pushing as hard as you can against a fixed resistance, you strengthen your power of push. In the supper table confrontation between stubborn father and stubborn daughter described above, she has pushed as hard as she can against a stronger resistance, losing for the moment, but now stronger than she was before and more resolved to win the next encounter. The strong-willed parent has only increased his daughter's strength of opposition.

## Losing Control to Get Control

"I just lost control," apologized the parent for having said some ugly things in anger to his daughter, when the child wouldn't immediately interrupt her video game to give help the parent had requested. But angry words and the damage they inflict cannot be undone by an apology. At most, they will not be repeated as part of the amends the apology makes. Now both parent and child feel hurt because of what Dad said to get what he wanted.

Strong-willed parents who are determined to win at all costs are most at risk of losing control to get control. The parent or child or both end up sorry for how the parent overreacted. A parent, no matter how strong-willed, is not always going to get his way, right away, exactly the way he wants it. That is not a problem to fix; it is a reality to accept.

Yelling is a good example of a bad parenting practice. *Yelling* is losing control to get control. The battered child ends up in control because she is given the power to provoke the parent into acting so loudly upset. Parents who regularly yell to get their way give away far more power of control than they ever get.

 **Fact**

Power struggles are losing propositions by definition. One party prevails at the expense of the other. When it comes to parenting a strong-willed child, it's better for a parent to establish a working collaboration than to compile a winning record.

## Excessive Needs for Control

Although actual parental control of the child is an illusion, some strong-willed parents insist on believing that control of their child actually exists. To prove this illusion true, they will often go to excessive lengths to prevent what they don't want or to get what they do want. A common example is the fear-prone parent who wants to protect the child from possible harm by reducing exposure to potential risk. Driven by fear, this parent is in danger of becoming overprotective and inclined to excessive control. The best kind of control is being in control of motivating your child to do what is best for him in the long run. This is the ultimate of being in charge.

### The Fear-Prone Parent

Growth requires trying oneself out in ways one has not tried before, and trial and error learning always offers potential harm.

The toddler can't learn to walk without risking falling down, the eight-year-old can't learn to cook without risking getting burned, the thirteen-year-old can't have a peer group without risking getting in trouble, and the sixteen-year-old can't drive a car without risking having accidents. Growth is an inherently risky process. The book *Free-Range Kids: How to Raise Safe, Self-Reliant Children* (listed in the resources at the end of this book) offers wonderful suggestions for fearful parents.

## Alert

Parents preoccupied with fear of potential harm to their child can become extremely cautious and overprotective. In consequence, they may raise a child who is anxious or raise a willful child who is rebelliously risk-attracted, too defiantly adventurous for his own good. Instead, parents should simply teach the child how to assess and safely manage risks that come with normal growth.

Parents who cannot bear the thought of exposing their growing child to possible harm can let fear cause them to hold on to the child too tightly, micromanaging the child's behavior, holding growth back instead of letting go so healthy expression, activity, association, and exploration can occur. Of course, letting go is the hardest part of parenting because putting the child at the mercy of his immature decision making, much less at the mercy of an unpredictable and dangerous world, is scary for most parents. What excites the child ("I can't wait to swim over at the neighbor's pool!") can terrify the fearful parent. Suppose no adult is supervising?

### Constructive Worry

To help ease the fear of letting go, the overprotective parent needs to use fear not as a warden who says no to every new freedom because it entails risk, but as an advisor who helps make it safer to let go. Overprotective parents need to avail themselves of constructive worry. Constructive worry asks "what if?" questions to anticipate possible risks and come up with strategies for preventing some and for coping with others should they occur. Asks the parent, "What if the supervising adult was called away from the pool for an emergency, what would you do?" Answers the child, after thinking ahead, "I'd get out of the pool and wait until the parent or another adult came back." Constructive worry can help the child be prepared.

Rather than protect against risks associated with their child's normal growth by forbidding any uncertain exposure, parents can use worry to assess risks, to help the child foresee them, and to teach the child to use worry to think ahead and make plans for dealing with problems that might occur.

Fear-prone parents are high-control parents who have excessive information needs: "I need to know everything that is going on in my child's life to protect him from harm and to feel secure myself." If they get into toxic worry, the more extreme and urgent their need to know becomes, the more their worry discourages the communication they are desperate to have from their child, the more anxious from ignorance they become. For his own protection, the child reduces contact and limits conversation to keep this poisonous anxiety away. If you tend to be fearful, work on increasing your trust in life in general instead of covering every possible angle with your child. You will be a happier person.

Strong-willed parents can be their own worst enemies or their own best friends. To be the latter, take your strength of will and invest it in patience, persistence, and perspective, three parenting characteristics that shall serve you very well.

## CHAPTER 7

# When a Willful Child Runs the Family

For many parents there are times when power becomes reversed, and instead of the parents being in charge, it seems as if the strong-willed child is running the family. They constantly react to her impulses and respond to her ultimatums. They keep waiting to see what kind of mood she's in, stay worried about her becoming upset, and continually endeavor to keep her happy. They struggle to get her agreement, trying to convince her to make cooperative choices. They strive to establish a family structure into which she will fit and to set a family agenda she will follow. This chapter describes some of the telltale changes in parental behavior that signal the presence of a child in the family who has too much power for everyone's good.

## Parental Authority

Parental authority is what you insist upon as the grownup in the family. It's not something you ask for from the willful child. It is yours by right. Authority comes from confidence and your right of entitlement. If you *know* you are in charge, your child will respect that. One way to keep this attitude in the forefront of your awareness is to imagine your child grown in twenty-five years. How does she live and behave? Is she functional, cooperative, and happy? These are your end point goals.

Following are some authoritative actions that indicate your strength for now:

- Making demands for actions to be taken. "This needs to be done by 3 o'clock."
- Repeatedly insisting that something be done.
- Advising the child on the best course of action.
- Being in charge of what you will do and not do.
- Giving conditional support. "You may go when your room is clean."

You may want to think about whether your style of authority is dictatorial or approachable. If you require absolute control, you may be in for some heavy resistance. If you are flexible and willing to adjust parameters when it seems necessary, you may have an easier time with your child. It does a child a disservice to abdicate authority to her, creating an unfortunate individual who cannot function in society.

## Parents Lose Their Sense of Priority

When a willful child is allowed to rule the family, parents primarily focus on problems posed by the child's dominant behavior and ignore what should be higher priorities. Overwhelmed by concern for the child, parents think and talk of little else. They set everything else aside to focus on the child, soon feeling trapped by the child, usually growing angry and resentful.

Actually, they are not trapped by the child. They are trapped by their preoccupation with the child and sacrifices they have made. Now they begin to blame the child for what lack of adequate self-care and lack of marital care are starting to cost—stress on each of them and erosion of the marriage relationship. "You're driving us crazy and ruining our marriage with all the conflict you cause between us!" No. The parents are electing to drive themselves crazy and to neglect the marriage on the child's behalf.

 **Alert**

One risk of parenting a strong-willed child is neglecting other siblings. Parents must not become so absorbed in coping with the demands of their strong-willed child that they ignore the less urgent but equally important needs of other children in the family.

There are certain functional priorities that a healthy family should have. The first priority is for both parents to take adequate care of their individual selves so that each has enough energy and positive attention to devote to other members of the family. The second priority (if there are two parents in the home) is to take good care of the marriage so their partnership is nourished and their parenting remains united. And the third priority is taking care of the children's needs and wants.

 **Essential**

Parents frequently set aside their needs to attend to those of their child. The child is best served when the individual and marital needs of parents are taken care of first. Stressed, divided parents are unlikely to create a stable and supportive consistent family structure on which their child can securely depend.

By elevating the willful child to number one, he is inappropriately empowered, parental energy gets run down, and the marriage becomes more estranged and conflicted from lack of adequate attention. Take good care of yourselves first and your marriage second, and healthy family functioning, upon which the child's welfare ultimately depends, tends to follow. To take good care of your children, put them last.

## Parents Can See Nothing but Negative

The most telling, and the most damaging, characteristic of parents who are ruled by a strong-willed child is an overwhelming negative attitude toward her. This negativity has massive damaging effects. It discourages the child from making efforts to self-correct, because there is nothing positive to work for in the relationship. "All you ever do is get angry, threaten, criticize, or punish, so why should I do what you want?" It discourages the child, who comes to see herself fitting the terms parents describe. "My parents say I'm nothing but trouble. They're right, I am!" It discourages parents because the more negative they feel, the more negative they act, and the more negative their willful child usually acts in response. "The more we punish, the more determined she becomes not to do what we ask!"

It diminishes your self-esteem because as you grow more negative toward your child, you grow more negative toward yourself. "We're just lousy parents; that's the bottom line!" This dynamic is extremely destructive. What both parents and child need at this point is to be pumped up with positive regard. When parents cease to recognize and reward the good in their willful child's behavior, they end up losing the greatest power of influence they have— positive caring.

It is the responsibility of parents to keep the broadest possible picture of their child so that any problem that arises is kept in a larger perspective. Unhappily, embattled parents of a strong-willed child often cannot see the forest for the trees. They can't see all that is going well because they are so focused on what is going wrong.

Particularly when the willful child's choice seems self-defeating (falling grades from not completing some homework) or potentially self-destructive (engaging in periodic substance use), parents may equate the problem with the person, even though the willful child protests against this restrictive and unrealistic identification. "Bad grades are not all I am!" "Using pot is not all I do!"

 **Fact**

> When a willful child makes wrong-headed choices, parents must remember that any problem is a small part of a large person who performs well in other areas of life. Without this larger perspective, both parents and child are at risk of ignoring positive functioning and personal strengths that could otherwise be helpfully called into play.

The first step parents need to take when working with their child to help correct a persistent problem is to list everything else that is going well, to appreciate all the good choices the child is making and all the bad choices that she's not making. "Your attendance, class work, and test scores are good; it's just not doing homework that is bringing your grades down." "You're taking care of business at school, you're driving responsibly, you're holding down a part-time job, you help out and do your chores at home, you do so much that we appreciate. It's just that your smoking pot on some weekends with friends is causing us concern."

## Parents Are Scattered and Distracted

When a willful child is allowed to rule the family, parents become increasingly disorganized in the structure and discipline they provide. This disorganization only creates more freedom for their child. The more disorganized and scattered they are, the more confused they become, and the more they lose touch with their parenting priorities. In a confused, disorganized family, the willful child gains more ruling power. One way for parents to minimize this negative trend is to make certain they are following and developing their own interests. This takes the heat off the child.

## Scattered Attention

When a willful child rules the family, urgently pushing here and intensively resisting there, parents can move into crisis management mode, just coping with incidents and outbursts as they occur. Parenting moment to moment in this way, their attention becomes scattered as they try to cope with the latest outburst or incident at the expense of sustaining important child-raising priorities. "Sure, we know teaching him habits of picking up after himself, asking for instead of taking what he wants, and following rules for safety are all important, but when he's always throwing tantrums, we forget the bigger picture." Do whatever you need to do to regain your objectivity and perspective. Back off a little and regain your vision of what you want for your family and your child's future.

### Essential

Parents must keep their larger training objectives clearly in mind and not allow themselves to become scattered by the multiplicity and intensity of the willful child's demands. When they get lost in coping moment to moment, they will lose touch with larger parenting priorities, and the willful child will only gather more power.

Living in chaos is confusing. It's hard to keep your focus. It's hard to remember training issues that matter most. It's hard to keep a sense of priority. Out of confusion, comes uncertainty about what happened and what should happen. "What did I really say? I can't remember." "What should I do? I can't decide." The outcome of uncertainty, begotten by confusion from crisis management, is hit-or-miss parenting—just doing something, anything, to respond to the moment. The willful child is definitely in charge.

It may seem artificial, but it is worth writing down your priorities. To remain clear about your parenting priorities, and to not fall prey to confusion from becoming scattered, post a list of your most important objectives where you can see it each day. For example, "Our priorities each day are to (1) Teach our child to speak in respectful and not hurtful language; (2) Teach our child not to hit or take; (3) Teach our child to stop and listen when we speak; (4) Teach our child to fit into the family schedule." A written reminder can refocus attention.

### Becoming Distracted

It takes consistency to maintain discipline, to train a child to live within family rules and to act according to family values. Because a willful child can test parental tolerances and contest their authority on so many fronts, it is easy for parents to be distracted from attending to one issue when the child raises another—a strategy willful adolescents use all the time.

"I was in the process of checking to see if homework had been taken care of when he began arguing about his right to privacy. Then, when I shifted focus to address the issue of privacy, he turned on the TV, which he knows is against the rules until after his homework is done!" Push, push, push! Keeping parents off base is one way a willful child is able to rule the family. It's not that discipline breaks down so much as that it is never given enough consistent application to take hold. In this case, the parent should have remained on the topic of homework and ignored other distractions until the checking was complete. No matter the distractions, deal with one issue at a time.

## Parents Focus on What They Can't Control

When a willful child is allowed to rule the family, parents suffer two common losses: loss of self-consciousness and loss of responsibility. In each case, they focus on what they can't control at the expense of attending to what they can.

## Loss of Self-Consciousness

Consider the parents who are in constant struggle to put their willful child to bed on time. They're very clear about where the problem lies: "It's her bedtime behavior that's causing all the trouble. She refuses to stay put. She's always getting up to ask for one more thing. It's infuriating! But no matter how angry we get, she fights us every night until she's finally so exhausted she falls asleep. By then, we're so tired from the struggle, we end up bickering between ourselves!"

By placing the problem on the child's behavior, the parents have lost focus on their own, which they do control. What's going on here is an interaction between parents and child at bedtime that is resulting in the child's refusing to stay in bed.

Perhaps, if they would focus on their own conduct, they might identify some changes in themselves that might make a difference. For example, instead of acting angry and unloving, which may cause the child to act frightened and cling for additional parental contact, putting off dreaded time alone, they might want to create a playful ritual that would help bedtime feel welcome, peaceful, and secure.

## Alert

When they focus on the willful child's conduct in a problem interaction (refusal to talk) and ignore their own (criticizing a decision), parents reduce their capacity to influence what's going on. Often the best way to get a change in their child's behavior is to change their own. Suppose, instead of criticizing, they asked, "Can you help us understand how you came to make that choice?"

## Loss of Responsibility

Good advice for parents of a willful child is "Don't play the blame game." Overwhelmed by insistent demand and stubborn refusal, parents can get fed up and run down, venting their displeasure by blaming the child for their unhappy state. "Of course we're irritable. It's our daughter's fault! If she weren't so obstinate and demanding, we wouldn't be so cranky!"

Blame casts off responsibility, empowering the person blamed and victimizing the blamer. When a willful child is allowed to rule the family, parents usually concede this domination through casting blame.

## Parents React

When a willful child is allowed to rule the family, parents react too much of the time. Of course, when a child is born, parents are immediately put on the reactive. They respond when discontent and distress are expressed; they try to figure out what the infant wants and needs; and they often feel the little child is calling the shots as they adjust to the fussing, feeding, playing, and sleeping patterns of this newcomer in the family. As the child grows older, parents are gradually able to conform his schedule to better suit their own, and the child increasingly responds to the demands of the parents.

### Essential

Although parents should hold the willful child responsible for choices he makes and the consequences, they must be careful not to shift responsibility for their feelings to the child through blame: "Our unhappiness is our child's fault!" By victimizing themselves, they arm the child with the belief that he is in charge of their well-being. This is not a good thing for the child to believe.

When the child is by nature or nurture strong-willed, however, parents can remain on the reactive and get in the habit of putting their own initiatives on hold, waiting to see what their willful child wants or does before deciding how to act. When this habit of parental reactivity takes shape, they have given that child too much ruling power. "We rarely make family plans anymore because we don't know what kind of mood he'll be in or how he'll act. Mostly we base what we do on what he's done, is willing to do, or will do next. A lot of times it's easier to let him lead the way." This is a dreadful way to run a family.

## Taking Initiative

Willful children are more demanding to live with in two ways. They literally tend to make more demands than other children do, and they are more intense about the demands they make. In the face of the rate and intensity of these demands, it is understandable that parents would become focused on responding to what the child wants and doesn't want to do.

To take back initiative with their willful child, parents have to bravely become more demanding in the relationship. For example, consider the prickly fourteen-year-old who is currently ruling the family. "He's always arguing and up for a fight at the slightest question we ask or request we make, and gets really impatient with us when we don't do what he wants right away. So for the sake of peace and quiet, we've learned to tiptoe around his bad moods, which are most of the time, and approach him just when he seems approachable, which isn't very often. We can usually tell how bad his day has been by how hard he slams the front door when he gets home and by how quickly he storms off to his room to be left alone."

How can parents take back the initiative? They can greet him at the door with questions and demands, and when he tries to back them off, they can brush his intensity and objections aside in determined pursuit of the information they want and the tasks they need accomplished. Often some conflict is provoked for parents when they move to take initiative back, but if they are resolved to show they mean business, if they don't back off or back down, and if they keep up their demands, the child will come around. He will grudgingly accept that, when it comes to interaction in the family, parents are going to initiate the most demands.

## Setting the Agenda

What happens when the child begins to increasingly set the agenda for the family? As parents become more reactive to the child, their loss of influence is the child's gain. "I want us to go out to eat tonight!" declares the child to parents who had been planning for them all to eat at home. Then they explain and he complains. They become firm. He starts to whine and soon becomes upset. They begin to waver. Now he sweetens up to soften them up. And finally, to avoid a tiring conflict at the end of a long day, they let him have his way. The child's agenda has prevailed.

Taking back control of the family agenda requires proactive parenting. Parents have to plan what they want to have happen, declare that plan to the child, and stick to that plan even when the child objects. To get control of the family agenda back where it belongs, parents can start each day informing the child about the schedule of planned events and arrangements that have been made. Certainly they can ask for the child's input to better encourage his cooperation, but the main point that preplanning makes is that the parents, not the child, are in charge of organizing the flow of family events.

## CHAPTER 8

# Building Blocks for Getting Back in Charge

There are pervasive ideas in our culture that lead parents to be overindulgent toward children. Maybe it's some sort of collective guilt because everyone is working and feeling neglectful of the next generation. However, you are not responsible for what everyone else thinks and does. You can separate from that and get your own house back in order. What can you do to regain the family reins? There are steps to take that clear up communication, reset boundaries of responsibility, assess consent, assert authority, and regain a positive outlook. Be forewarned: This will feel like turning around the *Titanic*.

## Getting Communication to Work

By the time a willful child is ruling the family, parental communication with that child has usually fallen into considerable disarray. What you say and how you say it often incites the child to become more entrenched in acting in ways you do not want. Since verbal communication is chosen behavior, not genetic or fixed, parents can change the tone and content of their speech. You always can improve what has gone wrong.

## Communication That Doesn't Work

Here are some don'ts to consider:

- **Don't be critical.** Willful children are extremely sensitive to criticism. Because they get so much of it, they are on guard against it. Rather than receive what you have to say, they will block it out or fight you back.
- **Don't be overly emotional.** Willful children are already intense. Adding your own emotion, particularly when in existing conflict, only arouses more emotion in the child.
- **Don't be abstract.** Using vague or general terms to express your disagreement only communicates disapproval without clarifying specific charges that are causing you offense. "You are a day late taking your belongings out of the living room as you promised," is better. Focus on the behavior only.
- **Don't be inconsistent.** Selective enforcement of significant rules only communicates that sometimes you mean business and sometimes you do not. Given this mixed message, the willful child will gamble that you don't.
- **Don't be locked in.** Don't stick to disciplinary decisions that don't work only because you are too tired to think of anything else—this only demonstrates how discouraged you have become. You must keep trying something different until something works—for a while.
- **Don't be impatient.** Most willful children are already too impatient for their own good. Don't encourage this trait by modeling impatience of your own. Impatience only speeds up a sense of urgency and empowers impulse when both parent and child would be better served by more deliberate decision making that slows things down.
- **Don't get distracted.** Stick to the issue at hand until it is settled, and don't let your child shift the focus to something else. Distraction is the enemy of resolution. Distraction favors your willful child by throwing you off the subject of discussion. Be alert!

- **Don't be negative.** The more negative you become, the less willingness—cooperation and consent—you will motivate in your child.
- **Don't be accusatory.** The more you attack your willful child for not doing what you want, the more defensive she is likely to become, and the more counterattack will ignite conflict between you. This does not make a happy family.
- **Don't use extremes.** Better not to say "You always" or "You never" when describing misbehavior, because such statements deny or discount those times when willingness you want has been given. "You never do what you're asked!" may feel emotionally true, but it is factually false. You want to be sure to reward with recognition every act of cooperation your child gives you.

## ⓔ✓ Fact

It's not what hardships parents and willful child go through with each other that count most in their long-term relationship; it's how they go through them. And the key to that "how" is communication. Parents and children who openly and effectively communicate through turbulent times end up closely connected. Those who do not, end up estranged.

### Communication That Does Work

Here are some dos to consider.

- **Be careful of using labels.** Even positive labels such as Mommy's Little Man can be limiting. Your aim is to rear a whole person, not an actor in a small play.
- **Do be nonevaluative.** When disciplining, remember that, for your willful child, correction is criticism enough. Any additional judgment is only likely to arouse more resistance. So when some misbehavior has occurred, say, "We disagree

with the choice you have made; here is why; and this is what we need to have happen in consequence."

- **Do be reasonable.** When you model the use of reason in disagreement, and do not resort to emotion, your example encourages the child to adopt a reasonable approach in response. Explain why you want what you want, and then try to negotiate an agreement.

- **Do be operational.** When describing what you want or do not want your child doing, talk contractually in terms of specific behaviors and events. "What I need to have happen is for you to be home by the curfew time on which we agreed."

- **Do be consistent.** If you want to train your child to follow your rules, then you must faithfully articulate and enforce those rules consistently.

- **Do be resourceful.** Keep thinking up new approaches for influencing your child when old ones lose their persuasive power. If your child knows you will never run out of choices, then she knows you will never give up.

- **Do be patient.** Don't get upset or give up if you don't get your way with your willful child right away. Just act like you have all the time and energy it takes to keep insisting until your request is met. The patient message is "I will not be defeated by delay."

- **Do stay focused.** Keep your mind on what matters most. If you don't stick to your parenting priorities, then your child won't either.

- **Do be empathetic.** Show your child that no matter how you may disagree with her actions, your first concern is how she feels. "Before we deal with what happened, I want to hear about what caused you to feel so upset."

- **Do be moderate.** Extreme statements and measures by parents tend to provoke extreme statements and measures in response from the willful child. To keep interactions on an even keel—follow the middle way. "A lot of times you do, sometimes you don't, and this time you didn't."

**Fact**

Old-fashioned courtesy in your communications will go a long way to clean up the relationship between you and your strong-willed child. Use a respectful tone of voice. Ask instead of giving orders. Freely give compliments, praise, and affection. Say "thank you" when your child does well and acts in an agreeable way.

## Clarifying Responsibilities

To get back in charge, parents must be clear about what they are in charge of and what they are not in charge of. Simply put, they are responsible for only their own decision making. They are not responsible for the decision making of their child any more than the child is responsible for the decision making of the parents. This means that parents must be very clear about who is responsible for which behavior. This requires thought.

### Giving Away Too Much Responsibility

Beware the willful promise. When a willful child wants something very much, he will make all kinds of extreme promises to get parents to give permission or to relent.

"If you get me the puppy, I promise I'll do all the care and you won't have to remind me or do any yourselves!"

"If you let me go to the party tonight, I promise I'll stay home the next month of weekends and help around the place with no complaints!"

"If you get me shoes like my friends have, I promise I'll do my chores without having to be nagged!"

Willful promises can sound very persuasive; that's why you might be easily taken in. In most cases, the child promises to take some kind of responsibility in exchange for what he seeks. In many cases, however, the willful child lacks the self-discipline to keep the promises he makes. You end up taking care of the puppy, having to argue to keep the child at home on the weekends as agreed, or pursuing the completion of chores.

You are mistaken in giving in to promises of responsibility the child is not prepared to keep. From past experience, you recognize that the child won't keep his word, but you keep taking it anyway because he is so convincing that you think he means it at the time. Parental hope can be a great deceiver.

## Appropriating Too Much Responsibility

When parents believe that they are in charge of the child's decisions, they take over responsibility that properly belongs to the child. "It's our fault that he started experimenting with drugs. If we hadn't gotten divorced, this never would have happened!" No, their son decided to experiment with drugs. If he is using substances to cope with unhappy feelings stemming from parental divorce, he needs to know and own that he has other choices for managing his unhappiness. The more parents blame themselves, the more their son will deny responsibility, casting it off onto them. Parental guilt can be a great enabler, children gathering unhealthy power of irresponsibility by exploiting parental self-blame. This does no one any good.

 **Essential**

To get back in charge after a willful child has begun to rule the family, parents must clearly and consistently observe appropriate boundaries of responsibility—neither blaming their child for their own decisions nor blaming themselves for the child's decisions.

# Assessing Consent

In the extremity of their frustration, anger, and helplessness with a child who is ruling the family, parents' perceptions of what is going on can become distorted. "She never does anything we want, only what she wants!" This statement is both false and true. It is false because she *sometimes* does do what they want. It is true because the child, like anybody else, only does what she wants to do, even when she doesn't like doing whatever that is.

The first part of the statement can do a lot of damage. If they truly believe she never does anything they want, then they will feel totally defied, and the child will not get recognition or credit for the compliance she sometimes gives. In truth, no child is 100 percent defiant, no matter how it may feel to the parents, and no parents are totally without influence. To some degree, some of the time, even the most difficult child is cooperative. Call this willingness to go along consent.

To get back in charge, parents need to recognize and affirm that all is not lost. Although their willful child seems to be ruling the family, a lot of the time she is giving them consent of two kinds: doing what they want her to do, and not doing what they don't want her to do.

## Identifying Positive Consent

Take a time-out and list out all the things the child is doing that you want her to do. She may be a fussy eater, but she is eating. She may not be doing much homework, but she is going to school and doing class work there. She may sometimes use rude language to you, but she is polite to adults who come over and to adults away from the family. She may be breaking some home rules, but she is following rules at school and social laws. The point is, you are not bankrupt of influence. You are just not having as much influence and getting as much cooperation as you would like.

## Identifying Negative Consent

Next, list out all the things you can think of that she is not doing that you don't want her to do and have told her not to do. The world is full of dangerous and forbidden possibilities open to your child, and you can't change the world. More than that, you are operating a home, not a prison. The child could experiment in all kinds of ways but is not. Why not? Only her choices are keeping her from trying out these negative possibilities. So when assessing consent, credit the child for the dangerous risks and forbidden temptations she is resisting.

For example, although she sometimes comes in after curfew, she is not late for school. Although she sometimes borrows her mother's clothes without asking, she does not shoplift from stores. Although she hangs out with friends who smoke, she is not smoking herself.

### Alert

When parents are in the process of getting back in charge, they should identify and appreciate the positive and negative consent they are being given, because that is the basis on which more consent can be built.

# Asserting Authority

A willful child cannot rule the family unless parents have backed off because of the child's relentless demands over a long period of time. For parents to get back in charge, they must reclaim authority.

There are two criteria for parental authority: parents must say what they mean and mean what they say. "Before you get to play with friends on Saturday, all your weekend chores must be completed." If words fail to convince, parents back up their words with actions to show they mean business. "I'm not driving you over to your friend's until your chores are done."

When a willful child is allowed to rule the family, he has learned that parents don't mean what they say and won't back up what they say with actions. "So what authority is there to respect?" thinks the child. And at the moment, the answer is "not much," since parents caved in to his complaints once again, letting him go without chores accomplished, just as they did last weekend. Rules without enforcement earn no respect. Two kinds of authority need to be restored: corrective authority, which asserts parental influence the child dislikes, and contributive authority, which demonstrates parental powers that the child values receiving.

## Corrective Authority

There are many assertive acts through which parents communicate corrective authority. Consider just a few:

- Requesting information
- Holding the child accountable
- Asking questions
- Confronting issues
- Checking performance
- Giving directions
- Setting conditions
- Applying consequences
- Advising choices
- Stating prohibitions

Through these and other corrective acts, you establish strength with the child. When you start practicing these acts, you can create or reclaim an authoritative presence in the child's life—as long as you mean what you say and are committed to backing up your words with actions if it's required to convince your child that you are serious. When words alone don't work, you must take action to show you mean business.

## 🗸 Fact

In adolescence, the parent as rule maker is more frequently in conflict with the teenager who acts in the role of rule breaker. Just because he doesn't like your rules, doesn't agree with your rules, and sometimes doesn't follow your rules, doesn't mean that he doesn't need the security of your rules to depend on for support and direction. He does, more than ever.

## Contributive Authority

An equally powerful source of authority, which the willful child may take for granted because demanding makes it so easy to get, is contributive authority—acts that demonstrate how parental authority can *benefit* the child. Parents have the power to do many things for the child that the child, no matter how willful, is unable to do for himself. When children experience and appreciate what parental authority is good for ("My parents can help me figure out my homework when I get stuck"), they realize that it is not all bad. Consider just a few of the ways contributive parental authority can be of use:

- For protection
- For advocacy
- For getting help
- For encouragement
- For approval
- For support
- For instruction
- For problem solving
- For providing permission
- For providing resources

So, when going through a parental passage that requires more corrective authority, be sure you find ways to mix into this negative period some times when contributive authority comes into play. "I know I'm on your case a lot to get off the phone to get your school work done, so let's take a break from the supervision and arguments and go out for something to eat." The more you rely on corrective authority, the more you need to maintain acts of contributive authority so your bad influence is lightened by the good.

## Keeping a Positive Perspective

Probably the hardest challenge when parenting a willful child is maintaining a positive attitude in the face of stubborn self-determination and ongoing resistance. Your sense of effectiveness can be worn down to the point that you feel frustrated and helpless a lot of the time, and you may feel isolated and angry.

Anger is an inherently critical emotion. It responds to perceived violations of one's well-being. "This is wrong. This is unfair. This shouldn't happen. This is not what I want. This isn't right." Anger also empowers an expressive, protective, or corrective response. Under the influence of anger, parents can make the situation with their child worse by allowing themselves to become excessively negative.

### The High Cost of Negativity

"After a while we get tired of the constant struggle for compliance and we just wear down," parents confess. And with the use of the term "wear down," they announce the other cause for their discouraged state of mind. They are exhausted. Fatigue can act like a mood-altering chemical that casts a pall of negativity over perception and motivation. "It's all going downhill; there's no point in trying." From chronic negativity grows pessimism.

Negativity lies. It keeps you from recognizing the intermittent consent and cooperation the child gives, and makes you feel like giving up when what's really necessary is keeping on. On the receiving end of this stream of negativity, the child becomes discouraged, too, discouraged from working with parents who apparently believe that all he is good at is doing something wrong. Negative parental outlook becomes self-fulfilling as the child decides to act more headstrong and obstinate than ever. "If trouble is all you think I am, then trouble is how I'm going to act!"

## The Persuasive Power of the Positive

When parenting a willful child, there is a slogan that is helpful to remember: "No deposit, no return." If you will keep contributing positive responsiveness to your child, even when going through a stormy passage, then your child will see the relationship as having positive personal value and will be more inclined to respond well to you. If the only attention the child receives from you is complaints, criticism, and threatened and actual punishment, then you have removed any positive incentive for the child to cooperate with you. "There's no pleasing my parents, so why try?"

Remember that animal trainers do not train animals to do tricks by applying negative reinforcement when the animal fails to perform. Instead, they relentlessly repeat the training exercise, always rewarding effort to keep up the creature's will to try, and rewarding desired outcome when it occurs. The same principle applies to gaining cooperation and consent from a willful child. "It's time to practice putting back your toys again. This is hard to learn, and I appreciate your trying. When you get them all put back on your own, we will celebrate!"

Consider every positive response you give your child as putting money in the bank of his long-term willingness to cooperate with you. And keep positive and negative responses separate from each other. Be negative when you have to, but don't allow the fact that you are going through a prolonged corrective time in pursuit of some behavior change to cause you to diminish the ongoing positive responses you invest in his willingness to work with you.

# 🔔 Alert

To keep from becoming unduly negative with your willful child, practice the rule of two for one. For every negative or corrective response you make, within the next hour find an authentic way to make two positive responses to show how you value the child and appreciate his efforts.

When parents assume authority ("We are in charge because we are the parents"), when they clearly define the family rules ("This is what you can and cannot do"), when they expect compliance ("We know you will behave as you've been taught"), and when they consistently reward consent and correct infractions ("This response is in consequence for what you did"), they will reestablish their leadership role within the family.

## Seeking Outside Help

Sometimes you have exhausted your inner resources and need assistance in coping with a strong-willed child. Ministers and mental health clinics often offer services at a nominal fee. Social service agencies may be of assistance, as well as marriage and family therapists. Psychologists and psychiatrists offer help, and the expense will be greater. When you meet with a counselor for the first time, ask lots of questions and try to determine whether you really feel comfortable with that individual. It's your prerogative to ask about the level of education, specialties and whether the individual has experience with the specific issues you face.

Do not hesitate to shop around a bit and ask for referrals from friends and other professionals in your life. The fit has to be correct in order for you to make progress in your family. Insurance may or may not cover therapy, but then can you place a financial value on mental health for yourself and your family? Is it equal to a new TV or an upgrade on your car? A luxurious vacation?

CHAPTER 9

# Roadblocks to Getting Back in Charge

We live in a time when adults have forfeited some of the rights and responsibilities of being grown up. We have a pervasive youth culture, and lines between youth and maturity become blurred. However, to regain authority in your home, forceful, clear actions must replace formerly ambivalent actions and words. In the case of the violent child, this requires willingness to confront the child in ways that teach nonviolent choices for managing strong emotions and urgent wants. In these cases, parents have to change their attitudes and behavior to bring about acceptable conduct in their willful child.

## The Intractable Child

The intractable child is one whose determined willfulness makes him extremely difficult to govern, to the point that parents often feel it is the child who is running the family. Parents typically feel frustrated, angry, helpless, and even negatively toward the child. Parents in this quandary feel bad about themselves; and have lost the ability to establish a respectful family structure.

It is much easier to give a child power than it is to take it back, and the intractable willful child who is now calling the shots has little incentive to give up the freedom of choice and unbridled influence he has gained. Letting a child become a little dictator does him a disservice in the long run. Such an individual will have a very difficult time in relationships and in the normal functioning within society. Life can be very hard on someone who always expects to be indulged.

Consider parents with an intractable eight-year-old who, among other acts of willfulness:

- Eats snacks when he wants to and doesn't eat meals when he doesn't want to
- Refuses to pick up after himself
- Won't do household chores
- Uses hurtful name-calling when angry
- Takes siblings' belongings when he wants to use them
- Won't come along when parents ask
- Throws tantrums when parents deny him what he wants
- Routinely puts off homework so it rarely gets done

Changing the habits of the intractable child will not happen overnight. It will take concerted effort, and the result will still be a willful child, but one who goes along more with what you want than he did before.

With retraining, you must recognize that your goal is to change habits—patterns of behavior learned through repetition over time until they have become automatic. Your goal is to teach the child a new way to manage frustration, positively rewarding each incident of changed behavior often enough so that more constructive habits are established. The rewards should be emotional, not material, giving the child appreciation, approval, affection, or praise each time he shows improvement.

Of course, prevention is always the best way to approach difficulties with intractable children, but that isn't apparent, except through hindsight! Once better behaviors are in place, however, they will become ultimately precious and worth keeping.

In fact, parents can let the child know during the period of retraining how much they appreciate the changed use of language when frustration has occurred. And when the name-calling recurred, they should have let the child know that now this is the exception, not the rule, and that they are aware of that. The goal of recovering from harmful habits is progress, not perfection.

## Retraining the Intractable Child

It takes clarity and consistency for parents to retrain a child. Retraining takes concerted effort and considerable time. It is not a quick and easy fix. It is worth it to regain your authority.

### Clarifying Structure

The opening step in retraining your freedom-loving child is to clarify the basic parental rules that children in the family are expected to follow. Write out on large paper the five or ten most important rules, explain them to your child, and post this paper in a conspicuous place where it can catch her attention daily. State the rules specifically, not abstractly. Not, "Treat each family member respectfully," but "Ask and be given permission before using another family member's belongings."

Each morning before or after breakfast for the next three months, or for however long it takes for the child to mostly conform to these rules, you and the child will read them aloud. This exercise is partly to remind the child about the behavior you want, and it is partly to represent your renewed seriousness about having rules followed. This exercise not only clarifies what you expect; it shows that you mean business. The specific written statement has symbolic value: the child has been put on notice that you have changed.

### Committing to Priorities

The intractable child is usually acting out of parental bounds in so many areas that it's hard for parents to know where retraining should begin. If you try to change everything at once you will end up changing nothing because the efforts are too scattered to be effective.

Instead, follow the rule of three. At one time, commit to consistently address no more than three behavior areas you'd like to change, and accept that you will only intermittently, as remaining energy permits, keep after the others. This means setting priorities. Which of the misbehaviors do parents consider most in need of change? If they select putting an end to hurtful name-calling as the most important, then patrolling that verbal behavior, acting to discourage its occurrence and to encourage nondestructive alternatives, is where they invest their primary attention until their child learns a more constructive habit of communicating frustration. When the new habit seems mostly in place, then they can drop name-calling from their list of priorities and add another.

 **Fact**

Lack of consistency is the most common failure in parental discipline. Inconsistent discipline keeps parenting from being effective. Stay on your tactics like a broken record.

### Providing Consistent Supervision

When parents swear that they have tried everything to get back in charge, they are mistaken on two counts. First, no parents have tried everything, because there are an infinite number of influential choices they could try. Second, and most important, they don't give what they've tried a fair try—repeating it with enough regularity over time to convince the child to finally change behavior in response.

To retrain your intractable child, you must commit to consistency. If your priority is getting your child to stop using hurtful language when she's frustrated by parental denial, then you must address that expression each and every time it occurs with the correct response until the name-calling diminishes or ceases. You also need to provide constructive alternatives and praise the child when she makes a better choice. "I really appreciated how you took yourself to another room to calm down your frustration when I said 'no,' and then afterward talked to me about your disappointment."

## Connecting Choice and Consequence

At this point you may wish to post a list of daily privileges the child gets to enjoy at home. Privileges are any valued activities that require parental provision or permission. This list may include having a certain snack food, watching a favorite TV program, playing a video game, shooting hoops in the backyard, instant messaging on the computer, or whatever activities the child likes to do.

Then explain, "We want you to get to enjoy your full list of privileges each day, and you can, so long as you follow the rules. That's your choice. Follow the rules and get all your privileges. Break a rule and lose a privilege for that day. If there's no time left that day, then lose a privilege the day after. Choose to follow the rules, and full privileges will be enjoyed for the day. Choose not to follow the rules, and some privilege will be taken away that day. Our wish is that each day you start with full privileges and end up choosing to enjoy them all."

# The Violent Child

Willful children may resort to violent actions to assert power and strengthen dominance in the family. Acts of violence may be used to get his way or to protest not getting his way. They may be used to impulsively act out extreme emotion. They can demonstrate inability or unwillingness to abide by the rules that others follow.

Acts of violence are very serious. If they are allowed to continue, the willful child becomes too powerful and dominant for his own and the family's good, and family members feel too threatened and act too intimidated for their own good. With the willfully violent child, parents must find ways to discourage physically destructive behavior. Hitting, pinching, kicking, biting, hair pulling, threatening harm, throwing or breaking the possessions of others, and the use of abusive language are unsafe behaviors for everyone in the family.

What are some behaviors to watch for that indicate that physical violence could be next?

- Name-calling
- Throwing or destroying objects
- Interrupting and insulting
- Carrying over previous grievances

## ❓ Question

**What's the most important attribute of a healthy family?**
In a healthy family, emotional and physical safety for all concerned must be maintained. Any family violence, by child or adult, must be turned into a public act. Influential outsiders and extended family will be notified and consulted about the problem to help prevent violence from happening again. There will be no secrets.

## Encouraging Nonviolent Behavior

Parental confrontation is the key to discouraging violent behavior in willful children. These approaches are listed in rough order of severity and are generally best used in the order in which they are presented here, going to the next level if less powerful confrontations have not had influential effect.

### Confronting Feelings

Violent children are usually emotionally upset at the time violence is committed. Anger appears to be the driving force, but it usually is not. Anger commonly acts as a protective cover to conceal more vulnerable feelings hidden underneath—sadness, disappointment, betrayal, jealousy, anxiety, rejection, hurt, frustration, embarrassment, humiliation, or shame, for example.

Bypass the action for the moment to penetrate beneath the anger. You need to empathetically confront the child, not with disapproval or punishment, but with emotional concern, to draw out underlying feelings. "You must be feeling terribly hurt to act like that. Please tell me what is going on." By empathetically connecting, you can open up emotional disclosure and discuss what is really going on. Immediately after a violent episode is not the time to talk with the child about what happened, why it happened, and any consequence to follow. When the child is still emotionally upset, there will be no thinking person home. A parent's first step is helping the child to calm down enough so reason and rational discussion are restored.

Violence is acting out strong emotion. Parents want to teach the child to talk out these feelings instead. Turn a destructive act into a constructive discussion about alternative ways to manage whatever unhappiness was going on. Identify any triggering conditions or events that tend to set the child off, like being teased or put down by an older sibling, because there may be mistreatment from others that is involved that needs to be identified and stopped. "I hate it when he calls me fat and stupid!"

Identify and help establish an early warning system so the child can notice when she might be at risk of escalating to a violent response and so can have a plan in readiness for doing something else. "Next time I start feeling left out or put down by the older kids, I will come and talk to you."

Give an emotional reference to the child that expresses how she feels when such an act of violence takes place. "I feel really sad for the family when any one of us acts to hurt each other." If parents grew up in a family where physical abuse was part of life, they may also want to talk about that. "You know, I grew up in a scary family where violence happened and people were physically hurt, where it was hard to trust and difficult to love, and so I really want a family of my own that is violence-free."

### Confronting the Victim

Having the child confront people who are impacted by her violence can catch the child's attention and cause her to rethink her violent acts. Confronting the victim of violence, the child can hear what it felt like to be on the receiving end of what she did. The victim might say to her, "You threw my favorite toy and broke it, the one I worked to buy with my own money! When you hurt my things, you hurt me!" The child can apologize if she genuinely feels sorry, describing the behavior she is sorry for. If not, ask her to give his idea of how she thinks the victim of her violence felt. "You must have felt angry for what I did." And finally, the child can then be expected to make amends for damage done. "I'll do some work to earn the money to buy you another toy just like it."

 **Essential**

> Help the violent child understand the emotional damage done by the violent act by reversing roles. "Tell me how it would feel if someone bigger knocked you down and kept hitting on you."

## Confronting the Consequence of Public Knowledge

In most occasions of family violence, the perpetrator (in this case, the willful child) does not want news of what happened to be broadcast outside of the family because reputation with significant others could be affected. "Don't tell my grandparents!" pleads the child. "I don't want them to know." Make the violent child understand that significant outside others—extended family, close family friends,

other important adults—will be t
lence that he commits. Explain, "V
enough to discourage you from act
outside of family to others who car
we can do." The child learns that priv
receive public attention, that attention

One of the most powerful respon
a willful child engages in family violer
world by letting significant others outsic        ....my know what has
happened, soliciting their advice, and letting the child know his
violent act has become more widely known. Secrecy only enables
family violence.

The long-term consequences of family violence are severe.
Children who are allowed to be violent will become statistics of
crime and domestic abuse in the future. This is not what you wish
for your little one.

## Confronting Concerned Others

If the previous confrontations have failed to persuade the willful child to cease his violent ways, assemble a circle of caring. To
his surprise, the child finds a circle of significant adults assembled
at home, all of whom are there to express caring and support for
him. Include a grandparent, an aunt, an uncle, a couple of close
family friends, a valued teacher, a coach, the parents of a close
friend—any adults whose good opinion would matter to the child.

Like an intervention, these adults are all there to express positive regard and sincere concerns, and what they have to say is non-
critical, only caring. Their mission is:

- To express concern over specific violence that has happened
- To express all the positive regard in which they hold the
  child and why
- To express how they each stand ready to be of help to the
  child in any way they can

o more communication and contact with the
keep up with how he is coming along

### nfronting Social Reality

If the previous confrontations have failed to persuade, you can
put the child on notice that any further acts of violence will cause
you to call in social authority by reporting a family disturbance
to the police. When the police arrive, describe the incident to the
officers, the officers will speak to the child, and the child will have
a chance to speak to the police and hear the trouble that additional
acts of family violence can bring.

### Confronting Outplacement from the Family

If all the previous confrontations fail to persuade the child to
cease his acts of family violence, let the child know that you're considering temporary placement outside the family in a highly struc-
tured situation to teach him nonviolent ways of living. This could
be a treatment facility. It could be a strict residential home. "We
want you to be able to live with us, but if you continue to be a danger to the safety of other family members, then you forfeit the right
to live among us until you have learned better self-control."

 **Fact**

Sometimes extended family can provide the external placement and
learning the violent child needs. For example, a child who is violent in
his immediate family may never resort to such destructive acting out
while living with grandparents, because he respects them too much
and does not want them to see his violent side.

The first step is giving the child this notification. The second
step is to visit a treatment or residential facility. And, if the violence continues, the final step is to exit the child from the family

for outside help for some period of time. The first step should not be considered unless you are serious and feel temporary outplacement from family can teach the child self-discipline that cannot be taught at home.

If you are going to confront the violent child with the possibility of outplacement, it must be presented as a necessary change to preserve safety in the family and not used as a threat, punishment, or rejection. It must be done with love and hope that the child can learn to live by nonviolent choices and very soon be back in the home.

## Confronting Acts of Self-Violence

Of course, when a willfully violent child turns to self-harm or attempted suicide, this calls for a confrontation with a mental health agency or psychiatric unit at a hospital for an immediate risk assessment. The child needs to know that you will take any self-destructive behavior so seriously that you will immediately seek outside intervention.

Most self-cutting occurs in early and midadolescence (between ages nine and fifteen) and is actually not suicidal. It is done for drama, to attract attention and impress friends, or to socially fit in by copying what friends are doing. It is also done to create and control physical pain as a way to manage existing emotional pain. The child needs help developing healthier ways to get attention, socially belong, and cope with pain.

A child's suicide is the act of violence parents most dread. Four common conditions, singly or in combination, in the child's life that can trigger suicidal thoughts need to be taken seriously:

- **Isolation**—the child does not communicate about personal problems or hurt feelings with others
- **Distortion**—the child does not keep a realistic perspective during adversity or stress

- **Despondency**—the child becomes depressed in response to a performance failure or relationship loss
- **Substance abuse**—the child relies on self-medication to escape from unhappiness or pain

Suicidal talk, threats, plans, or attempts must be taken literally and confronted by the consequence of an external risk assessment. "I didn't really mean I was going to kill myself," protests the child. "I was just kidding to get you upset." Reply the parents, "Suicidal talk is no joking matter. We will check out the seriousness of your intent." Make it known that violence to oneself, just like violence to others, is not an acceptable option.

## CHAPTER 10

# Handling Discipline

D iscipline is the combination of parental instruction and parental correction through which a child is taught to live according to family values and to act within family rules. Since no two families subscribe to exactly the same values and rules, every child learns a unique pattern of behavior and carries a unique code of personal conduct into adulthood. Informed parents adjust the types of discipline according to the age of the child, shifting from the loving guidance for a two-year-old to the more contractual negotiation appropriate for a teenager. However be wary when negotiation veers into the realm of bribery. This creates an atmosphere of uncertainty for the child.

## The Goal of Discipline

The ultimate goal of parental discipline is to work parents out of their job. Effective discipline needs to be 90 percent instructional and positive and no more than 10 percent corrective and negative. When this ratio becomes reversed, as so easily happens with a willful child, particularly with a willful adolescent, the child's behavior becomes worse, not better. Keep in mind that your goal is to raise a person who is capable of comfortably functioning in society at large. Being in charge of your domain may bring on feelings of fear that your child will no longer like you or that you're not necessarily the nice guy you imagined. The end result is worth it.

Relying exclusively on corrective measures to change your willful child only encourages more resistance. "And we'll keep punishing you until your attitude improves!" But the outcome of your efforts is a more sullen child. The most powerful incentive for desirable behavior you can provide is ongoing affirmation for who and how the child is. Everyone hungers for affirmation of self, and you are in a position to give that, daily, to your child.

Strong-willed children often test parental rules because they are so independently inclined. The realistic hope is not to get 100 percent compliance. That is not a realistic expectation. The parents' job is to keep asserting those family rules and values in order to encourage the child to follow a healthy path in life. When parents give up on disciplinary leadership, they deprive the child of the opportunity for healthy choice. Parents who relinquish this leadership, by default, give their child other, less caring and reliable influences (like peers) to follow. This is not what you want for your child's future.

 **Essential**

> With a willful child, the best parents can do is work for compromise. They must accept that they will not get their way all the time, only some of the time, to some degree. This is a realistic expectation: some has to be enough. The same expectation holds for the willful child. Only some of the time, to some degree, will he get his way.

## Respecting Choice

Strong-willed children want to be self-directed. They want personal choice. So, when your child is acting most obstinate or insistent, it is always worth questioning her: "Tell me why, help me understand why making this decision is so important to you." Sometimes your empathy with the child's intense desire for self-determination can avert automatic acting out by opening up a discussion that allows you to influence the choice being made.

Instead of immediately censoring a clothing decision, the mother asks why the child is making that decision. So the child explains, "I'm going to tear my jeans at the knee because that's the different look I want to take to school. I don't want to be like everyone else." "Thank you for helping me understand," replies the parent. "Now I understand that you are not just trashing your new jeans. You want to dress in your own individual way. How about this? Suppose I help you bleach the knees so they look worn, but are untorn? Would you be willing to try that?" And so understanding mother and willful child reach a working compromise—more than the mother wanted but less than the child desired.

 **Fact**

> A big part of effectively parenting a willful child depends on the parent's skill at finding the middle way in disagreements where absolutes, such as "must" or "can't," are not at stake.

## Separation of Powers

Your willful child needs to know that the only choices you, as parent, are concerned with controlling are your own. When the child says "You can't make me!" or "You can't stop me!" you need to immediately agree. "That's right. Your choices are always up to you, just as my choices are always up to me."

Then you need to repeat one more time the parent rules—the rules you are duty-bound to follow in order to be a responsible parent. You can preface the rules by saying something like this: "Being a responsible parent isn't always easy, popular, or fun, because I sometimes have to make decisions you don't like. Because these decisions will sometimes be opposed to what you want, you may think I am not on your side. But that is not true. When I take a stand against what you want, it is for what I believe are your best interests." Then state the parent rules:

"I am supposed to:

- Set limits to keep you safe
- Tell you information and teach you skills you need to know
- Keep after you to get tasks done and to build healthy habits
- Set a good example for you to follow
- Determine which freedom is okay now and which must wait
- Give you more work and responsibility as you grow
- Provide for your care until you are able to support yourself
- Listen when we disagree and be willing to have the final say
- Commit to the fact that, no matter how we disagree, you will always have my love."

## 🅔❗ Alert

A rested child is more inclined to cooperate than an exhausted child. A calm child is more inclined to listen than one who is emotionally upset. Therefore, it is in the interests of effective discipline to keep your willful child adequately rested and to encourage calmness by acting calm yourself. Take care of your own rest, as well.

### Choice-for-Choice Contracting

"Why should I?" asks the willful child, objecting to a request or a demand. Sometimes, in response, the parent can persuade: "Because I'm busy doing the cooking and I need your help." At other times, however, you need to appeal to the child's self-interest by connecting her personal choice with your parental response if she does not comply as asked. While respecting the willful child's power of choice, you must also teach the child to respect your power of choice. Parents can explain choice-for-choice contracting like this:

"Your choices are entirely up to you."

"My choices are entirely up to me."

"If you agree to do what I ask, this is what I will choose to do."

"If you refuse to do what I ask, this is what I will choose to do."

"Which response I give depends a lot on what you do."

To be effective, choice-for-choice contracting should not be done in anger or as a threat. State it matter-of-factly, as you would when describing how some household mechanism works. You are giving information and notification. "It's pretty simple, really. If you choose this, then I choose that." After your child makes her choice—to do her chores, to give you help, to abide by your rule—follow through as stated. "Because you chose to help me, I choose to do what you asked." You empower the child by respecting her choice and giving her influence over your response.

 **Fact**

> During early adolescence (ages nine to thirteen), earning and warning systems become less effective, as the more rebellious child now sees these tactics as power plays by parents and refuses to go along. "When you tell me what you'll give me if I do what you want, that's not a reward, that's a threat! If I don't do what you want, then I don't get what you promised! No way!"

## Earning Systems and Warning Systems

With preadolescent children, up to about age eight or nine, two time-honored kinds of choice-for-choice contracting are earning systems and warning systems. Both systems give children a chance to think ahead and weigh personal choice in light of consequences—the kind of choice parents will make in response.

Earning systems attach credits to cooperative choices; warning systems attach penalties to noncooperative choices. Using an earning system, the parent can promise, "If you feed the dog every day this week, by the weekend you will have earned a lunch out for you and a friend." Using a warning system, the parent can promise, "If by the count of three you have not ended your game and started setting the table for supper, you will get no dessert." In each case, the child has the choice to make the system work in her favor or not.

## Consistency Matters Most

What is the most important principle for disciplining a strong-willed child? Consistency.

Consistently clarify what you want and do not want to have happen. "You will come home at the time we agreed and you will not be late."

Consistently commit to back up what you want. "If you are late, I will come and get you, and for a while you will have less freedom to go out than you had before."

Consistently continue to restate and back up what you want. "As before, when you go over to a friend's, I set a time for your return."

Parental consistency does not guarantee 100 percent compliance from a strong-willed child, but it does help maximize the influence you have. It is in the nature of a willful child to test rules to see if they are firm or flexible, to see if you are just making noise or actually taking a stand. It is as if the willful child is thinking, "The only way to know if my parents mean business about what I can do is to disobey and see what happens. If they don't back off or back down, then I know they're serious."

When it comes to respecting parental demands and limits, willful children are often not one-trial learners. They will contest what they are told to see if it holds true. Say it and show that you mean it, and you stand a good chance of turning your willful child into a believer.

## Making Rules Stick

It is tiring to repeatedly state and stick to what you say when you're tired and feel like slacking off. But being inconsistent with a willful child is even more exhausting because of the double message you send: "Sometimes we mean what we say and sometimes we don't." Just as a willful child comes to respect the firmness of "always," he can find it hard to resist exploiting the weakness of "sometimes."

 **Essential**

> Parental inconsistency is an invitation to the willful child to test his willful way. When parents create an exception to a requirement by upholding it inconsistently, the willful child often will use that opening to break the rule.

## Identifying Compliance

When tired parents become discouraged into believing that they have lost all influence with their willful child, it can be helpful to locate a baseline of compliance. To do so, parents need to answer a simple but significant question: "Where does our willful child regularly and without protest do what we ask?" It seems like never.

On sober reflection, they will be able to find some area of discipline where the child always seems to give compliance. Because this area feels like the exception to the rule of argument and resistance, the parents have paid it scant attention. What a mistake! They ignore where their discipline is working.

The parents may grudgingly admit, "He never gives us trouble at bedtime. He gets right in, on time, with no delay or complaint." Why is that? "Because," they explain, "he knows that by the end of the day we're in no mood to put up with any nonsense and we want some adult time by ourselves." And how does he know? "From experience," they say. "One thing we've never given an inch on is his bedtime. We've made our expectations clear from the beginning. He takes it for granted because that's how we've always been."

And once they realize that, they can recognize that as the baseline model for getting compliance. That's the one area of discipline they've consistently shown to be nonnegotiable, and therefore not worth challenging. So now they must apply this to other areas of his behavior to get compliance. Make it clear what is nonnegotiable.

### ✅ Fact

There's a learning curve for everything, including discipline. Parents who learn to teach discipline the fastest, and children who learn to accept discipline the fastest, both depend on one factor more than on any other: consistent parental instruction and correction.

## Principles of Noninflammatory Discipline

With a willful child, the first guideline for parents is to not inflame the situation by unwittingly increasing the child's tendency to resist. To this end, there are four principles of noninflammatory discipline that parents should consistently follow.

### Keep Discipline Nonemotional

The more calm, reasoned, and matter-of-fact parents act, the more they encourage that quality of response. "As we agreed the last time, if you take and break your brother's toy again, you will have to use what money you've saved to buy him another." Mix discipline with emotional intensity and a willful child will become emotional in response.

### Keep Discipline Nonevaluative

The less critical and judgmental parents act when giving a correction, the less likely the willful child will become defensive in return. Practice this mantra of correction until it becomes second nature: "We disagree with the choice you have made; this is why, and this is what we need to have happen in consequence." Correction is criticism enough.

### Keep Discipline Nonargumentative

The more you debate whether a behavior was wrong, the more argument you encourage. The more invested in changing your mind the willful child becomes, the more she believes resolution is a matter of competition, and the angrier she feels when she discovers it is not. Explain, but don't debate. Be willing to discuss to understand. Don't argue with a child.

### Keep Discipline Noncoercive

The more you try to emotionally or physically force your way, the more you threaten to take away or overwhelm the willful child's decision-making power, the more determined to fight to preserve that power the child becomes. Instead, simply explain the choice you need the child to make, and then explain what will be your responses to compliance or noncompliance. Force makes things worse, not better.

## Guidance

Of the four major delivery systems for discipline—guidance, supervision, structure, and working the exchange points—guidance is the most influential because it offers the most instructional power. The purpose of guidance is to guide the child with the best understanding you can provide. This is accomplished by giving constant feedback about which choices the child is making that are working well and which choices are not. Emphasize the child's range of choice and you are likely to receive cooperation.

Guidance is how parents support good decisions, to discourage bad ones, to advise, to inform, to editorialize, and to educate about life. Children who are blessed with a parent who is not afraid to speak up always know where that parent stands, always have an adult reference to guide them, and always can count on an honest response to how they are conducting their lives.

 **Fact**

Communication is the most powerful source of parental influence in general, and it's the most powerful response to an infraction that parents have to give. Your constant guidance is not designed to control the child's choice but to continually inform the child's choice about what good lessons can be learned from bad experiences and what is wise. The best parents never abdicate their rights of speaking up.

## Why Children Resist Guidance

With a strong-willed child, parental guidance can be resisted and resented on the principle of independence. "You don't have to tell me! I know all about it! I don't have to be told! I don't need your opinion! I can figure it out!" Self-determined to be left to his own devices, the willful child doesn't want the parent butting in. But interfering with a mature perspective is a parent's job. Otherwise, the child will be left at the mercy of personal ignorance and the ignorance of peers.

"What's the point of giving guidance if my child doesn't want to hear what I say, doesn't understand the importance of what I say, doesn't agree with what I say, and doesn't do what I say? Why waste the words?"

It is never a waste to give guidance to your child, because children always listen to their parents. Whether the child wants to hear what you have to say, understands the importance of what you say, agrees with what you say, or actually does what you say has no bearing on the value of the guidance you give. The value of parental guidance is the mature, caring, adult frame of reference for making decisions and the perspective for sorting out what is happening in the child's world. The first purpose of guidance is for parents to define for the child what they believe and where they stand.

## ⊛ Essential

Parental guidance is in the business of informing the child's understanding, not controlling the child's choice. Your wise, informed experience carries weight.

How to give guidance to a willful child is the issue. You don't want to give guidance in any way that is likely to make the child defensive. So refrain from criticism, argument, worry, anger, threats, and emotional upset in general. These will not keep the child from hearing what you have to say, but they will reduce the likelihood of following what you have to say.

Effective guidance is not in the business of forcing your opinion or changing the child's mind. Thus, instead of challenging the child's belief, formed by trusted middle school peer informants, that inhalants can't do any harm, simply offer an alternative perspective: "I understand what you've been told. Here is another way to think about huffing inhalants. Good scientific research has shown that those chemicals can permanently damage the brain. Just so you know."

### Creating Talking Points

Because the willful child is so insistent on self-determination, he is apt to be defensive when making a mistake or having a problem, treating the parental response as a criticism for not taking care of business effectively. "I know, I know! Just get the punishment over with. I don't want to talk about it!" The willful child just wants to be done with the correction, omit the discussion, and go on about his business.

But correction should never be the primary consequence when a willful child gets into difficulty or commits an infraction. The primary consequence needs to be communication and instruction, extracting guidance from an unhappy situation by turning what happened into a talking point so the child can learn from hard experience. "I will let you know later about what restitution you need to make for what you did. First, you and I will discuss how you got into that situation, what led you to make that decision, and how you can avoid getting into that kind of trouble again. Although I wish this hadn't happened, since it did, I want you to be able to learn all you can from the experience so you'll be better informed from now on."

## Supervision

The second major delivery system for discipline is supervision—the willingness of parents to relentlessly keep after the willful child to do what she has been asked or has agreed to do.

Supervision is nagging, honorable, and onerous work, the drudgework of parenting. If there are two parents in the home, it can be shared; otherwise unequal supervision can divide the marriage. The nagging parent is resented for her thankless efforts and feels resentful toward the more popular parent who is better liked because of how he lets supervision slide by.

When parents supervise, they demonstrate with their repeating and reminding that they mean business about what they asked or to what the child agreed. "And I'll keep after you and after you and after you until your chores get done."

Effective supervision requires emotionally sober insistence. Keep emotions out of it. When parents get frustrated in their pursuit, the child learns that delay has the power to get them emotionally worked up. Therefore, when in the process of supervision you feel yourself emotionally heating up, pass supervision on to the other parent, or take a break, cool down, and then take up the pursuit later. Remember, part of being a willful child is a dislike of being directed, interfered with, or interrupted. When it comes to supervision, effective parents never give up.

You will find that the degree of supervision changes as the child matures. Little ones may need a lot of measures for safety and simple routines around the house. As your adolescent is preparing for independent living, the amount of supervision and the type will change. Your goal is to relinquish all supervision so the child is ultimately on her own.

## ⊕ Alert

In general, don't assign more chores than you have energy to supervise. If you commit to more demands than you can supervise, you risk encouraging your willful child to exploit the inconsistency of your attention because it appears that you didn't really mean it.

### Supervision as Pursuit

The most common supervisory issues that parents pursue are those in which ongoing performance of basic responsibilities is required—like doing chores and homework. Sometimes parents punish a willful child for not discharging one of these responsibilities. This is a mistake. Punishment is applied where a child has chosen to violate a family rule. The parent says, "Since you chose to disobey, there will be a consequence for your choice."

Not discharging an ongoing responsibility, however, must not be treated as a matter of choice. The child cannot choose to get out of doing chores or homework. She can only delay the inevitable, because eventually parental pursuit on these matters will catch up to her and she will get them done. The willful child needs to know that parental supervision of basic responsibilities is like death and taxes—inevitable. There is no escape.

## Supervision as Surveillance

One form of supervision is surveillance. This means being willing to invade the child's world to make sure she is where she said she would be. You may call the parents of the child's friend to see if the child is really there as promised, or whether she is only using that destination as a cover to escape elsewhere. Or you may make sure that your child and friends really went into the movie theater as agreed and didn't just duck in and then skip out to wander the mall.

Supervision is also checking up on your child. It is invasive of privacy, and the more willful your child, the more she will resent this intrusion. "You should respect my right to privacy and not go snooping through my room, computer, and personal belongings!" But privacy is not a child's right. It is a privilege of personal freedom that parents grant the child based on trustworthy behavior. If the child is showing signs of trouble but refusing to communicate, parents may want to exercise their right of search and seizure and inspect what she holds private to discover clues to what is really going on.

# Structure

The third major delivery system for discipline is structure—the willingness of parents to specify major rules of social conduct that the child is expected to obey. These are the limitations and obligations that you intend to hold your child responsible for observing. For example, "Within the family there is no hurtful name-calling, no hitting, and no taking of other people's belongings allowed; and you will keep your promises, tell us the truth, and communicate in a respectful way." These prohibitions and obligations communicate basic parental values and provide a basic structural framework within which good habits of behavior can be learned. The structure of rules that parents provide is only as strong as the parents' determination to enforce these rules with consequences when children violate them. When it comes to providing structure, parents have three responsibilities: to explain the rules, to enforce the rules, and to express appreciation for following the rules.

Willful children, because they are inclined to play by their own rules, often question parental rules. You must expect these questions, answer as honestly as you can ("Because we want to keep you safe," "Because this is a value we believe in"), and then stand by your rule when the child pronounces your explanation not good enough.

## Consequences for Violations of Rules

When a child breaks a rule, you apply consequences to catch the child's attention, cause him to rethink what happened, and hopefully discourage him from repeating that choice again. The goal of punishment is to teach a lesson that convinces the child not to repeat the infraction. Three powerful consequences are natural consequences, a good talking-to, and reparation.

Natural consequences are often enough to teach a corrective lesson without parents' having to add any additional consequences of their own. Going against the rules, the child plays with fire and gets burned. Lesson learned.

A good talking-to is often the most disliked consequence of all. "And you're going to sit here and listen for as long as it takes me to say everything I want to say about what I feel and think about what you've done." After ten minutes, the chastened child asks, "Are you done?" Replies the steadfast parent, "Honey, I'm not even warmed up yet!" Children hate a lecture most of all.

Reparation is giving the rule breaker some work to do he would not normally have to do before he gets to do anything else he wants to do. Reparation is much more influential than taking something away because the child has to do particular actions to work off the offense. Some parents keep a list of jobs in need of doing around the home posted on the refrigerator door—jobs that can be accomplished through reparation work should major violations occur.

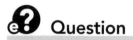

## Question

**Why isn't spanking listed as a consequence for rule breaking?**
Because spanking just teaches that hitting is okay if you are bigger than the other person and want to get your way. If you get physical with a willful child, you will get more determined opposition back than you had before, from a child who now feels humiliated and resentful for being pushed around.

Reserve the application of punitive consequences for major rule violations. Delaying chores, forgetting homework, playing music too loud, talking too late on the phone, leaving the refrigerator door open again, and other similar infractions are not grounds for punishment. These are simple guidance issues. Parents who punish for every offense end up losing disciplinary influence. "Big deal, you're going to punish me again."

In general, unless the situation is an intractable one, refrain from using deprivation like social grounding or withdrawal of household privileges to punish a willful child. Because freedom is so important, taking some away will only cause resentment and increase resistance, as happens when parents ground a social child for falling effort and failing grades in middle school. Performance usually gets worse. In adolescence, punishment for falling grades reduces academic motivation. Supervisory support is what is needed instead.

## Alert

If you feel you must use deprivation, never, ever punish a willful adolescent by taking away a pillar of self-esteem—an interest or activity or relationship in which the child invests and gains self-affirmation. Causing a child to feel bad about himself takes away any chance of cooperation. Pillars of self-esteem are sacred and should never be subject to deprivation. Take away something else less important.

"If you can't bring your homework home, I will meet you at the end of school and together you and I shall walk the halls to pick it up and bring it home. If you don't turn your homework in, I will go to school with you and together we shall walk the halls to turn it in. And if you are unable to sit still, not bother other students, and get class work done, I will take time off from work and sit beside you to help you do what the teacher asks." Many of the common causes of achievement drop-off in early adolescence (from not doing homework or not behaving in class), which often occurs in upper elementary and middle school, can be corrected when parents extend their supervision into the child's world at school. "Coming to school with me is embarrassing!" complains the child. Replies the parent, "Take care of business and I won't have to come to school."

## Object Lessons

Because the willful child is so self-determined, it sometimes takes a hard lesson to teach the child the error of his ways. Object lessons can sometimes provide this education in powerfully convincing ways. With an object lesson, you set up a situation in which the child learns from experience what words alone are unable to teach.

### ⦸ Alert

Object lessons can be tricky. Showing the little child what it feels like to be slapped by slapping back can not only hurt the child, but can encourage him to use parental example to justify hitting. "Well, you hit me back, so that means I can keep on hitting you!" The risk of object lessons is that they can teach the opposite of what you intend.

Imagine a child who insists he won't do anything his parents ask unless they pay him. "Why should I work for you for free?" So the parent, who understands that arguing the issue of free family service with such a willful child is doomed to failure, agrees to this, saying, "This has to go both ways. I'll pay you a dollar for doing everything I ask, and you pay me a dollar for everything I do for you. Okay?" And the child happily agrees, collecting several dollars that night for clearing the supper table, for changing the cat's litter box, and for picking up his clothes that had been thrown on the floor. What a great system!

Next morning, the child asks for a clean shirt to wear to school. "That will be a dollar," says the parent. Then the child wants some shampoo to wash his hair. "That will be a dollar," says the parent. Then the child comes in for breakfast. "That will be a dollar," says the parent. Then the child, now out of money, wants lunch for school. "That will be a dollar," says the parent. "But I haven't got a dollar," complains the child. "I paid them all back!" "Then," explains the parent sympathetically, "I guess you'll have to go to school without lunch." "But this isn't fair!" objects the child, now that the system of paid service is working against and not for him. "Well," suggests the parent, "why don't you think about the system of freely doing for each other we had before, and we can talk about going back to that when you get home from school, at the free supper I'm going to fix for you tonight."

## Constructive Cooperation

The fourth major delivery system for discipline is working exchange points—using the child's dependency on parents to encourage cooperation with parents by withholding daily services, resources, or permissions until the child does something they requested first. This is neither a threat nor a punishment. If anything, it is a kind of object lesson that teaches the child how giving is required for getting.

"I'd be happy to drive you over to your friend's house, but before I do, please take out the trash as I asked." To which the impatient child responds, "I promise I will when I get back!" No. Promises are false currency. They have repeatedly been used to get the parent to make a bad bargain—to do for the child only to have the child renege on the agreement later on. So the parent holds firm. "I'm happy to drive you, but the trash must be taken out first."

If your willful child is highly resistant to doing chores, just wait for the next likely situation where you can make a logical trade. When it comes to working these trades, effective parents make sure they get what they want before they give what the child wants.

By working these exchange conditions, parents not only encourage the willful child to meet some of the parents' requests, but they also teach the child to appreciate that relationships work two ways, satisfying the needs of other people as well as her own. Parents who refuse to teach their child to live in two-way relationships unfortunately are preparing the child for an unhappy, lonely future.

## CHAPTER 11

# Handling Conflict

If you have a child who is by nature willful, or if you have a child who is growing through a willful phase like adolescence, it is realistic to expect more conflict with that self-determined boy. Keeping in mind that from birth, it is the ultimate aim of parenting to nurture the child to independent functioning, there should be no surprise that conflict will arise with the inevitable clashing of aims and personalities.

## Conflict in Action

Willful children want choice. If you obstruct that choice, conflict is likely to ensue. "You can't go over to a friend's house on school nights." "You have to do your chores before going out to play this weekend." What seem like reasonable and responsible requests to you often strike your willful child as arbitrary and unfair.

"Give me one good reason!" demands the child, opening the door to an argument he hopes will change your mind. If he can't persuade you with logic, at least he has a chance of wearing down your resolve. But as a parent, you know that for your willful child there is no reason good enough to justify refusal of what he wants. Thus you are not surprised when he objects, "That's not a good enough reason!" You simply steadfastly reply, "It may not be good enough for you, but it's good enough for me." Sometimes it takes determination to parent a strong-willed child. And it's not necessary to engage in fruitless debate.

Storming off to his room, the boy mutters loudly enough to be overheard, "That's all parents are good for—keeping you from doing what you want!" And you let your frustrated child have this parting shot because you understand that it is part of a working compromise. The child gets to have his say, and you get to have your way.

## The Nature of Conflict

Conflict is the process through which people clarify, confront, and resolve inevitable human differences. The more human diversity there is in families (and stepfamilies have even more than the biological kind), the more likely there will be conflict. Conflicts between parents, parents and child, and child and child are built into family life when any of four categories of common questions are raised.

- **Cooperation creates conflict.** Who gets to do what? Who gets to get what? What is a fair share?
- **Control creates conflict.** Who is in charge? Who makes the rules? Whose is the right way?
- **Competition creates conflict.** Who wins? Who gets the most? Who goes first?
- **Conformity creates conflict.** Who sets the norm? Who has to fit in? Who gets to act different?

 Fact

In families, differences are inevitable; conflict is necessary; but violence is not. The first rule of family conflict is safety: neither parents nor children have the right to do anyone deliberate harm when contesting differences in wants, beliefs, or perceptions that arise between them.

## Conflict Takes Cooperation

"Our child is so stubborn, she fights with us about everything. It's just exhausting. How can we stop her from fighting with us all the time?" The answer is simple: stop fighting back. It takes two to make a conflict. You've heard the question, "What if they gave a war and nobody came?" You can decide not to participate. There is no battle without two participants. Suppose the willful child wants an argument, but neither parent is so inclined. To stop arguments, simply refuse to argue back.

Contrary to common sense, conflict is not about disagreement. Conflict is a matter of agreement—two parties agreeing to disagree over some common issue at difference between them. Should homework be done immediately? Your twelve-year-old thinks texting is more urgent. You take a stand for homework first. She argues. You insist. She grudgingly consents. A conflict arose because you both agreed to disagree about homework. In this case, resolution was in your favor.

### ⏺ Alert

Conflict usually stresses parents more than it stresses the child. Afterward, parents want to collapse and rest, whereas their child isn't even breathing hard. Therefore, don't cooperate in more conflict than you have purpose to justify and energy to afford.

Conflict is always a matter of agreement—parents agreeing to contest a difference that their willful child agrees to contest with them. Parents don't have to cooperate in any more conflict than they want to. They always have a choice. Since parents cannot afford the energy to fight over every difference that arises, they must pick their battles wisely.

## Conflict Is Informative

Many parents do not appreciate the educational value of conflict with their willful child. Verbal conflict is an act of communication. The child is speaking up and sharing information about what she wants, what she values, how she thinks, and how she sees the world. Conflict is just two different ways of looking at the same issue. It provides a window into the other person's point of view.

For example, consider the battle over posters on the bedroom wall. "We are not having you decorate your room with posters of any rock group called Nasty Manners!" The child shouts, "I want those band posters in my room because the music matters to me. Don't you understand? When I look at the pictures and listen to the music, it helps calm my feelings down!"

Parents who consider conflict with their willful child only a matter of winning or losing miss out on using conflict as a great point of discussion, a chance to understand their child more deeply than before, and as a chance to become better known themselves. Conflict creates an opportunity for dialogue.

## ⓔ✺ Essential

Parental guidance is in the business of informing the child's understanding, not controlling the child's choice. In caring relationships, the primary goal of conflict is not supremacy, but intimacy. There are two avenues for intimacy. First, by sharing similarities, people create commonality. And second, by being willing to disagree, people create understanding about natural differences between them. People who never fight are people with half an intimacy—they either avoid or ignore important diversity in their relationships.

When parent and willful child declare, after a conflict, that they understand each other better than they did before, then conflict has fulfilled its function. A deeper intimacy has been established. "I can see why you got so upset at my fooling around with alcohol," the child says. "I never knew before about all the problems it caused in your family growing up."

## Conflict Is Formative

Conflict is not something you have with your willful child. It is something you do with your willful child. Conflict is a performance act. Every time you do conflict with your child, by experience, example, and instruction, you teach your child how to conduct conflict. So, when you model sticking to specifics, staying on the subject, avoiding extreme statements, keeping in the present, speaking for yourself, taking responsibility for your position, hearing the other person out, and being empathetic and nonjudgmental, you give your child productive behaviors to follow. In addition, when she interrupts or calls names, you intervene. "I'm willing to continue talking, but you may not interrupt or call me names."

Another formative part of conflict has to do with the equation that now equals later. How your child learns to do conflict with you now is how she will conduct conflict with other people later on. When you engage in conflict with your child, you are training her in how conflict can be productively and safely conducted. Thus, you explain to your willful child, who, frustrated by your opposition, has just behaved in a physically threatening manner, how this behavior can not only hurt you now, but also can hurt her in the future.

"When I tell you that acting like you are going to hit me is unacceptable because it is unsafe, I am telling you this not just for my own good, but for yours. If I let you get away with this behavior now, there is the possibility that further down the road of life, when in conflict, you will repeat this behavior with someone you really care about. And that person, finding you unsafe to disagree with, may choose to end the relationship, and you will end up hurting yourself, perhaps losing a friend or someone you love."

If you commit verbal, emotional, or physical injury in family conflict, the trustful nature of that relationship can be seriously damaged or lost. This is why the first rule in family conflict is safety. In family conflict, words do most of the damage. Like other animals, people fight with their mouths. So watch what you say. "I'm sorry" cannot undo the damage done. The only acceptable amends is never committing such injury again.

# Responsibility in Conflict

Conflict is a mutually agreed upon opposition over an issue at difference between two or more parties. Parents may disagree over how to correct their child for breaking a family rule. Parent and child may disagree over the necessity of the child's doing a chore. Children may disagree over whose turn it is to play with a toy. In these cases, each party is responsible for contributing to the active opposition between them.

The problem is, responsibility can be hard to take. Parents and child often like to blame the other person for the conflict. "We're only arguing because you're wrong," says one parent to the other. "If you'd just do what you're told, we wouldn't have to fight about it," says the parent to the child. "He started it!" protests one child about the other. In each case, the speaker is disavowing responsibility for the conflict and assigning it to the other party. Keep in mind that it is normal to have more conflict during the adolescent phase of your child's development. He needs to assert himself in order to become a separate individual.

## Placing Blame

In the short run, blame can make a person feel better by excusing him of any part in his own trouble or unhappiness. In the long run, however, it only attacks the blamed and victimizes the blamer. If the trouble or unhappiness is entirely the other person's fault, then the other person is both accused and empowered, and the blamer is helpless to stop or influence what is going on.

# ❗ Alert

Some parental blame statements cut children to the core. "How could you do this to us?" "You really let us down!" "You've disappointed us!" "You should be ashamed!" "You've ruined your life!" "You're nothing but a problem!" Blame can do a lot of harm.

"Our child keeps the family in a constant state of upset!" With this statement of blame, parents cast off power of responsibility to change an unhappy situation. To improve the situation at home, they have to reclaim their share of responsibility. "Just because our child is constantly acting out doesn't mean we always have to get upset in response. In fact, our response may be only encouraging his acting out." During adolescence, it is common for parents and teenager to blame each other with the same complaints. The other party:

- "Never listens to what I say"
- "Never appreciates all I do"
- "Never does what I want"

Blame and complaints, as natural as they are, do not resolve conflicts; they only intensify them. The blamed party often blames the blamer back, and soon the conflict over who is going to do or get what, or over who is right and who is wrong, has escalated into accusations over who is the sorrier human being.

# ✅ Fact

Learning to fight well is the work of a lifetime. By victimizing the blamer and offending and empowering the blamed, blame only makes conflicts worse, never better. By accepting personal responsibility for one's share in conflict, each person is best able to resolve it.

## Replacing Blame with Responsibility

Anytime you find yourself blaming, or about to blame, your willful child for a conflict, remember that when you do you only empower him and reduce your influence. Instead, ask yourself these questions:

- What degree of cooperative responsibility are you willing to accept for your share in the conflict? "As soon as he gets home from school, I tell my child to begin his chores and we immediately get into an argument."
- What are you willing to do differently to change the interaction? "I might ask him how his day was and suggest he take a break to relax before helping me around the home."
- What are you willing to give in order to get what you want? "I might give him more choice over when the chores get done, later than I ideally would like but delayed enough to encourage his cooperation."

# Conflict Resolution

Resolution of conflict is how you and your child come to agreement over what to do about the difference on which you both have agreed to disagree. Who is responsible? Which is the right way? What needs to happen? When will it be done? Why is that necessary? How much should be allowed?

Every conflict can be stated as a question, and every resolution is an attempt to answer that question in a way both parties can accept. This doesn't mean that both parties necessarily like the resolution, only that both agree to accept it. If the resolution is a compromise, for example, this means that, on a personal level, resolution is going to be a losing proposition. Each party agrees to take less than 100 percent of what each ideally wants to settle the divisive issue between them. So the willful thirteen-year-old pushes to stay out longer than parents really want, but agrees to come home earlier than other friends who have been allowed a later curfew. On a relationship level, compromises are a winning proposition because conflict over a difference has been successfully resolved, and the relationship has been strengthened by reaching a settlement both agree to honor.

 **Essential**

> Do not get into proprietary conflicts with your willful child, trying to change what only the child can control. "I'll go potty when I want!" "You can't make me eat!" "Going to sleep is up to me!" Simply explain why you believe it is in her best interests to do what you agree only the child can ultimately decide to do, and encourage the child to try.

### Strategies for Resolving Conflict

Left to her own self-preoccupation, the willful child often thinks that there are only three options for resolving conflict: "my way," "your way," or "no way." Left to their own frustration, parents can think in a similarly limited way. Maybe all the family members can think about "our way."

There are many ways for resolving conflict, and with a willful child, with whom conflict is a frequent occurrence, parents need a variety of resolution strategies at their disposal. The more choices they have, the more freedom of flexibility they will feel. Consider just a few of the more common choices.

### Change

You and your child are in conflict over picking up her backpack where she has dumped it in the hall when she and a friend came home from school. After ignoring your demand, she says she'll do it later. "Do it now!" you command. And when she refuses, you take her into the other room to discuss the problem. "If you'd ask instead of tell, I might," she says. "I won't be ordered around in

158

front of friends." So you decide to make a change in your approach. Ten minutes later, you interrupt the two friends with a request for your daughter: "I'd really appreciate it if you'd take your backpack to your room." "Sure," she agrees. She saves face, and you get cooperation.

## ⊘ Alert

When you are about to engage in conflict with your child, instead of going for control, try expressing concern. Rather than make a critical response, try making an empathetic response instead: "Is everything okay?" The child may feel less defensive and more receptive to discussion.

## Concession

You have a rule that, until your child is in the fourth grade, she can't walk to school without you. But in third grade, her friends from the neighborhood are now walking to school unaccompanied by an adult, and she wants to, too. "I feel stupid walking with my parent when all my friends can just go with each other." Weighing your concerns for safety with her needs for social belonging, you decide to make a concession. "I think this issue is more important for you than it is for me, so I agree to let you have what you want, so long as you remain mindful of the rules of safety you've been taught. Another time when we have a disagreement, when the issue is more important to me, I'd like you to go along with me."

## Chance

Your two children are fighting over who gets to go first. Rather than get into an endless discussion to determine what is fair, you offer to resolve the issue by chance: "I'll flip a coin, and the winner gets to go first." And both children agree to abide by that decision.

### Compromise

Your child wants your help on a school project but doesn't want to start working on it until the night before, using last-minute deadline pressure as a motivator for overcoming resistance to completing what she doesn't want to do. You don't want to give last-minute help because that feels too stressful. So you reach a compromise. If she agrees to begin work two nights before it's due, you will agree to give help under somewhat less stressful conditions. You each sacrificed some self-interest to get what you could both live with.

### Creative Alternative

You've offered to take the kids out to eat, but they immediately disagree on what restaurant they want, and the outing has become obstructed by the conflict between them. It seems like an either/or situation, either one child's choice or the other's, until you reframe the choice in a larger way. "Why we are really going out is not just to eat, but to have fun together. So rather than get bogged down in where to eat, let's think about some other activity that would be fun for us all." So you end up going bowling instead. You opened up a choice that was outside the limited alternatives posed by the original opposition between them.

### Avoid Emotional Extortion

A willful child, or a willful parent, bent on winning a conflict can resort to manipulation, which works in the short run but builds ill feeling into the relationship over time. Either party can choose to use emotional extortion to get her way.

What is emotional extortion? Rather than declare what she wants and discuss and negotiate a resolution, the willful child or willful parent can try to force agreement by using the strong expression of emotion to get the other person to relent.

- She can use the expression of love to cajole and flatter.
- She can use the expression of anger to communicate rejection.
- She can use the expression of suffering to elicit guilt.
- She can use the expression of helplessness to play on pity.
- She can use the expression of apathy to signify abandonment of caring.
- She can combine anger and suffering into a tantrum to intimidate.
- She can use the expression of violence to threaten physical injury.

When parent or child gives in to any of these emotional ploys, she ends up feeling manipulated and resentful and ultimately distrustful. And the relationship suffers. So don't use emotional extortion yourself, and if your willful child ever uses it on you, simply respond by saying, "Expressing strong feeling is not going to get me to change my mind or cause me to agree. Tell me what it is you want or do not want to have happen, and we can talk it out." Take the child out of an emotionally manipulative mode and into a rationally declarative one.

## Conflict Avoidance

Because conflict takes so much energy, parents cannot afford to become embroiled in every opportunity for conflict that a willful child offers. "It's bedtime," declares the parent. "No, it's not," disagrees the child. "It's too early and I'm not tired yet." "Your bedtime," explains the parent, "isn't just about your need for rest. It's about my need for rest, too. Right now I am tired enough for you to go to bed and too tired to discuss the point. So, good night." And the child, being given no further opening for argument, wearily gives up the fight for the night, but not for tomorrow.

It's not just that willful children have more energy for conflict than their parents do; willful children are energized by conflict in ways their parents typically are not. For willful children, conflict is challenging and stimulating. It provides an opportunity to assert self-interest that many willful children value. "Parents are good to practice my arguing on. And there's always a chance that I can change their mind."

So when it comes to conflict, the keys for parents of a willful child are to be selective, to not engage in any more conflict than they have energy and purpose to confront, and to avoid those invitations (or provocations) into conflict that are not worth their while.

### 🅔✴ Essential

If you lack adequate conflict-avoidance skills, you risk getting entrapped in more conflict than you have energy for. To avoid excessive conflict: let angry provocations go, refuse to further justify demands you have already explained, and back up your stands with firm insistence, refusing to back down.

Be watchful of a walking-on-eggshells atmosphere in your home. Don't let yourself be backed into a corner with conflict avoidance, just to keep the peace. Ask yourself, "What is being avoided here?" It might be something as simple as the temporary displeasure of your child. You can handle that.

### When to Avoid Conflict

Sometimes a willful child, feeling up for a fight, will challenge parents by throwing out an extreme statement about what he is going or not going to do: "I'm going to run away, and you can't stop me!" "I'm never going back to that school, and you can't make me!" Willful challenges are either statements of frustration or invitations to conflict.

For parents, such extreme statements can be scary. Taking them literally and becoming frightened, they can be seduced into taking a stand over a threat or making extreme statements in return ("If you refuse, I'll ship you off to military school!"). And the willful child gets the angry outlet or argument he was after. So what should parents do when a willful challenge comes their way? Leave the challenge on the table. Don't argue with it. Don't credit it with truth. After all, if the child were really going to run away or refuse to return to school, he wouldn't waste time putting you on notice. He'd be doing it. He just wants to create a forum for frustration or a conflict around this issue.

So, say something like this: "Well, it seems to me that decision would cause you more problems than benefits, but your choices are certainly up to you. Of course, if there are feelings behind this decision you would like to discuss, I'd be happy to hear what you have to say."

You let the child know you don't think the proposal is a good idea, but you take your opposition off the table. You place responsibility for carrying through with the decision firmly on the child. You make no emotional reaction to the proposal. And you offer to listen if there are any feelings attached to this proposal that the child wants to share. At the same time, threats, especially empty threats, are best avoided. They teach the willful child that the parents will not follow through, which is the same as a broken promise.

# 🄴❗ Alert

There are two conditions under which parents should not avoid conflict with their willful child. First, if parents are doing so out of intimidation, because then they will end up giving their child extortionate power over their fear. And second, if by doing so parents run the risk of escalation—the longer they delay confronting an issue, the more volatile it gets.

## When Not to Avoid Conflict

Some parents may say, "I would rather put up with what I don't like than fight about it with my child." But there are definite dangers to avoiding conflict.

- If you tiptoe around sensitive issues that get your child angry, you increase your fear of the child's anger. This is an unhealthy balance of power in the home.
- If you let some of your child's unacceptable behavior go, you will increasingly choose to live on your child's unacceptable terms.
- If you keep quiet about your child's offensive behavior, you will store up resentment toward the child.
- If you avoid talking out differences, you will tend to imagine and distort what is really going on with the child.
- If you stuff your own declaration of anger, you risk building it up for a later blow-up over something not related to the first offense.
- If you don't dare talk about a divisive issue, you will lose an opportunity for dialogue and intimacy that conflict has to offer.
- If you keep avoiding conflict, you will develop a habit of avoidance that can be hard to break.
- If you keep avoiding conflict, you will weaken your capacity to resolve differences in a satisfactory way.

## Blustering Tactics

Parents of a willful adolescent need to expect several common blustering tactics designed to discourage parents from raising issues the teenager doesn't want to discuss. To escape discussion, the teenager tries to bully the parent into avoidance.

Protective belligerence: "Don't mess with me, I'm in a bad mood!"
Protective busyness: "Not now; can't you see I'm doing something important!"
Protective unavailability: "I've got to leave; we can talk about it later!"

So when is a good time to have a sensitive talk with your willful teenager? There isn't one. You are often going to be given a hard time dealing with something the teenager doesn't want to discuss. So don't let adolescent blustering tactics scare you off. Brave your adolescent's disapproval and choose any old bad time to have your say.

## Sibling Conflicts

"Our two daughters never get along," complain the parents. "They're always bickering and fighting." But that isn't a sign that their daughters don't get along—bickering and quarreling is how they get along. Sibling rivalry increases the will for conflict because it arouses the will to win. This is why some parents, wishing to avoid the constant push and shove between multiple children, elect to have only one child.

 **Fact**

More powerful than getting angry to stop children from hitting each other, you might try this: "I appreciate how well you both usually get along. When you start hitting, I feel sad that you would want to hurt each other, because I want our family to be free of deliberate harm." Get mad at them and they become defensive. Feel sad for them and they may respond to your concern.

Maximum rivalry occurs when children are the same sex and close in age, where the need for dominance and differentiation create ongoing conflict. (The exception to this pattern is identical twins, who often develop unusual closeness based on sharing a single definition between them, needing continual contact with each other to feel adequately connected and individually complete.)

So why do siblings have the will to fight? Partly because there is a natural competition for shared family resources, parental attention, and parental approval. When parents appear to play favorites in response, the seeds for rivalry between adult siblings can be sown.

"My parents always liked my sister better than me when we were children, and now that we're grown up, they still do. She can do no wrong in their eyes, and whatever I do is never good enough!" Favoritism is family discrimination, and it intensifies sibling rivalry with resentment, the less favored child taking anger out on the favored sibling for what parents have unfairly done.

For most siblings, however, there is plenty to fight about even without parental favoritism. Siblings typically engage in conflict:

- To test power (Who is dominant?)
- To establish individuality (Who is different?)
- To ventilate emotions (Who needs to relieve a bad mood?)

What is satisfying for siblings, however, can be exhausting for parents. The children's conflict is one more unwelcome source of stress in the parents' stressful world. It can feel unpleasant, irritating, and upsetting. In response, the parents' attitude can be affected. They become more negative, they become more fatigued, they become more prone to getting into conflict with each other, and they have less positive energy to give to other children who were not party to the conflict to begin with.

### The Parental Role in Sibling Conflict

You can minimize sibling conflict by frequently reiterating family rules, such as no hitting and no taking other people's things without asking.

Parents have four roles in dealing with sibling conflict. They act as separator, keeping children apart to reduce fighting and the stress it causes parents. They act as monitor, making sure that conflict is conducted within safe limits so neither party gets hurt or feels abused. They act as governor, intervening to control the conflict when it is threatening to escalate to harmful effect. And they act as mediator, settling differences the children are unable to settle themselves.

Because conflict is cooperative, parents must never get sucked in to the trap of figuring out who started the fight in order to punish the guilty party. If they try to determine who started the conflict, they will go back to year one. Since it takes two parties to create a conflict, hold both siblings cooperatively responsible. You can try and mediate the conflict if you choose, but remember the saying, "Blessed be the mediator, for he shall be hated by both sides." Because your solution will give the children less than 100 percent of what each wants, both will consider your resolution unfair. "Just because we couldn't agree over which TV show to watch, now you've decided we don't get to watch TV tonight at all!" Or you may just separate the combatants for a prescribed cooling off period for them, and a rest for you.

Mediate or separate; however, you must hold each sibling accountable for individual behavior in the conflict. "You need to know that, although I hold you both responsible for creating any conflict between you, I hold you separately responsible for how you treat each other during the conflict. If either of you acts in deliberately hurtful ways, then that person is going to have some business with me. You will conduct your disagreements with each other safely because safety is the rule for conflict that everyone in this family is expected to follow. Do you understand?"

## Older/Younger Conflicts

There is a natural jealousy built into sibling relationships based on the age difference and birth order between them. The first child gets to be treated as only child for a while, with exclusive claim to all attention parents have to give. The second child comes along as a spoiler, taking attention previously devoted to child number one, creating demands for sharing that did not exist before. The second child resents the first child for getting grown-up freedoms first; the first child resents the second child for getting older freedoms earlier than they were granted before. The second child sees the first as "bossy," and the first child sees the second child as "spoiled." It's the age-old battle between who will dominate and who won't.

The older child often engages in teasing to put down the competition and to assert supremacy: "You are my inferior." The younger child often imitates the older to provoke attention and gather power: "I am your equal." Given these natural tensions, putting older in charge of younger when parents are away can create an irresistible opportunity for sibling conflict, with the older determined to give orders and the younger determined not to be ordered around. If the older child is particularly willful, he may abuse his power. If the younger child is particularly willful, she may seriously challenge the authority of the older.

Sometimes parents can encourage siblings to suspend normal hostilities and accept a childcare relationship by giving them something special to do together they do not ordinarily get to enjoy. If in your absence they both cooperate with the arrangement you have made, be sure to reward them each with your appreciation for a job well done.

 **Fact**

Expect it. The more willful your child, the more opportunities for conflict there will be between you, and the more intense that conflict is likely to be. How much conflict you choose to cooperate in is always up to you. Through insistence and example, your job is to teach your willful child how to conduct conflict in a safe and productive way.

Occasionally siblings will insist they can't help fighting. One parent designed an object lesson to test this assertion. "All right, if you can't help fighting, you can both go fight outside so I don't have to hear it. The one who wins gets to come back inside." And she shuts the door behind them. After a few minutes, there's a knock. "Can we come in?" "Sure," she says. "Which one won the fight?" "No one. We decided not to fight," they reply. "Oh," says the parent feigning surprise. "Then I guess you can help fighting after all. That's good to know. Now why don't both of you come back inside."

Despite what tired parents are prone to think, siblings who fight a lot are usually not enemies in the family. They are loyal adversaries and sometime friends. Fighting together does not signify that they don't get along. It is just how they get along.

## CHAPTER 12

# Maintaining Emotional Sobriety

Emotions can be intense in a family with a strong-willed child. Everyone in the family is affected by the willful child in a variety of ways, and often you might let high emotion get in the way of effective decision making. Making the right decisions about how to behave, how to respond, how to react, and how to teach your willful child is best done when you are thinking rationally, not emotionally.

## Emotions Running High

Emotions can be intense in a family with a strong-willed child, because everyone concerned is easily upset. Siblings of the strong-willed child may resent how much attention their willful sibling gets and the exceptions to family rules he seems to get away with. Parents may grow weary and impatient trying to keep up with the child's demands and resistance. And the willful child can bridle with frustration against parental restraints that stand in the way of what he intensely wants to do. Maintaining an unemotional stance is important in being effective and exerting positive influence over your strong-willed child.

When the willful child becomes intensely emotional, for a short while there is no thinking person home. This is not the time for parents to jam the child with a demand to declare what is going on. Lost in the emotional moment, the child may not know what is really going on. Time-outs can be a protective cooling off mechanism for both parents and child. Set the situation aside for a while. Go for a walk. Call a friend. Suggest a change of scenery for the child, and resume the discussion later.

Give the self-willed child time and space to calm down, to restore thought, to identify what he is feeling so it can be safely and productively talked out. When the child says, "I need to think about what I'm feeling," he isn't lying. For the willful child, feelings are often confusing, and he needs time to figure them out.

## 🅔 Alert

Beware emotional loading—labeling objectionable behavior with insulting, inflammatory language. When parents angrily call their four-year-old, who has regressed to thumb sucking, a "baby" for acting infantile, this only increases the emotional power of the interaction. The label offends the child and upsets the parents, perhaps encouraging the willful child to act babyish with a vengeance, crying for a bottle and maybe breaking toilet training, too, making a difficult situation even worse.

## Emotions: Good Servants, Bad Masters

As consistently as you can, maintain your emotional sobriety: Stay calm, cool, and reasonable, and help your willful child to do the same. If you start thinking with your feelings, you will make poor decisions. Emotions are good informants but bad advisors. As informants they alert us to what is going on. Fear alerts us to dangers. Frustration alerts us to obstructions. Anger alerts us to violations. But as advisors, emotions can make matters worse, not better. Fear can advise us to run from what is scary, rather than face it. Frustration can advise us to force a situation, rather than be patient. Anger can advise us to retaliate, rather than negotiate. Emotion is for sensing what is going on; thought is for deciding what to do.

It is the parent's job to teach the willful child to separate the functions of emotion and thought. For example, hurt and angry from being teased, the willful child decides to never play with her best friends again. To which the parent responds, "First tell me all about what happened and how you feel; then afterward, we can think together about what is wise to do."

## Thought Mediates Emotion

How you interpret what happens to you is often more important than the happening itself. Imagine a middle-school-age girl who has just lost her best friend of many years because early adolescence has caused the two young girls to grow their separate ways, to grow apart. Now her best friend wants different friends instead. Knowing that her daughter is suffering because of this loss of intimate companionship on which she has relied for many years, the parent attends very carefully to the interpretation her unhappy daughter puts on this adverse event.

Will her daughter say, "This just goes to show what a loser I am! Nobody could like someone like me! I'll never have a friend again!" Or will her daughter say, "This really hurts to lose my friend. She wanted a change, but not because there's something wrong with me. In fact, having had a best friend just shows that I'll be able to make another good friend again."

**🅔✓ Fact**

Since mental set affects emotional state, help yourself and your willful child maintain a realistic attitude by remaining mindful of the facts of life. "You only get one life. It goes very fast. It's very precious. It's not always fair. You won't always get your way. You can choose to dwell on bad times or you can hope for better times ahead. You won't get all you want, but you can be grateful for everything you have."

The first interpretation leads to insecurity, low self-esteem, and despair. The second interpretation can lead to confidence, self-assurance, and hope. If this were your daughter, which interpretation would you want her to make? The lesson for parents is this: Notice your child's perceptions about what is happening and ask questions about her interpretations. How she chooses to think affects how she is going to feel.

Terrible interpretations of adverse events are dangerous because they can drive exhausted parents or willful child to emotional extremes. When either parents or child are becoming upset, they need to ask themselves, "What am I thinking?" To change how they feel, they can change how they think. Instead of assuming, "You did that on purpose," the parent or child could choose to suppose, "You did that by mistake." Your example as a rational role model helps the child act accordingly.

## Objective and Subjective Responses

Or consider a casual interaction between parent and willful child at the end of the school day. You ask your child for household help as she passes you on the stairs, and she appears to ignore your request. What do you choose to think about that response? You could choose to take it personally and make a subjective response: "She just treated me rudely by not responding, that makes me really angry, I'm going to let her know I don't like it!" Or you could choose to take it impersonally and make an objective response: "She didn't reply to my request; I need to ask again for what I need. Maybe she didn't hear me because of being preoccupied with her own life."

How people perceive and interpret what is going on makes an enormous difference in how people respond to each other emotionally. The more realistic, operational, and objective your thinking is, the less emotionally upset you are likely to become. The more evaluative, distorted, and subjective your thinking is, the more emotionally intense your family interactions are likely to be.

Keep in mind, as well, that anxiety increases in very close relationships. It's because you *care* that you overreact. The same with your child. Therefore when your willful child enters adolescence and discloses less to you and more to peers, which interpretation of this changed behavior do you choose to make? "She is more private now than as a child, needs more separation from her parents, and would rather confide in friends." Make this interpretation and you will feel calm and accepting, maintain perspective, and stay available to your less communicative teenager. Or do you choose a different interpretation? "She is rejecting our relationship; she doesn't love me anymore; she is trying to make me feel bad." Feeling hurt and angry by choosing to think like this, the parent may punish and push her daughter further away. Such gloomy thinking can cause painful feelings that can motivate a negative response.

 **Fact**

Both alcohol and drugs use can affect a person's mental attitude and emotional sobriety. Parents who get mean when they drink at the end of the day often do so because, under the influence, they get in a mood to review grievances or decide to perceive themselves as treated unjustly. Then they start looking to provoke a fight so they can retaliate and feel better.

## Taking Emotional Responsibility

"He makes me so angry!" storms a parent when describing her willful child. But this is untrue. The parent is responsible for her own feelings. If her child can make her angry, then the child is controlling her emotions. People often externalize the cause of their anger with blame: "That made me angry," "You made me angry." Only by internalizing the source of our anger—"I am choosing to feel angry because of how you treated me"—can we keep it under responsible control. Choose to be a leader in your family, showing that you alone can moderate your emotions and behavior. It does wonders for everyone.

## The Anger-Prone Parent

There is a type of parent who is sure her anger is everybody else's fault: the anger-prone parent. "Well, if the kids would just do what they're told, I wouldn't get mad!" "Well, if the kids just did things correctly, I wouldn't get mad!" "Well, if the kids wouldn't deliberately provoke me, I wouldn't get mad!" The anger-prone parent is willful in three potentially damaging ways.

- She has a high need for control. She has to get her way and gets mad when she does not.
- She is highly judgmental. She believes she knows what's right and gets mad when others do or see things incorrectly in her estimation.
- She is highly sensitive to insult. She takes personally what is not personally intended, getting mad because she believes others are deliberately out to upset her.

Combine within the family an anger-prone parent and a willful child, and there is potential for an explosion every time the child challenges or resists parental authority or a conflict of interests occurs. To anger-prone parents, there are no small offenses or disagreements, because each can contribute to an abiding sense of grievance: "Something is always going wrong!"

For the willful child, anger-prone parents teach a constant lesson that not getting what one wants merits becoming angry. Anger-prone parents, by example and interaction, train their willful child to become anger-prone in response. "I learned my temper from my mother. When things didn't go the way she wanted, the first thing she did was blow up about it. Now I'm the same way."

One sure formula for creating unceasing power struggles in a family is pairing a willful child with an anger-prone parent. If, as the parent, you want to change the formula, then you have to change yourself.

Fortunately, if anger-prone parents want to change their volatile ways, they can. This change requires ceasing to blame the object of their anger for their anger, and reclaiming responsibility for their own emotions. They can choose to change their emotional set points by altering beliefs that justify an angry response.

To become less controlling, they can practice saying to themselves, "I don't need to get my way all the time."

To become less judgmental, they can practice saying to themselves, "I don't have to be right all the time."

To take events less personally, they can say to themselves, "I don't have to assume that actions I don't like are deliberately meant to upset me."

What actions can you take when you feel the temperature rising?

- Inform your child that you're taking a time-out and do not wish to talk.
- Do something physical away from your child—jogging, calisthenics, heavy cleaning. Plug in to your favorite music and detach. Dance or walk energetically.
- Develop and use a support group of like-minded parents. These friends can take an emergency phone call or chat with you online or by text to hear you out and calm you down. Cultivate these relationships *before* you are in crisis, so the help is there when you need it.
- Keep hotline numbers near the phone to avert family violence. Use them.

- Enlist the help of your partner, neighbors, and extended family to provide a time-out of several days, if needed. The more open you are about your stress, the more help you will receive. You might ask the grandparents to keep the child for a weekend, or you might want an overnight stay in a friend's house in order to chill out over coffee and sympathetic conversation.

### Anger Interferes with Thinking

Anger makes it hard to delay action and consult judgment (what is reasonable, ethical, and wise) before making a decision. When the recovering anger-prone parent is able to change her emotional set points and engage in logical thinking, the results can be dramatic.

What if your son took your camera without asking and returned it broken, excusing what he did by saying you never said he couldn't borrow it, and it was old and falling apart anyhow? Well, you could blow up, and that would take the place of dealing with the offense. What if you take the time to stop and think, and in a calm voice, matter-of-factly explain that taking your things without permission is theft. It's disrespectful, and stealing is not allowed. He will have to pay to get the camera repaired. No blow-up. Just feedback, rule setting, and consequence. Without anger, he may hear what you are saying and agree to do as asked.

# The Function of Anger

Anger, like any emotion, is functional. The purpose of anger is to identify violations to our well-being. "You took what was mine!" "You hurt me on purpose!" "You broke your promise!" "You shouldn't have done that!" The angry person feels wronged, that she was mistreated, that she was dealt with unfairly. Anger helps adults and children identify these kinds of violations.

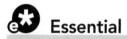 **Essential**

If your spouse and children say your facial expression is scary when you get very angry and you don't believe them, check it out. Next time you feel in a rage, go look in a mirror and see what the rest of the family is talking about. Maybe you wouldn't like to be around a person who looks like that.

After anger identifies a violation of our well-being, it can then bring empowering energy for an appropriate expressive response. Breathe deeply and think about what you want to change.

Since anger can be a dangerous emotion when it motivates aggressive behavior, children must be taught nonviolent ways to manage anger. When a child's sibling takes a toy from her and the child then gets into a hitting fight with her to get it back, parents intervene. They try to help the warring children move from acting out to talking out to working out their conflict. To this end, parents declare a time-out to stop the acting out, to create a break to calm emotions down so talking out and then working out can occur.

Willful children, because they are so easily frustrated, are at risk of becoming prone to anger. "I get mad when I can't get what I want or do what I want or have to do what I don't want!" When parents question the child's right to anger now, the child is likely to get angrier later on. It's more productive to confirm the anger and lead the child through it. Use everything you have within your maturity to be a role model and calmly help the child through the rough time.

**Alert**

Don't hold on to hurt feelings. The longer you do, the more resentful you will become. Keep in mind the adage from Alcoholics Anonymous: "Resentment is like taking poison and waiting for the other person to die." Your hostility may be offensive to others, but you are mostly poisoning yourself.

By example and instruction, parents need to discuss with their willful child the nature and management of anger. At a relaxed time—not an upset time—they can choose to raise some of the following points:

- You can become angry when you decide that something has been done to you that you believe should not have happened.
- Your anger is not involuntary; it is a matter of your personal choice. How you think about what happened is what makes you angry, not what another person did.
- No one can make you angry without your permission.
- Blaming someone for making you angry only shows that you have given control of your anger to that person. This is not a good idea.
- Take responsibility for deciding to get angry and we can use that emotional energy to make an expressive, protective, or corrective response.
- Anger is always an expression of caring. People don't get angry at what doesn't matter to them.
- When you decide to get angry, ask yourself what you really care about in this situation, then discuss with the other person what matters to you about what just happened, why you need it to stop, and see what you can do to work it out.

## Emotional Escalation

Emotional reactivity is your worst enemy in relationships, and it does you harm in relating with your willful child. Emotions do run high when you love someone, but they don't have to be out of control.

Two common ways that parents and willful child can escalate emotion between them are when parents get into yelling cycles and when the willful child throws temper tantrums. Parents need to know how to reduce the likelihood of both events.

## Yelling Cycles

Parental yelling is usually an expression of frustration with their willful child's repeated delay to do what they asked or to stop doing what they forbid. They didn't start out yelling, but they ended up that way, and the more often they have to get to the yelling point to get compliance, the sooner they get to yelling the next time around.

Parental yelling is definitely a loss of emotional sobriety. It shows the child how delay can successfully provoke parental upset, and it shows the child that parents have reached the point where they are finally serious about what they asked. This is how yelling cycles work: now the child waits to be yelled at before complying, while parents yell when fed up with the delay.

Parents who yell place their faith in increased volume of speech: "The louder I speak, the more I can force you to hear and obey what I have to say." Parents believe that they are talking out when they yell, but they are not. They are acting out of frustration and training their child to delay compliance until parents have reached the high frustration point. This is how yelling cycles are learned. Yelling is counterproductive for several reasons.

The child who is yelled at can feel angry, hurt, or frightened as the yelling parent causes the relationship to feel unsafe. The message parents want to send is obscured by the intensity and volume of frustration and anger they express. By modeling yelling, parents often encourage the child to yell back in return.

The parents have lost control to get control, and the child ends up in control by being given this emotionally provocative power.

Stopping a yelling cycle is very simple: Stop yelling to get what you want. Calmly and insistently pursue what you want. Some parents who are recovering from being yellers find going to the other extreme to be very effective. They actually talk more softly.

Not only does the child not predict this response, but he now has to listen carefully to hear what is being said. And now a new cue for parental seriousness is created: "I know my mom really means business when she lowers her voice."

It may help you avert out-of-control anger to inventory your belief system about family interactions. Just take a journal for a few minutes and write down your beliefs and expectations about family rules and communications. You may surprise yourself with what flows onto the page. You may be repeating the dynamic of your own childhood without meaning to. If necessary, therapy can do wonders to deconstruct those outdated ideas.

## Temper Tantrums

A temper tantrum is equal parts an intense expression of frustration or hurt, an increased emotional clamor to attract attention, and a calculated manipulation to get one's way. The willful four-year-old who is head banging and screaming on the floor is sincerely upset. He is also commanding parental attention. And he is using upset, loudness, and acting out to try and change their minds. Because a tantrum is an honest expression of suffering and anger, parents should try to hear the feelings out, but they must insist on civil communication and they must not give in to extortion. How can you do this?

- **To the expression of discomfort or hurt, make an empathetic response:** "You are feeling really upset; please tell me about it, I want to know."
- **To the use of clamor to attract attention, make a limiting response:** "When you yell, I can't hear you for all the noise. I can hear you better if you speak quietly."
- **To the acting out of suffering and anger to get one's way, make a negating response:** "No matter how extremely unhappy you act, that is not going to change my mind."

Some people advise parents to ignore a temper tantrum and let the child rage and cry out his upset. It's better to respond to the tantrum with empathetic, limiting, and negating responses because of good lessons those responses have to teach: to learn to talk out emotion, to learn to do so in a calm and civil manner, and to forsake using intense emotionality for manipulative gain.

To help a child recover from a tantrum, first ask, "Tell me what you feel; I want to hear." Second ask, "Tell me what you think; I want to understand." Third ask, "Tell me what you need; I want to know." Fourth ask, "Tell me what you could do to feel better, even though you can't have what you want. Maybe I can help."

## Expectations and Emotion

Mental sets have emotional consequences—how people choose to think affects how they come to feel. Nowhere is this truer than with expectations, those mental sets people create to anticipate what is going to happen in the immediate future. When parents hold unrealistic expectations about how their willful child is going to be, the emotional consequences can be intensely upsetting.

"I never thought you'd do something like this!" explodes the parent who had never caught her willful twelve-year-old in a lie before. This is not what the parent expected from an oldest child always known to tell the truth. In consequence of this unexpected change in behavior, the parent can feel a painful combination of betrayal, anxiety, and disappointment.

If the parent had factored lying into his expectations about changes in his child's early adolescence, however, he might have anticipated an increased incidence of dishonesty to get away with doing the forbidden for freedom's sake. Expect does not mean accept. The parent is still obliged to deal with the misbehavior of lying, but expecting that possibility would have kept him from being caught off guard, being emotionally thrown for a loop, and risking overreacting and making the situation worse.

To repeat, *expect* is not *accept*. There is much conduct of your willful child that you may not accept, but by expecting the possibility of these behaviors, you reduce the likelihood that such willful choices, changes, and characteristics catch you unprepared and cause you to compound your corrective response with emotional upset.

## The Nature of Expectations

How do expectations work? Expectations are beliefs you construct to move through life with its experiences and changes. Without the capacity to form any expectations, we would be in a state of ignorance and consequent confusion much of the time, which would be very frightening and cause significant insecurity. The price for this confusion is anxiety.

 **Fact**

For a lot of willful children, many expectations must be met before happiness can be enjoyed. There are predictions to fulfill, ambitions to be satisfied, conditions to be lived up to. The older such children grow, the more discontent comes their way because, as the world grows larger, their command is reduced. They need to become less controlling, not more, or more unhappiness will be their consequence.

Consider three common kinds of parental expectations.

- **Predictions are what you choose to believe will happen.** "I will be able to count on my child's cooperation." As long as this prediction works, you feel secure.
- **Ambitions are what you choose to want to have happen.** "I want my child to be considerate of my needs." As long as this ambition works, you feel fulfilled.
- **Conditions are what you choose to believe should happen.** "My child should always follow family rules." As long as this condition works, you feel satisfied.

As long as expectations you choose to hold fit the reality you have, even when you don't like that reality, you will be prepared for what happens.

## When Expectations Are Unrealistic

Suppose the expectations described above held up with your first child, who has generally been compliant and easy to parent. Now along comes your second offspring, a willful child. When you apply expectations of child number one, for whom these expectations have been realistic, to your willful child, they do not seem to fit.

- **Now your prediction is more frequently violated.** Your willful child is at least as often resistant as she is cooperative, and on these resistant occasions, you find yourself feeling surprised, insecure, and anxious.
- **Now your ambition is more frequently violated.** Your willful child is often more focused on her own wants than she is considerate of your needs, and on these self-centered occasions, you find yourself feeling disappointed, sad, and hurt.
- **Now your condition is more frequently violated.** Your willful child is more often focused on testing and breaking rules than she is compliant, and on these oppositional occasions, you find yourself feeling betrayed, offended, and angry.

Violated expectations are a good example of how mental sets can have powerful emotional consequences. If you continue to hold unrealistic expectations about your willful child, you will be in a state of upset most of the time. Better to adjust your expectations to fit the reality of this self-determined child: sometimes she will be resistant, sometimes she won't be as considerate of your needs as you want, and sometimes she will refuse to follow family rules. Again, this doesn't mean that you accept resistance, self-centeredness, and rule breaking and let them go. You do not. But when they occur, you are not blind-sided; you expected some of these behaviors, so you don't double up, adding your own emotional upset to your disciplinary response.

It is one purpose of this book to propose realistic expectations about what it's like to have a willful child and to reduce the emotional costs of holding unrealistic expectations, so you can more calmly and effectively cope with the challenges involved in raising such a child.

 **Essential**

> Parents need to keep their own expectations of their child's interests in line with those of the child. When parents develop higher expectations than the child's (because of their own investment in the activity), if the child loses interest, they may feel anxious, disappointed, or angry, because their expectations have been violated. "I guess we cared more about her being involved in soccer than she did. That's why we got so upset when she quit."

## Emotional Overreactions

For both parent and willful child, sometime it's bound to happen: someone overreacts emotionally. For no apparent good cause, usually in response to something too small to merit such an intense response, either party will explode, and the other will wonder "What's going on?" Even the overreactor may be puzzled: "Why did such a minor event set me off?"

The other person didn't hear what you said; so what? The other person didn't show up exactly on time; so what? The other person mentioned what you said to somebody else; so what? Little things shouldn't cause such major upsets, you may believe. Oh, yes, they often should. And both parties need to understand why, to profit from that understanding.

## Little Things Are Big Things in Disguise

When a little event sets off a disproportionately large emotional reaction for you or your willful child, you know that the small happening was really a "big thing" in disguise. The person who explodes is amplifying the significance of a small event into an emotional reaction for a number of common causes—from stress, from suppression, from symbolism, from similarity, or from surprise.

Already exhausted from overdemand at work, one small additional thing to do at home is enough to carry you over your emotional tipping point and you explode. "I've been cleaning up after people all day at work, so wash those snack dishes in the sink, and I mean now!" Overreactions from stress are usually a result of exhaustion.

Having spent a whole day at school being teased and saying nothing back, your child explodes at you for criticizing his messy room. "Why don't you just get in line with all the other people who don't like me? Now leave me alone!" Overreactions from suppression are usually the result of emotional buildup from unexpressed irritations, insults, or injuries.

Waiting for your spouse to arrive an hour late without calling, you explode when he finally walks in the door. "Not calling when you knew you were going to be late just goes to show how you never consider my feelings!" Symbolic overreactions are usually the result of what specific actions come to signify and represent.

Giving the first child home from school first chance to play with the new computer infuriates the older child when he gets home from sports. "This is just like what has happened a million times since he was born. My younger brother gets favored over me!" Similarity overreactions are usually the result of a current occurrence that reminds someone of something painful that has happened before.

You did not think to tell your child that your weekend plans have changed and you won't be able to provide transportation he assumed would be available; he reacts like he's been betrayed. "You never tell me anything! I'm just left to find stuff out at the last minute, when it's going to mess up my life!" Overreactions from surprise are usually from an unexpected turn of events that prove disruptive.

## What Overreactions Can Teach

Although at the time overreactions command a lot of attention, once over, they tend to be ignored. People just want to forget the unpleasantness and put it behind them. The person who overreacts feels foolish for having blown up at something so small, and the person blown up at doesn't want to revisit the discomfort. This immediate dismissal of an unhappy event, however, is a mistake. Overreactions can be very informative if people will take the time to learn from what hidden issues have to teach. Understand the reasons behind the other person's unreasonable behavior, or your own, and you can gain valuable insight. Do this by asking clarifying questions that can unlock what is really going on.

- Ask the stress question: "Have you experienced a lot of other demands today?"
- Ask the suppression question: "Has there been another hard experience upsetting you?"
- Ask the symbolism question: "What does how I just acted represent to you?"
- Ask the similarity question: "What does what happened remind you of?"
- Ask the surprise question: "What were you thinking would occur?"

It is a wasted opportunity to let emotional overreactions go. Use clarifying questions to tease the meaning out. Although both parent and willful child might wish the episode had never happened, since it did, learn from it all you can. Moderation of emotion will carry the day, and keep your voice modulated, even when discussing uncomfortable events.

Keep a healthy awareness that children can sometimes be a mirror for the parents' issues, humbling as that may be. A degree of openness with your child about not always having the answers and being willing to learn softens the tone in the household.

Whenever possible, realize for yourself that mental and emotional expectations have a way of eventually outwardly manifesting in your life. Take care, then, to consciously keep good, positive pictures of your child, yourself, and the healthy family emotional tone in your mind. This way you'll be experiencing that, not the opposite.

## CHAPTER 13

# ADD and ADHD
# Children and Willfulness

P arents often wonder to what degree a child should be held responsible for her strong-willed behavior. After all, suppose the child can't help it? Suppose there's some mental condition that is beyond the child's power to control? Suppose some kind of special help is needed for the child to effect any behavior change? Just because they're frustrated by the child's mental condition and associated behavior, they won't correct it by correcting the child. The child needs understanding and help, not impatience and punishment, which will only make matters worse. "If you don't stop squirming and fidgeting and won't sit still, you can spend the rest of the day in your room!"

## The Wandering Child and the Wild Child

There are cases where children are easily distracted because of attention deficit disorder (ADD). Maybe the wild child who is exploding with energy and breaking rules has a limiting condition, a predisposition to impulsivity from hyperactivity disorder (HD). Or maybe the child suffers from some combination of both limiting conditions: attention deficit/hyperactivity disorder (ADHD).

What are the signs of attention deficit? Children who, over a six-month period or longer, suffer from an attention-deficit condition commonly display difficulty concentrating on low-interest tasks, listening to what they are told, following directions, completing assignments, getting and staying organized, keeping track of belongings, and remembering important information, because they are so easily distracted by changing stimulation.

What are some signs of hyperactivity? Children might be hyperactive who, for six months or longer, suffer from difficulty being still, staying quiet, keeping silent, slowing down, delaying gratification, thinking before acting, abiding social restraints, not acting restless, and not rushing through tasks because they are so impulsively driven.

Exactly how many millions of children in the United States have ADD and ADHD is hard to determine, but based on the increase in medical prescriptions given for the condition, the number appears to be growing.

# Separating the Condition from the Choice

When the willful child shows signs of either an ADD or ADHD condition, parents need to assess to what degree these behaviors are subject to his control. Don't try to make this assessment at home, because freedom in the family often gives a false picture of what is a matter of the child's condition and what is a matter of the child's choice. Consider, instead, your child's behavior in locations outside the home.

## Making a Social Situation Assessment
Remember, growth is just a gathering of power from dependence to independence, and a willful child gathers it any way he can. A wandering willful child may choose not to attend to what parents are saying for freedom's sake. A wild willful child may choose to break rules at home to see what she can get away with. In either case, parents may excuse the inattention and the disobedience by ascribing these actions to the child's mental condition, not to the child's choice.

How can you tell if the troublesome behavior is a matter of condition or choice? Make a social situation assessment. Ask this question and then honestly answer: "Can my child pay adequate attention to directions and instructions, and exercise adequate control over urge and impulse, so he is able to stay in communication and act within prescribed social limits at school, at Scout or church groups, at his grandparents' and other relatives', at the homes of friends, at school field trips, at sports activities, at day camp, at overnight camp, at the mall, at the daycare, or with a babysitter?"

## Alert

All diagnoses, including ADD and ADHD, are extremely finite and should be treated that way. A diagnosis describes only some of a person's human condition in terms of a particular cluster of behaviors. And those behaviors are just a very small part of an infinitely larger person. It is the responsibility of parents to always keep that larger person in mind. Never let the diagnostic label define the total child. Do not succumb to the temptation of labeling the child as a way of forever excusing his and your mistakes. This is not a happy road to follow.

### Evaluating the Data

If the data show that the child can choose to attend and consent to the social limits away from home, then hold him to that responsible account within the family. Do not let him in his willfulness exploit ADD, HD, or ADHD conditions to authorize behaviors that should be out-of-bounds or to earn exemptions from normal family rules and expectations.

Expect that the child who is capable of attentive and compliant behavior apart from family can choose to act that way at home. You can explain how the same reasoning applies to you as parents. "If we can get tired at our jobs and still manage to act in a patient and courteous manner, then you have the right to expect that when we are tired at home, we can make the same effort to treat you with patience and courtesy, too."

## The Cultural Contribution

Parents must also factor in two formative cultural influences that may contribute to ADD, HD, and ADHD behavior. One factor common to all three conditions is the need for constant stimulation, hence the child's wandering attention or need to be in constant motion or both. Are these characteristics innate, or can they also be taught or learned through culture? You may want to experiment with having quiet nights at home when nothing electronic or digital is allowed—no cell phones, no texting, no TV, no laptops, and no video games. Slow the pace down and have some normal conversation.

Parents may want to factor in cultural conditioning because then they can reduce the effect of that conditioning if they so choose. In the United States today, children tend to become acculturated to a high degree of personal choice and to an extremely varied menu of sensational stimulation from electronic entertainment. Make some effort to moderate this overstimulation and sense everyone calming down. Turn off your own iPod and digital planner and attend to the humans in your family.

### Too Many Choices

The more choices children are given, the more control over choices they want, the less content they are to live in terms of choices other people make. If a child is continually given many choices, from what she can play with or get to do to what she will eat for breakfast, then having a lot of choices is something she will expect.

Just consider the entertainment culture in which your child is growing up—all the choices for stimulation she has on a regular basis. Every choice is a potential stimulant because it creates the opportunity for change—adding something new and different and unfamiliar to the child's world. How many toys does your child have to play with? How many TV channels are available to watch? How many destinations on the Internet are there for the child to visit? How many computer and video games are available? How many apps on the iPad? Every entertainment choice a child makes is a choice for fresh stimulation.

The more stimulation children get to choose, the more stimulation they need to have to feel okay. To make matters worse, the more passively they rely on entertainment, the less initiative children develop to entertain themselves and the less self-discipline they have to do without entertainment and engage in uninteresting work. "I can't make myself do what isn't exciting and fun!"

 **Essential**

Clutter can cause confusion by creating too much distraction. So help order and simplify your ADHD child's personal surroundings, and you will simplify her choices and help organize her world. Reducing room clutter can reduce overstimulation, confusion, and loss of focus.

By late elementary school and middle school, unless they can be watching television, talking on the telephone, instant messaging on the computer, texting on the phone, listening to music, or doing all at the same time, many children can't get their homework done. "It takes a lot of distraction to concentrate on doing something so boring!" They need enough stimulation to keep dreaded boredom away. "I hate having nothing to do!" They have become adjusted to stimulation overload, and that adjustment is often expressed in ADD and ADHD behaviors—wandering attention and a body needing to be constantly on the move.

No wonder there is a disconnection between the cultural experience of society and the educational experience of school, where so many children are identified as candidates for ADD/ADHD evaluation. By comparison with the entertainment culture they are used to, many children have a hard time concentrating on low-interest tasks and sitting still for an hour at a time in a world where choices and variety of stimulation are more limited.

Think of ADD/ADHD as a cultural problem. Today, a minority of children are identified and treated for ADD/ADHD; in another generation, it may be the majority. Do your best not to be at the mercy of cultural pressures to label and categorize your child. There are ultimately no shortcuts to the relentless responsibility of parenting. The route of labeling and medicating may be appealing for the short term but it does nothing to enhance a future, happy adult life for your current strong-willed charge.

## Alert

If your child is identified as ADD/ADHD, it is probably not a good idea to sit her in front of the TV for long periods of time. This may seem to calm or settle the child down, but actually it only increases the child's reliance on passive entertainment and the need for excessive stimulation. The short visual bytes also feed in to the short attention span.

Parents can mitigate some of these ADD/ADHD effects by moderating the amount of passive electronic entertainment choices they allow, by teaching their children to actively entertain themselves, and by having them get used to doing some regular amount of routine, boring work.

### Electronic Brain Training

One effect of TV watching and playing video or computer games that many parents ignore is the electronic brain training they are providing their young child. They are plugging the child in to an activity that assaults the mind with swiftly changing, frenetic, and exciting stimulation in order to hold the child's attention. In the process, her attention span is being electronically conditioned. Mental functioning is being shaped as the child's brain is fired and wired to keep up with this onslaught of extremely fast-changing and sensational electronic stimuli.

 **Fact**

> Sometimes a change in environmental factors will shift a child's attention or hyperactive difficulties. Improvements in diet (fewer sweets and processed foods) as well as minimizing chemicals in household products can result in a calmer child.

So, starting at around age one, maybe you use TV as an electronic babysitter for an hour or two a day, and by age three, the child is watching three or four hours a day. You believe you are calming the child down when, in fact, you may be laying the electronic conditioning foundation for ADD/ADHD behaviors. Be deliberate about how much TV and video/computer game exposure you allow your child. Think of it as high-stimulation brain training. If you believe your child is already in overload, reduce this electronic brain training. Your child doesn't need any more.

Because, through excessive choice and electronic brain training, we acculturate our children to short attention span and stimulation overload, the question parents need to ask is not "Does my child have ADD or ADHD?" but "How much ADD or ADHD does my child have?" The more of these characteristics that your strong-willed child has, the more intensely willful she is likely to act, the less easily she will be able to tolerate a less stimulating environment like the classroom, the demands of repetitive work, and the restrictions of rules.

**Fact**

For ADD/ADHD children, psycho-stimulant medication and electronic brain training can both have the same effect. The increase of chemical or electronic stimulation calms the child down by temporarily meeting her high stimulation needs, but in the long run, it just perpetuates dependency on high stimulation and short attention span demands to feel okay.

## Problem Solving

What can parents do to help their willful ADD or ADHD child learn to constructively play the mental condition she has been dealt by inheritance or acquired experience? Commit to very labor-intensive parenting that takes the time for daily problem solving and makes the time for daily practice.

Why should parents make this commitment? Because, at school for example, left at the mercy of insufficient stimulation, the child can become quickly bored. To cope with this discomfort, he may disengage from classroom involvement, daydream, ignore instruction, oppose limits, forget directions, give in to restlessness, give up on uninteresting tasks, refuse to complete work, and act out to get attention. No wonder ADD/ADHD children have a higher-than-average rate of school failure, not to mention other problems to which they are also statistically more prone: alcohol and drug abuse, accidents, trouble with the law, even suicide. When you can't comply with the demands of social systems like family and school, when you continually get criticized and punished for not conforming and not complying, it is easy to feel disconnected and alienated and suffer a loss of esteem.

Because of proneness to distraction (ADD) and impulse (HD), ADHD children have a high incidence of offending the regulatory powers that be at home, at school, and out in the world. Each time one of these encounters occurs, a disciplinary response needs to be made, and correction is not the one.

Remember, discipline is a combination of instruction and correction and to remain effective needs to be 90 percent instruction and no more than 10 percent correction. Reverse this percentage, as tired and frustrated parents of willful/ADD/ADHD children are often tempted to do, and disproportionate correction often encourages the misbehavior it is trying to stop. "And I'm going to keep punishing you until you cheer up!"

Correction and instruction are two different approaches to behavior problems. Correction is allowing or applying consequences to discourage repetition of what should not have occurred. "For acting without thinking and doing what you did, you're grounded for the weekend." Instruction is extracting learning from misbehavior to inform better choices the next time around. "We need to talk about the kind of thinking and decision making that caused you to act this way so you can understand how not to let this happen again."

The instructional approach has the most disciplinary value with ADD/ADHD children because you are trying to educate them to better manage their susceptibility to distraction and impulse. To this end, you turn every problem into a discussion, the purpose of which is to help your child learn how to manage his choices in more constructive ways. So the child comes to anticipate that the major consequence of any misbehavior is communication: "When I get in trouble for doing what I shouldn't, I know there's going to be a talk to figure out what went wrong and how to do it right." This approach to discipline is very labor- and time-intensive, but it is worth it. As a parent, you are most concerned with helping your ADD/ADHD child learn to manage well the condition the child has developed or been dealt.

# Question

Does being ADD, HD, or ADHD mean there is something psychologically wrong with my child?
No. These designations do not mean your child is emotionally troubled, learning disabled, socially hostile, personally unhappy, or intellectually deficient. They just mean your child's brain is prone, through nature and nurture, to working in a highly distractible and impulsive way.

## Practicing Self-Management Skills

ADD and ADHD children need parental help to learn from problems that distractibility and impulsivity can cause and to practice self-management skills that can increase concentration and self-restraint. The occupational therapy approach through which children practice and develop specific capacities through many hours of repetition is a good model for parents to follow. They can daily work with their child on listening, remembering, organizing, and completing tasks, and they can daily work on themselves to provide a clear and consistent family structure, to reward compliance, and to simplify the child's personal space so spatial chaos does not add to personal confusion. Help with delayed gratification increases the child's comfort level in a variety of settings.

Parents can help the child learn to manage distractibility by practicing tolerance for boredom. This is one instructional value of homework and chores. They teach the child to concentrate attention on completing undesirable, uninteresting, and boring tasks. In the process, a work ethic is developed—learning to do what one does not necessarily like to do just to get it done. ADD and ADHD children can benefit from learning some self-discipline.

Parents can help the child learn to manage impulsivity by practicing tolerance for delay. Teach the child to defer immediate gratification through such activities as planning, earning, and saving. In the process, the child learns that he can control impulse and that there are benefits to being able to do so. ADD and ADHD children can benefit from learning some self-denial.

Probably the best thing for parents to give to their child with ADD/ADHD, besides love, is the ability to entertain himself. When children with ADD/ADHD learn to manage their energy and focus so they can depend upon themselves to initiate activities that cause them to feel good about themselves, they gain a sense of control over their own behavior and satisfaction from being who and how they are. They gain freedom to follow an agenda of activity of their own making, tailor-made to fit what actively works for them. In this regard, regular physical exercise can be extremely beneficial because it can relax the mind instead of overstimulating it. Artistic activities can do the same.

The ADHD child who spends untold hours shooting hoops, the ADD/ADHD child who gets absorbed in tinkering with machines, the ADD/ADHD child who cannot seem to read enough science fiction each has found active, focused outlets for his heightened need for stimulation. Through creativity, practice, athletics, socializing, interest, or study, they learn to direct themselves. Where they can, parents need to support these activities. Of course, parents also have to be prepared for these children to hyperfocus on what they love and so have difficulty disengaging from or interrupting these activities.

## Using Medication

Medications deliver their effects more like shotguns than rifles. While they target a precise symptom or objective, they impact the entire system. So parents need to understand that when their child is receiving medication to moderate ADD/ADHD behavior, other areas of the child's functioning can be affected.

Treatment with prescriptive medication should be the intervention of last, not first, resort, after training through problem solving and practice has been given a systematic and consistent adequate trial. Do not treat medication as a quick and convenient fix. Training before treatment is the key. If training seems insufficiently beneficial, then try treatment with medication, but continue the training!

## The Benefits

The data clearly indicate that, for many children with ADD/ADHD, medication helps. Talk to some of these children and they will identify a positive difference. They will describe how it calms their frantic energy, how it creates an internal measure of choice that allows them to control impulse better than before, and how their capacity for sustained focus and concentration, even on boring tasks, has been improved. In addition, as they quiet down and attend more, and fit into family and social systems with less difficulty, they get treated in more positive ways by adults in authority and therefore feel better about themselves.

## The Risks

What kinds of risks are associated with medication? Some are known—and your prescribing physician will describe them—and some are not. There are some side effects that are immediately apparent, and there are some long-term effects that may not be identified until many years of research data can be mined to tease them out.

An example of an immediate side effect of a psycho-stimulant can be the child's eating behavior. Remember that stimulants have a long history in the diet industry as appetite suppressants. So as your child loses appetite, she may also lose weight, or not keep up normal weight gain with years of growth. Parents often report one effect of taking the child off stimulant medication is return of appetite and weight gain.

Ultimately be wary of medication as a shortcut for controlling your willful child. Although it takes more effort to shift around environmental factors and teach the child calm, controlled ways of behaving at home and away from home, the end result is worth it. Being drugged is not a worthy state at any age. It cuts one off from life and the richness of inner knowledge and the process of character development. Becoming acquainted with one's inner life and resources is a worthy endeavor, regardless of age. It's a way of achieving security and competency in life.

You may also want to consider changes in diet that can moderate your child's behavior. There is growing research that shows that a simple, pure diet, without sugar and chemical additives, calms a person down. This may require considerable effort, concentration, and shift in family lifestyle, but it could be worth it in terms of a calmer child.

## Fact

According to Dan Kindlon, author of *Too Much of a Good Thing*, research reveals five factors present in the homes of well-behaved children—eating dinner together; parents are not divorced or separated; the children have to keep their room clean; there is no phone in the child's room; and the children do community service.

## CHAPTER 14

# Introducing Education

C hildren are required to go to school, and since requirements of any kind can grate against a willful child's independent spirit, school is not always that easy for him. Consider a few aspects of precious self-determination that the strong-willed child must give up when entering the classroom. He must follow a schedule, take directions, do class work, do homework, be graded, be treated as one of many, comply with authority, sit still, do as told, speak only when called upon, get up only with permission, not talk back, and not challenge rules or the adult making them.

## Issues with School

In addition to adjusting to the limitations and demands of school itself, the child has to deal with parental involvement in his social conduct and academic performance there. Now school not only complicates the child's personal life, it complicates his relationship with parents, too. Certainly the child is responsible for his choices at school, but parents are responsible for monitoring conduct and performance and intervening when those choices go awry. You can make life easier for yourself and your child if you enroll him in preschool and other play programs at a young age. That way the sting of enforced cooperation in a school setting is not so severe. He will learn patience and delayed gratification.

Much normal conflict, particularly between parents and a willful child, is directly related to disagreements over school. There is the elementary school child who clings to parents and doesn't want to separate for school. There is the middle school child who starts forgetting homework. There is the high school child who skips classes to hang out with friends. There is an infinite array of conflicts that school demands create between parents and child.

 **Fact**

> Willful young children who have free rein in the family can have a hard time starting school because they have to give up much of their freedom. If parents foresee a difficult educational adjustment, they should prepare the child for unaccustomed changes that school will likely bring. For example, "You won't be allowed to get up and wander around when you feel restless."

## Setting Academic Expectations

It is the parents' responsibility to set the child's standards of academic performance at school because they know their daughter best. They have a sense of the child's innate capacity and potential. Parents have to estimate the first and set expectations for the second. However, be careful not to make the child over in your own image. It's *her* life and education, not yours.

### What Are Your Standards?

Statements parents commonly make to encourage appropriate academic performance include, "Just do your best," "Just try your hardest," "Just work up to your potential, that's all we ask."

That's asking too much. Abstract, vague standards are impossible to reach. Who among us does our best, tries our hardest, or works up to our potential? And how could we possibly know? The only outcome of these discouraging admonitions is to cause the child to feel any effort is deficient because more effort could always be made.

Instead, specify standards in terms of the grading system the school uses to evaluate performance. First set a performance ceiling, and then set a performance floor. "We think you have the ability to get straight Bs and maybe a few As if you totally dedicated yourself to your studies. We believe it is reasonable for us to expect you to earn all Bs, so that is the minimal level of performance we will accept. Get below a B, and we will do whatever we can to help you bring that grade back up." Now you have set your expectations for your child in terms of a specific outcome she can understand.

But how can you be sure that your standards are realistic? After all, you don't want to set them unrealistically high, pressuring an average student to excel beyond what she is truly capable of, any more than you want to set them unrealistically low, causing the more academically able child to under-perform. The answer is, you need to get an academic benchmark, and you usually have to get it twice—once in elementary school and once in secondary school.

### Getting a Benchmark

An academic benchmark is an accurate measure of the child's operating capacity, which she earns for one grading period during which the child gets all homework done, turns it in on time, studies for all tests, attends all classes, and finishes all projects and class work on schedule. To get this measure, you supervise as much as necessary to see what the child's level of performance will be when all work is completely and consistently accomplished—your definition of when a 100 percent effort is made. Now you know what your child is capable of—be it As, Bs, Cs, or some combination thereof, and you have a basis for holding the child to that standard of performance.

However, just because a child was able to get all As with a full-faith effort in elementary school does not mean the same standard automatically holds for middle school or high school. Why the difference? As your child moves from elementary to secondary school, not only do the knowledge and skills taught become more complex to master, but the curriculum, and the tracks through that curriculum, becomes more diverse. Academic placement can dramatically alter the group of peers with whom your child is competing. Degree of difficulty is increased from remedial, to regular, to gifted and talented, to honors, to advanced placement classes, so you may find it realistic to lower performance expectations if your child moves into a faster academic track. Now the curriculum is enriched, the instructional pace quickens, the amount of homework increases, and the concepts become more difficult to learn.

 **Question**

**Do report cards really matter?**
Yes! A report card is like a mirror for your child. You want her to be able to look in that mirror and see a faithful reflection of how she is capable of performing with a reasonable effort. "How well I have done shows me how well I can do." Adjusting to an underperforming report card can lower self-esteem.

Secondary school brings new academic conditions, and you may want to reset your academic benchmark. Getting this new benchmark in secondary school is also important because so many children go through an early adolescent achievement drop as rebellion and disaffection negatively affect their motivation to perform well in school. You have to be able to say to your older child, "When you consistently took care of all your business at school for that marking period, you achieved on a B level. So we are holding to that level hereafter."

**Fact**

By resisting instructional demands, doing less work, and performing adequately without effort, a willful child may think she is beating the teacher, winning in the classroom contest for control. But, of course, the child is really losing—losing out on the chance to learn, to achieve up to capacity, to lay academic groundwork for future mobility.

## Writing Off a Willful Child

Sometimes teachers find that managing a willful child takes all the energy they can afford to devote to a single student, and so they back off on making additional instructional demands. A teacher may write off a willful child academically by electing to leave bad enough alone, treating the child as too troublesome to teach, preferring to keep classroom problems down than to keep academic pressure up. Essentially, the teacher backs off on instructionally challenging the child to avoid the child's social challenges to the teacher.

The unhappy result is that your bright willful child ends up under-performing at school. Concerned by this unsatisfactory state of affairs, you schedule a conference with your child's teacher only to be told that low academic performance is the best the child can achieve.

- "Academics will always be a struggle for her."
- "She's more the athletic type than the academic type."
- "As the parent, you need to treat average achievement as good enough."

Don't buy it. You know this "pass don't push" approach to instruction is enabling your willful child to under-perform. But what should you do? Demand that the teacher push your child harder? No. Instead, tell the teacher you are ready to do some pushing of your own. And don't let your child be warehoused in a special class, even if behavior is a problem.

Tell the teacher you want all homework, tests, papers, and projects that receive a score of 79 or less sent home, where you will take the time with your child to go over what was left incomplete or done incorrectly to help improve performance back at school. You are bringing the instructional pressure home. You are also sending a message to your child: "The less adequately you do classroom work at school, the more you will be redoing classroom work at home." And you are sending a message to the teacher: "I expect you to expect more of my child."

## Collaborating with the School

"The problem with having almost thirty students in the classroom," explained the seasoned elementary teacher, "is that they've got you outnumbered. So at the beginning of the year, my job is to outnumber them. By the end of the first two weeks, either on the phone or in person, I have visited with every parent and formed an academic alliance.

"Now it's two or three adults teamed together for each student, and each student is told that this partnership is in place. If the parents have any concerns, they contact me for help, and if I have any concerns, I contact them. That's how I get to outnumber the kids."

 **Fact**

Sometimes it is the teacher's thankless job to give a normative reference on a child to the child's parents. "Compared with other children this age, I see some developmental issues that need to be addressed." It's not easy being the bearer of bad news, but one professional responsibility of being a teacher is to screen children in the classroom for possible growth problems relative to their larger group of peers.

It's important for a willful child to know that parents and teacher have a relationship that is not determined by what the child says to one party about the other. When everything parents and teacher know about each other depends on what the child has to report, then the child has enormous power to influence how the adults perceive each other. "The reason I got in trouble in class," the willful child tells parents, "is because I wouldn't take being picked on by one of the teacher's favorites." Believing this, parents write off the child's misbehavior, attributing it to unfairness on the teacher's part. "If you write me up for what I did," pleads the child, "my parents will get really angry and spank me again." Believing this, the teacher elects not to write up the child in order to spare the child severe punishment at home.

What is the willful child in each example doing? He is simply exploiting the brokering power the adults have given. Now they must depend upon what the child has to say to understand each other. Never give the child brokering power over the parent/teacher relationship. The concerned adults should always establish a line of communication independent of the child. Make a concerted effort to keep the lines of communication open and, at some point, you may want to inquire whether there are guidance counselors or resource teachers who might be available to your child.

## Secondary School versus Primary School

From infancy through childhood, through adolescence, and throughout adulthood, human beings become more complex. Growth gives everyone more development to manage than they had before. Part of a parent's job is to help the child integrate and cope with the complexity created by new growth, which includes learning to cope with an increasingly complex social world as the child enters adolescence and secondary school, usually close to the same time.

The entry into middle school is complicated because three changes occur simultaneously. By the sixth grade, most children have begun to separate from childhood and to differentiate into more resistant adolescents. A middle school is larger than an elementary school and demands more responsibility from students compared to elementary school. Parents who may have been intimately involved in elementary school find it harder to maintain that level of institutional intimacy and easy communication in middle school.

## The Transition to Middle School

Compare two classrooms of children—second graders and seventh graders. How are they developmentally different to teach? The primary school teacher might generally characterize her students as curious, industrious, attentive, enthusiastic, positive, cooperative, and friendly much of the time. The secondary school teacher might generally characterize her students as disinterested, restless, distracted, apathetic, negative, disorganized, and fractious much of the time.

Why such different descriptions? The primary school teacher has a classroom of children, whereas the secondary school teacher has a classroom of adolescents. And it is this second teacher that parents must work with in middle school, a teacher who has more natural frustrations with students than teachers do in early elementary school. As students enter adolescence, teachers have a harder time getting their basic role needs met.

What basic role needs? Consider three basic needs of teachers: to be liked, to be obeyed, to be effective. To be liked, it feels good to have students who are friendly. To be in control, it feels good to have students who follow directions. To be effective, it feels good to have students who work to learn. It is partly because adolescent students tend to more frequently frustrate these teacher needs that those teachers are less responsive to parents and stricter with students, particularly those who are strong-willed and need to be shown who is in charge. Resistant adolescent students can sometimes make secondary teachers look bad, feel bad, and act less responsively with parents than did those teachers with fewer and better behaved students in elementary school.

The adjustment to middle school can be hard for students, but it can be even harder for parents. In elementary school, parents felt invited in to be involved, to be informed, to have influence by teachers who could give more attention to the individual child because there were fewer students in each class. In middle school, parents can start to feel pushed away, so students can learn responsibility, independence, and self-regulation, by teachers who must give less attention to the individual child because there are more students to teach.

Protective parents can go through a sort of withdrawal from having to let go of a child they could still hold on to in elementary school and from the loss of comfort and security and familiarity that primary school provided both parent and child. Although the elementary school she attended might have been a neighborhood school within walking distance from home, the secondary student may now be bussed to a middle school farther away. Now their child is embedded in a larger, more diverse institution, and so are they.

 **Fact**

Looking back on elementary school compared with secondary school, on childhood compared with adolescence, many parents wistfully appreciate the ease, the availability, the responsiveness of communication with child and school that has been lost.

## The Middle School Curriculum

In size, structure, and mission, middle school is not elementary school. In size, a middle school can be two or three times as large as an elementary school. "This isn't Kansas anymore." The administrative structure is more hierarchical and there are more rules and procedures required for keeping this larger institution running. And the mission is different. Elementary school tries to teach very young children the instructional basics. Middle school tries to equip early-adolescent students, who now have a hard time fitting in anywhere, with the self-management, system adjustment, and political skills for successfully navigating high school. This is the implied curriculum of the middle school.

The self-management skills middle school tries to teach have to do with responsibility (owning the consequences and coping with the consequences of one's decisions), self-discipline (motivating oneself to do class work and homework), and organization (keeping track of and keeping up with multiple lines of instruction).

The system adjustment skills are the three Cs: compliance with rules, cooperating with authority, and conformity to institutional norms. Students who learn the three Cs in middle school are treated positively by the system; students who don't, are not. The institutional message to students in middle school is pretty cut-and-dried: learn to work with the system or the system will work against you, and the system always wins.

The political skills are getting along with teachers who may not get along that easily with them. Students need to learn to meet the three basic role needs of teachers, and to do so, students need to learn to act. They need to act friendly so the teacher will feel liked. They need to act obedient so the teacher will feel in control. They need to act industrious so the teacher will feel effective.

Willful children in middle school who don't learn self-discipline, responsibility, and organization (the self-management skills); who don't learn to cooperate, conform, and comply (the system adjustment skills); and who don't learn to act as if they like, will obey, and will work to learn with teachers (the political skills) will have a hard time catching hold and successfully completing high school.

# Public, Private, or Homeschooling

When it comes to type of education, some parents have the means to have a choice between public, private, or homeschooling. There is no right or wrong choice to be considered here, only understanding that each choice has some factors that recommend it and others that do not. When parenting a willful child, it can be useful to keep these factors in mind, since some factors can support objectives that parents are struggling to encourage the willful child to reach.

Consider fifteen comparisons among the three types of schooling:

| | Public school | Private school | Homeschool |
|---|---|---|---|
| Teacher training requirements | Most | Moderate | Least |
| Mandated curriculum | Most | Moderate | Least |
| College preparation | Least | Most | Moderate |
| Student diversity | Most | Moderate | Least |
| Attention per student | Least | Moderate | Most |
| Individualized instruction | Least | Moderate | Most |
| Size of attendance area | Moderate | Most | Least |
| Competition for grades | Moderate | Most | Least |
| Extracurricular offerings and special support services | Most | Moderate | Least |
| Parental influence on student experience | Moderate | Least | Most |
| Social sheltering | Least | Moderate | Most |
| Academic achievement focus | Moderate | Most | Least |
| Strictness of school rules | Moderate | Most | Least |
| Adherence to family faith/values | Least | Moderate | Most |
| Instructional resources | Most | Moderate | Least |

# ⓔ✪ Essential

Same-sex schools, particularly for young women, can have beneficial effects both academically and developmentally. There is less pressure from sex-role stereotypes about what a woman can and cannot do and so she is encouraged to develop herself more fully. Also, there is no social distraction from trying to attract, fend off, and manage day-time relationships with young men. Freedom from sex-role constraints and freedom for personal growth are some of what same-sex education has to offer young women.

Now tally up the "mosts" to form a profile of each type of schooling in order to begin assessing which kind of schooling might best fit the needs of your willful child.

Public schooling has the most:
- Teacher training
- Mandated curriculum
- Instructional resources
- Extracurricular/support services
- Student diversity

Private schooling has the most:
- Size of attendance area
- Competition for grades
- Academic achievement focus
- Strictness of rules
- College preparation

Homeschooling has the most:
- Attention per student
- Individualized instruction
- Parental influence
- Social sheltering
- Adherence to family faith/values

**Fact**

> Paying for private school does not guarantee influence. In a public school, if parents disagree with how their child is treated, they can appeal to the principal, superintendent, school board, even state board of education. But in a private school, there is no appeal. The principal can simply say, "If you don't like how we treat your child here, you are free to enroll him elsewhere."

## Coming to Conclusions

Assuming they can afford to have a choice, what parents have to ask themselves is which of these paths might most favor the development of their willful child. Public school creates the opportunity to cope with the push and shove and impersonal treatment that can come from being one in the larger world of many. Children learn to make their way in a crowd. Private school (whether nondenominational, religious, or charter) offers students a smaller, sheltered institutional experience with a more academic focus. Children learn the will to work when they don't want to study. And homeschooling creates the opportunity for having education tailored to the child's nature, needs, and interests. Children learn to discover and develop their individual interests. Parents who homeschool may need to plan for time-outs for themselves, so they don't burn out.

Also consider how location affects your child's learning environment. In public school, children are usually assigned from the same geographic attendance area and so can make friends who live relatively close by. Going to private school, however, means making friends with children from all over the community, and so it becomes harder to get together with friends after school and harder for parents to get to know other parents. It is within your rights to inquire of either a public school or private school about whether there are opportunities for independent studies for a highly motivated student.

# Additional Education

There are times when existing public, private, or homeschooling is insufficient to meet the willful child's needs, either because willful opposition has caused her to fall behind in schoolwork or willful ambition has caused her to forge far ahead. In either case, additional educational resources can be helpful.

## Essential

> Willful children who go through an early adolescent period of rebelling against their own self-interest by refusing to do schoolwork—to show parents and teachers who controls getting it done—may win the battle of resistance at the time. However, the price of victory is usually a loss of important knowledge. The child falls behind and often will need remedial help to catch back up, and tutorial support to keep up, at least for a while.

### Falling Behind

Sometimes, when there is an early adolescent achievement drop or energy has been diverted from school responsibilities to cope with family change such as a move, divorce, or remarriage, the child may process less schoolwork for a significant period of time. As a result, she may miss out on knowledge and skills required to master new instructional content. So when the child reengages with schoolwork, it's not that she isn't trying hard enough to do well, it's that she doesn't know enough to do well.

At this juncture, parents need to check for possible educational loss. This requires getting the child academically assessed by a supplemental educational facility in her community to determine if she is on grade level in all subject areas, and if not, obtaining remedial help to catch the child up with what was lost.

Another use of supplemental help occurs when homework becomes an intractable battle between insistent parents and deceptive child ("I did it at school," "I'll do it in the morning," "There wasn't any"). Then parents find out that the failing grades are due to all the zeros that were given for homework not turned in.

Rather than continue a losing battle at home that only further frays relationships, some parents turn to supplemental education. They announce to their willful child, "Fighting every night about homework is only stressing our relationship and does not seem to get the homework done. So, starting tomorrow, you and your homework will be taken directly from school to a supplemental education center. You will stay there as long as it takes for you to get the homework done and for supervisors to check that it is all complete. Then you can come home, homework-free."

**Alert**

If your child goes through an early adolescent achievement drop, forgetting or not doing or not turning in homework or class work, grades falling from failing effort, let her know you will personally supervise her conduct at school by picking up and turning in homework together with her, and even sitting with her in class if inattention or misbehavior is occurring. This is not to embarrass the child; it is to help her take care of business.

## Graduating from High School Early

Some willful children are very directed in their schoolwork and in a hurry to pursue their goals. By junior year in high school, they have most of their graduation credits, socially feel finished with high school, and are ready to move on. Holding back the child based on the belief that high school is a four-year obligation is not a good idea. If your child is ambitious and determined to move on, explore options for doing so. See if your child can take some classes at a local community college during her senior year to begin accumulating higher-education credits. If your child wants to enter a four-year college, explore early admission policies. If your child just wants to get out of high school, explore credit-by-exam and correspondence options for graduating early.

If your willful child has the will to do the work to graduate early and to move on in life, more power to her. Support the challenge of accelerating graduation; don't arbitrarily impose the frustration of hanging around to graduate with peers.

Some closing thoughts on education for your willful child would include: be aware of community resources that can supplement your child's education (private lessons, recreation programs, YMCA programs, museum classes), and ultimately remember that you are at the helm of your child's education. Don't ever become passive in this responsibility, turning it over to the experts. You're the expert in this situation.

## CHAPTER 15

# How Adolescence Increases Willfulness

A t least with their first child, and definitely with their only child, most parents are in denial about adolescence. "I know it changes other people's children for the worse, but it won't happen to my own." But it will, and you've got to be prepared for what to expect and know how to handle it effectively without empowering your willful child in unhealthy ways.

## What Changes?

To some degree, no matter what, your child is going to become more difficult to live with during the adolescent years.

- Your child will insistently demand more to be satisfied.
- Your child will become more stubbornly resistant.
- Your child will question your rules.
- Your child will become more competitive and combative.
- Your child will become more urgent and impatient.
- Your child will also become more possessive of personal rights and freedoms.

Factor in puberty, with all the hormonal energy required for this development change, and most adolescents become far more willful than they were as children. And if they were willful children to begin with, expect them to become even more strong-willed now. Once a strong-willed child, always a strong-willed person.

## ✅ Fact

During their child's childhood, parents are fed a lot of adoration. During adolescence, however, parents must get used to living on a low-affirmation diet. It used to be they could do no wrong. Now they can do little right. Welcome to thankless parenting.

During early- and midadolescence, ages nine to fifteen, your willful child may forget obligations, shirk homework, become argumentative, sneak out at night, and ignore household chores. During later adolescence, as the child essentially becomes an adult, he may become rebellious in his social life, form relationships you don't approve of, and mismanage his money (or yours). He may push against your curfew requirements and rules about use of the car.

## How Long Adolescence Lasts

Adolescence is that ten- to twelve-year process of change that transforms a dependent child into an independent young adult. Children are adults in training, and adolescence is the training ground on which young people go through the struggles of learning to become more grown up.

Adolescence starts between ages nine and thirteen and ends in the early- to mid-twenties. During these ten to twelve years, there is a lot of developmental work to be accomplished. The young person must separate from childhood and dare to venture out into the larger world of more grown-up experience. The young person must experiment with new self-definition, trying on and off different cultural images and social relationships, to establish an individual identity that feels authentic. And the young person must gather the knowledge and skills required to finally depart from family into a responsible, self-supporting independence.

# The Journey of Adolescence

Although confusing both for parents and for child, adolescence is a process with certain changes, tensions, and conflicts unfolding in an orderly progression as the child gathers more experience and responsibility and grows toward the independence of self-sufficiency and self-support.

## Common Stages of Adolescence

To establish your expectations for the larger process of adolescence, here is a brief outline of common problems and the order in which they typically appear. Consider four stages of adolescent problems.

### Early Adolescence (Ages 9–13)

In this stage, problems are characterized by:

- **A negative attitude**—increased dissatisfaction from no longer being content to be defined and treated as a child, less interest in traditional childhood activities, with more boredom and restlessness from not knowing what to do, carrying a grievance about unfair demands and limits that adults impose.
- **Active and passive resistance**—more questioning of authority, arguing with rules, delaying compliance with parental requests, a proneness to letting fulfillment of normal home and school responsibilities go.
- **Early experimentation**—testing limits to see what she can get away with, including such activities as shoplifting, vandalizing, prank calls, and the beginning of substance experimentation with tobacco, alcohol, and inhalants.

### Midadolescence (Ages 13–15)

In this stage, problems are characterized by:

- More intense conflict over social freedom with parents.
- More lying to escape consequences from wrongdoing or to get to do what has been forbidden. There may be less direct communication with you.
- More peer pressure to go along with risk taking in order to belong, including more pressure to use substances.

### Late Adolescence (Ages 15–18)

In this stage, problems are characterized by:

- More independence as a result of doing grown-up activities —part-time employment, driving a car, dating, and recreational substance use at social gatherings.
- More significant emotional involvement in romantic relationships and more sexual activity.
- Grief over the graduation separation from friends and family and more anxiety at feeling unready to be an adult.

### Trial Independence (Ages 18–23)

In this stage, problems are characterized by:

- Lower self-esteem from not being able to keep all the commitments of adult responsibility.
- Increased anxiety from not having a clear sense of direction in life.
- High distraction from cohort of peers who are slipping and sliding and confused about direction too, partying more to deny problems or escape responsibility, as the stage of highest substance use begins, hard drugs beginning to enter the picture.

## Willfulness in Each Stage

Adolescence energizes willfulness in different ways, depending upon the stage. Willfulness in early adolescence is typically expressed through more active and passive resistance, argument and delay, and rebelling against parental control. Willfulness in midadolescence is typically expressed through more confrontation and conflict over rules and more manipulation and evasion through lying. Willfulness in late adolescence is typically expressed through acting more grown-up by engaging in adult behaviors like drinking, dating, driving, and earning and spending money from part-time work. Willfulness in trial independence is typically expressed through more late-night partying and building credit debt to live beyond one's means.

 **Fact**

The more difficult half of parenting, the half known as adolescence, comes last, as parents and teenager struggle to keep their relationship together while separation is pushing them apart. And the hardest stage of adolescence, trial independence, comes last, when many young people lose their footing and need the mentoring of parents to recover from missteps and find their way.

What are some end point tasks that you want your adolescent to be able to manage before leaving the nest?

- Responsibility for earning her own money
- Competence with household tasks, such as shopping, cooking, and laundry
- Money management
- Managing time and work obligations
- Taking care of a car
- Balancing social obligations

# Parenting Challenges in Adolescence

Each stage of adolescence comes with its own parenting challenge. When you know what to expect, you can adjust your tactics of dealing with your willful adolescent.

## Changing Parental Focus to Support Healthy Growth

In early adolescence the parenting challenge is to withstand the youngster's lashing out at you. He is anxious over his developmental changes and frustrated with needing your permission for everything. You can't take this reversal of good humor at all personally.

In midadolescence the parenting challenge is to provide loyal opposition to the child's harmful wants for his best interests, without resorting to coercion or manipulation. Conduct conflict in a safe and constructive way.

In late adolescence the parenting challenge is to allow more grown-up freedom and to insist on commensurate responsibilities in preparation for successfully making the next transition into more complete independence, without sacrificing family membership requirements and cooperation while the child still lives at home. You will be giving more freedom and demanding more responsibility.

In trial independence your parenting challenge is to communicate full confidence in the child's capacity for more independence to give helpful advice when asked, without rescuing or criticizing when the child runs into trouble coping on his own. Let go managerial control while communicating confidence and offering mentoring support.

## Three Principles for Maintaining Perspective

Parents need to keep their perspective when their child enters adolescence. There are three principles to keep firmly in mind so you can maintain a steady course when your child becomes more unpredictable and troublesome to live with.

1. **Adolescence is not a punishable offense.** It is a process of growth toward individuality and independence. You don't blame the child for the process, but you do hold the child accountable for how he chooses to manage the process. For example, no insulting or demeaning language is allowed.

2. **Adolescence wears the magic out of parenting.** Increasing conflicts of interest make the child less captivating to be around. Enchanted by the two-year-old, you are more disenchanted with the child ten years later. Your twelve-year-old is no longer cute and cuddly, and that's as it should be. You are no longer idolized. Adolescent abrasion over so many differences wears down the mutual dependence, so that independent young adulthood becomes the logical next step. After all, if you were both as enchanted with each other at the end of adolescence as you were at the beginning, neither would want to let the other go.

3. **Teenagers are naturally offensive.** This is not meant to be an insult. It simply describes the antagonistic responsibility of adolescents. A healthy teenager pushes for all the freedom he can get as soon as he can get it, and healthy parents restrain that push for the sake of safety and responsibility. Teenagers continually feel obliged to fight for more freedom than their parents are willing to allow.

 **Essential**

The most important sense to keep about you while your child is journeying through the perils and problems of adolescence is not your sense of danger or sense of outrage, but your sense of humor. While fear and anger intensify parental upset over what is happening, making it more emotional, serious, and urgent, humor lightens and calms responsiveness with healthy perspective.

# Resistance to Rules

One parent described the relationship with her willful adolescent as between the rule maker and the rule breaker. Rules are always contested both for their specific and symbolic values. Specifically, the child challenges her curfew because "all the other kids get to stay out later than me!" Symbolically, the child challenges the parent's right to make rules at all. "You say you want me to learn responsibility, but every rule you make keeps me from having the freedom to prove how responsible I can be!"

Adolescence poses many obstacles to a young person's freedom, and parents are the most common obstacles of all. Taking stands for the teenager's best interests against what she wants earns parents no popularity with the child, only anger from frustration. "You never let me do anything! You're overprotective! You're ruining my life!" This is why the hard part of parenting comes last. Resistance to rules breeds resentment of the rule maker.

## Following Rules

Rules are everywhere, defining acceptable and unacceptable behavior at home and legal and illegal conduct out in the world. A willful child who can't play by the rules at home may get away with infractions if lenient parents are unwilling to stand up to their enforcement responsibility, but a willful child who can't play by the rules out in society may invite a swift and strict punitive response.

Children, particularly willful children, must be taught to follow rules when young or continued rule breaking will get them into serious trouble as they grow older. Building a habit of social obedience is important for all children but particularly for willful children, who often can't stand being told what they can and cannot do. Some willful children even claim immunity to rules: "Rules are for other people, but not for me!" Actually, rules are for everyone.

## ✅ Fact

As following rules becomes a matter of habit, following rules becomes automatic and rules themselves become internalized. The longer parents wait to teach compliance with rules, the more resistance to rules their child develops, the more serious consequences infractions can bring. Don't wait for adolescence to teach respect for rules.

Why do adolescents follow rules? Many of them reluctantly comply because the crime is not worth the punishment. "If I sneak out for a couple of hours, I get kept in for a whole weekend!" For willful adolescents, however, the reverse is often true: the punishment is worth the crime. "I'll do what I want and pay for it later if I have to." Fear of getting in trouble, fear of facing consequences for violating rules, is not much of a deterrent for a willful adolescent bent on freedom at any cost. So what can parents do? They can take advantage of the willful adolescent's vulnerability to her wants to teach compliance with rules.

### To Get What You Want, Do What I Want

Remember that a willful adolescent is intensely wed to what she wants, and that satisfaction of many wants still depends on parental giving—of permission, resources, transportation, of other kinds of support. So the key to teaching a willful adolescent to follow rules is to not give anything automatically. Unwittingly, when it comes to learning to follow rules, the willful adolescent provides parents the means for her own instruction.

The willful teenager wants so much, so often, so urgently, that parents simply use each want as an opportunity to teach responsible, rule-abiding behavior. "You want to go to the dance next weekend? You'll need to earn your way by coming home on time every day after school this week. If you can follow that rule all week, I'll let you go to the dance." To get freedom that the teenager wants, she gets to practice following rules that parents want, and practice creates habit as she develops a pattern of obedience to rules. It's not fear of getting in trouble that causes willful adolescents to follow rules; it's following rules in order to earn something they want. Treat each request by the teenager as a potential training point. Before any want of hers is satisfied, she must earn it by practicing some contributive, responsible, or rule-abiding behavior first. Hold the willful adolescent hostage to the satisfaction of her wants. "I want you to have what you want," explains the parent, "but I want what I want first."

# The Willful Push

Adolescence is a challenging time for parents because their child becomes more challenging to live with. Striving to break free of the limited family definition of being a child and eager to gather worldly experience to become more grown up, the adolescent is a larger person for family to deal with in lots of ways. He is larger because of size, because of growing more emotionally intense, because of claiming more living space, and because of contesting more differences with parents.

## Growing "Larger" in Three Ways

Of course, the adolescent is physically larger than a child, more adultlike in appearance, and more inclined to act as powerfully as size permits. This is the age when the teenager may crowd a parent in a doorway, get in a parent's face, look down on a parent from a greater height, and borrow or take a parent's clothes that now fit his adolescent body. Becoming more physically grown up encourages the adolescent to act more grown up and to demand more parental respect on this account. "See, I'm not your little child anymore!" Parents must constantly let the willful adolescent know that adult size does not confer adult status until it is accompanied by adult responsibility.

During these challenging months and years, keep in mind your desired aim for the adolescent—full, functioning, self-support on his own. You will need to keep that picture in your mind during the tough times. The end reward will be worth it.

## Alert

What do you do if your willful teenager responds to your refusal by crowding your personal space, getting in your face, and yelling to get you to relent? Ask yourself, "What does he predict I will do?" Look scared, back away, and give in? If so, violate his prediction. Move toward him with a smile on your face, place your hands on his shoulders, pull him toward you, give him a big kiss, and say, "I love you when you act like this." If that's how you're going to respond to his attempt at intimidation, then he may elect not to get in your face again.

Growth is a gathering of power, from dependence to independence, and it is the parents' responsibility to help their adolescent gather this power in appropriate, not inappropriate, ways. It is inappropriate for parents to allow their adolescent to gather willful power in three potentially bullying ways.

- Becoming more emotionally intense, the adolescent may intimidate those parents who don't want to say anything that will get him more inflamed. "Leave me alone!" "Not now!" "Can't you see I'm already upset?" Given storm warnings like these, parents may act on the belief that the better part of wisdom is avoidance. By doing so, they may give their adolescent inappropriate space to grow.
- Becoming more territorially expansive, adolescents may aggressively take up more space in the home by leaving belongings outside of their bedroom, leaving some part of the home a mess, daring parents to demand removal of these markings for the sake of picking up. "I will in a minute!"

"I just got home!" "I'm busy right now!" Unless parents insist that dirty dishes in the sink, laundry on the bathroom floor, and unfinished snacks by the TV are cleaned up, parents will feel like they live in an occupied territory, paid for by them but governed by their adolescent. By allowing this, they may give their adolescent inappropriate space to grow.

- Becoming more argumentative, adolescents assert stronger opinions and provoke more debate for its own sake. Keeping out of arguments can prevent parents from speaking up and the adolescent from hearing what he needs to know. "Give me a reason!" "That doesn't make any sense!" "That's not fair!" Parents who decline to explain their position and instead suffer disagreement in silence risk giving their willful adolescent the false impression that he is right when he is not. By doing so, they may give their willful adolescent inappropriate space to grow.

Parents have to brave emotional upset, repel spatial invasions, and take nonargumentative stands to keep the willful adolescent push from dominating life at home. A willful teenager cannot grow to dominate the family without parental permission. Don't give him yours.

## CHAPTER 16

# Freedom and Willfulness

Why do children in general, and willful children in particular, bolt through the door of adolescence? For freedom. Adolescence opens up more freedom from curfews and other restraints, more freedom to act older and try grown-up activities.

## Freedom at All Costs

Think of the onset of adolescence as a Declaration of Independence. The adolescent holds certain truths to be self-evident.

- "I should be able to do what I want."
- "I shouldn't have to do what I don't want."
- "No one has the right to boss me around."
- "All rules are unfair."
- "I know what is best for me."

Freedom rings for the adolescent, and she wants nothing more than to answer its thrilling call, while your restraint creates a cause worth fighting for—liberty! Your adolescent will want to form romantic relationships, even sexual relationships, have use of a car, and enjoy the power of spending money. It's up to you to moderate the child's unbridled enthusiasm. You are the voice of reason and experience.

## Contracting for Freedom

Growth is about breaking established boundaries of definition to create more room. In the process, a price is always paid. Growing up is giving up, and so to gain more independence, the adolescent must let some old dependence go. Explain the parents, "It's a tradeoff. To get to make more decisions as a teenager means we will be doing less for you than when you were still a child. Now you must do more for yourself. With new freedom you have new responsibilities."

This exchange of freedom for responsibility is the basis of all contracting that parents must do with their adolescent as he pushes for more experience to grow. Freedom creates risk, and responsibility moderates risk. So as the time approaches when the adolescent wants to drive a car, the parents are very careful about specifying the conditions of responsibility. When and where and with whom, state of sobriety and observance of traffic laws, and footing certain expenses may be part of the deal parents wish to make. Many parents even put these conditions in writing so there is no misunderstanding afterward about what they were and the agreement that was made. It needs to be clear who pays for gas, insurance, and repairs.

### ✅ Fact

Nothing increases willfulness so much as the desire for freedom, and the adolescent desires freedom more than anything else.

Contracting with a willful adolescent often entails serious bargaining; the resulting compromise often means both parties have to give up something they want. The parents may have given more freedom than they were ideally comfortable with, agreeing to a later hour at a party than they initially wanted. The adolescent may have agreed to give more assurances than he initially wanted, agreeing to report in by phone when that was not what he originally desired. The important thing is negotiating an agreement that both sides can live with and the teenager commits to keep.

## The Freedom Contract

There are six basic provisions to the Freedom Contract.

1. **Believability.** "You will keep us reliably informed by giving us adequate and accurate information about what is going on in your life and what you are planning to do."
2. **Mutuality.** "You will live in a two-way relationship with us, doing for us in fair exchange for our doing for you, contributing to the family as the family contributes to you."
3. **Predictability.** "You will honor your word, keeping agreements and following through on commitments you make with us."
4. **Responsibility.** "Your conduct will be your passport to permission by showing us responsible behavior at home, at school, and out in the world."
5. **Availability.** "You will be available for a free and open discussion of any concern we may need to discuss when we have a need to talk."
6. **Civility.** "You will communicate with respect when we have something to discuss with you, and when you disagree with what we have to say, you shall do so in a courteous manner."

## Accountability

When your willful adolescent pushes for more freedom, he must be held accountable. Before you discuss the specifics of the new freedom, review the degree to which he has been living up to the conditions of the freedom contract. If he has, proceed with the negotiation. If he has not, address where he has been falling short and how he needs to get his act together before you will allow him more freedom. You are interested in corrected behavior, not reassuring words. You are not interested in promises. You require evidence of performance. Promises have no bargaining power.

# The Matter with Money

As children grow into adolescence, they consume more family resources (like food), they want more possessions (like clothes), and they're interested in more worldly experiences (like entertainment), all of which cost parents more money. Adolescence is expensive.

One way that adolescence increases willfulness is by increasing material wants. In the marketplace, the adolescent is the ideal consumer—an easy prey to ever-changing fashion and fads that he feels he must have to fit the identity that is most popular at the moment.

### Money Conflicts

From this point on, having money to spend and the ways money is spent become major sources of conflict between parents and the adolescent. Consider just one: the "I don't have anything to wear that fits" conflict. It goes like this.

CHILD: "I don't have anything to wear!"
PARENT: "What do you mean you don't have anything to wear? You've got a closet full of clothes."
CHILD: "None of them fit!"
PARENT: "They all fit!"
CHILD: "No, they don't! Nobody wears those styles anymore. They're out of fashion!"
PARENT: "So what?"
CHILD: "Oh, get real! Do you want me to be laughed at?"
PARENT: "I won't laugh."

CHILD: "I don't mean you. I mean people that matter. My friends. Don't you understand anything?"

PARENT: "I understand clothes cost money and I'm tired of buying outfits that you refuse to wear more than a couple of months."

CHILD: "Fine! Then I won't have any friends!"

PARENT: "Friends? Who's talking about friends? I thought we were talking about clothes?"

Of course, they're both talking about the same thing, but from different perspectives. The parent is correct: physically his clothes do fit. The child is also correct: they don't fit the current "in" look very long. And how he dresses does affect how he is accepted. However, "image" is a concept many parents don't understand. To them, it's superficial. To the adolescent, however, it's fundamental. There are different material requirements for every experimental change along adolescence's ever-changing way, and each change is experienced with urgency. "I've got to have it now!"

Three considerations for parents to keep in mind when managing financial requests are these:

- Pressure of want is most intense just before it goes away, so sometimes you can delay your response and the urgency of the desire will pass.
- It is unwise to invest more money in a new gadget or activity than you are willing to lose when the adolescent loses interest.
- It is unrealistic to expect consistency of interest from someone passing through a period of experimental and experiential change. Expect him to change his mind!

# 📣 Alert

When your willful teenager approaches you for more money for a special expense or just for a "cost of adolescent living" raise, make a real-world response. "At my job, when I want more money, I have to justify my request based on my performance and responsibilities. I want you to do the same with me."

## Managing Money

It's like magic. Now you see it, now you don't. One moment your adolescent has some money, and the next minute, by some miraculous sleight of hand, it's gone. No wonder parents and adolescent get into conflicts over spending money. For parents, money is for later. For the adolescent, money is for now.

It's hard for parents to preach the virtues of cash accumulation to an adolescent bent on living like there's no tomorrow. And it's hard for the adolescent to persuade parents that, for every desire they defer into the future, they are forsaking present pleasure that may never come again. After all, you're only young once. How can you teach a willful adolescent discipline when it comes to money? Consider several sources of money and the lessons of responsibility for each.

- **Gift money** can teach the adolescent that he is respected enough by parents and grandparents to spend discretionary money in a responsible way.
- **Allowance money** can teach the adolescent that he is now old enough to learn how to manage a regular amount of income. This allotment may increase to include responsibility for budgeting and paying for basic living expenses, such as clothing and entertainment, as he grows older.
- **Saved money** can teach the adolescent that he has been able to exercise sufficient self-restraint to resist impulse

spending and to accumulate money to obtain something of important value and substantial cost, such as a car or college.

- **Earned money** can teach the adolescent that he now has the power to generate independent income through holding an occasional, part-time, or full-time job. Stay in close communication with your adolescent about the extent of work responsibilities in order to help him maintain a balanced life. Some teens are tempted to drop out of school after they get a few hefty paychecks.
- **Borrowed money** can teach the adolescent that he can honor a loan agreement with parents by paying back what he owes in a timely fashion.

## ✅ Fact

Parents should vote with their money. Do not financially support the purchase of items and tickets to entertainment that you believe are unhealthy for your adolescent. Parents who find it easier to shut up and shell out are really just giving up and selling out.

## The Power of Peers

In the process of seeking more separation and independence from family and differentiating from childhood, the adolescent is also seeking to build a community of understanding friends who are all becoming different the same way she is, in whose supportive company she can explore and experience the larger world. Adolescence is too scary for most young people to want to go it alone. Better to share the uncertainties, the adventures, and the risks with similar peers, who really become like a second family, rivaling the influence of the one with parents.

It is this competing influence that can be so threatening to parents who are fearful of their adolescent's getting in with the wrong crowd, which will exert peer pressure to harmful effect, causing their child to stray from family rules into social trouble. And this fear is not unfounded, since much serious difficulty that adolescents get into is in the company of friends.

## Pressures of Peer Acceptance

The willfulness of adolescents is usually amplified by membership in a group of peers because of social pressures to conform to belong. To be accepted in the group and maintain good standing, your adolescent is, in so many words, often told, "To be one of us, you have to believe like us, behave like us, back us up, agree with us, look like us, like us best, and not do better than us."

Now the adolescent can become more willful for social belonging's sake. She just must be able to do what other members of the group can do, or social membership is threatened. "They're all going to the concert, so I have to, too!" The willfulness of the adolescent is increased by the will of the group.

 **Fact**

At an age when the majority of young people are feeling unsure of how to act and feeling insecure about who they are, a strong-willed, self-assured adolescent who appears to have it all together and is self-confident and assertive has enormous attracting power among peers. Willful adolescents are more often leaders than followers, but when not interested in leading, tend to follow their own way.

Conformity is expensive in interpersonal ways because of the high costs of social belonging. The adolescent sacrifices some degree of personal freedom in a variety of ways.

- Some independence is often sacrificed for the sake of conformity, the adolescent going along with group decisions she may not really like.
- Some authenticity is often sacrificed for the sake of acceptance—the adolescent shutting up instead of speaking up for fear of disapproval.
- Some honesty is often sacrificed for the sake of image—the adolescent acting like an adventure is enjoyable when it is really not.
- Some individuality is often sacrificed for the sake of group identity—the adolescent adopting behavior that defines the group at the expense of personal taste.

It is important for parents to be mindful of these group membership costs because, by comparison, fitting in with family is far less stressful. When your adolescent is declaring she wants to be with friends only and doesn't want anything to do with family, it is advisable to insist on family involvement—the adolescent can resist at first, but then having saved face through protest, can enjoy it. Family membership is a given, but peer group membership must constantly be earned. Regular family times and special good times remind the adolescent of the social circle in which she will always have a place, will always belong.

### Saying "No" Without Saying "No"

The collective will of the adolescent peer group ("We're going to see what we can get away with just for the fun of it!") can definitely influence the desire and judgment of its individual members ("I just decided to shut up and go along, even though I really didn't want to"). In response to this dreaded scenario, parents often wonder why a willful adolescent who has little difficulty saying "no" to them is so unable to say "no" to peers. The explanation is simple. Say "no" to parents and they still love you. But say "no" to friends, and they may stop being your friends. Saying "no" to friends carries a social threat of criticism, rejection, and even exclusion.

The question for parents to address with their strong-willed adolescent, who does not want to risk the social consequences of refusal with friends, is how to decline to go along with peer pressure without actually saying the word. You can teach your adolescent some alternative strategies for saying "no."

1. **Create a delay.** Say "Not right now, later." And if pressure increases, get angry. "Cut it out! I don't like being pushed around. Not by you or anyone! I'll do it when I feel like it, and not before!" Adolescent peers tend to respect the principle of not being pushed around.

2. **Make a temporary exit.** Say "I have to use the bathroom." Use this pretext to create time to think about what is best to do and how to do it. Often, when you return, group thought has turned in another direction and impulse of the moment has passed.

3. **Make an excuse.** Say "I don't feel well," "I tried that before and I had a bad trip," "If I don't get home on time I'll be grounded for a week," "I'd like to, but my parents drug test me, and if I come up positive they'll yank my car." As it happens, each of these four statements may be a lie, but if the adolescent can't socially afford to say a truthful "no," then a dishonest "no" may be her next best choice.

Of course, anytime the adolescent reports saying an honest "no," parents need to praise that decision. "Good for you! Saying 'no' is an act of self-respect and can earn you the respect of others." But short of that, "Not right now," "I'll be right back," "I can't because . . ." are all part of the repertoire of indirect refusal to peer pressure of which every adolescent, even the willful kind, at some time has need.

**Alert**

Some tips for taking care of yourself as the teenager copes with peer influence:

- Increase your social support—spiritual groups, networking groups, online friends.
- Join online support forums where you can connect day or night.
- Increase your devotion to your own interests. This will make you happy, give your mind a rest from worries, and create a haven to prepare you for the time your adolescent leaves home.

CHAPTER 17

# Willfulness in Early Adolescence

Moving through adolescence is an act of courage. The child must dare to separate from childhood, rejecting some childish activities, relationships, and dependencies that made him feel secure in the past. The child must dare to assert differences that test parental patience and bring on their disapproval. And finally, the child must dare to push against, pull away from, and get around authority for more freedom to grow, creating more family conflict. Usually beginning between the ages of nine and thirteen, early adolescent change is accompanied by some anxiety, insecurity, loneliness, and loss. Growing up requires giving up, as the familiar is sacrificed to the unknown. And the more strong-willed the child was, the more willful his parents can expect the adolescent to be.

## Signs of Early Adolescence

You mark the beginning of adolescence by your reaction to changes in your child and by your child's reaction to changes in you. Adolescence isn't just a change that a child goes through on the way to adulthood. It is also how parents change in response, and how the relationship between parents and child transforms.

Expectations are violated on both sides. Observe the parents, "Our child used to be loving, obedient, hardworking, and helpful, and now he's become resistant, inconsiderate, unmotivated, and moody." But ask the child how he knows adolescence has begun and he is very clear: "My parents have changed!" And he's correct. "They used to be understanding, patient, trusting, and fun, and now they've become worrying, critical, suspicious, and tense." The onset of adolescence changes everybody. Looking more closely, you observe four categories of changes in your adolescent child.

- **Characteristics.** Now the child is physically and socially growing and acting more adult; for example, becoming larger and more willing to challenge parental authority.
- **Values.** Now the child's beliefs and tastes become more counter to the parents' culture; for example, listening to popular music that is often unpopular with parents or even offensive.
- **Habits.** Now the child's habits of behavior become harder to live with; for example, keeping a messy room and spreading clutter around the home.
- **Wants.** Now the child becomes more urgent about freedoms that are harder to grant; for example, pushing to socialize more away from home and be less forthcoming about what that socializing entails.

## ✅ Fact

Although from adolescence forward you will actually spend less time with your child, you will actually spend more time on that young person, weighing decisions about what to expect from the teenager, how to treat the teenager, and what new worldly freedoms are safe to allow.

Now, to a degree, parents find themselves living with a young person who is more dissatisfied, resentful, resistant, restless, bored, moody, intense, put upon, argumentative, uncooperative, defiant, uncommunicative, and combative than the "easy" child they once knew.

## Letting the "Bad" Child Out

Early adolescence is about letting the bad child out. "Bad" does not mean evil, immoral, or unlawful, but simply more abrasive to live with. The function of letting out this bad behavior is twofold: to differentiate oneself from the "good" (easier to get along with) child one was and to provoke parents into letting their bad side out by becoming more disapproving and disciplinary ("meaner") in their response. An early adolescent needs to have "bad" parents to complain about to friends ("You won't believe what my parents are making me do!") and to justify her own worsening behavior ("Well, if my parents can be harder to get along with, then so can I!"). Now the conspiratorial alliance with peers takes a more pronounced anti-adult, anti-authority turn.

 **Essential**

During early adolescence, the parents are kicked off the popularity pyramid. Before, they could do no wrong; now, they can do no right. An early adolescent needs "bad" parents to help justify letting her bad side out. Parents who can't accept this thankless role by continuing to apply healthy demands and limits only encourage more willfulness to grow. Your child's safety is more important than your child's approval.

Children who have been especially good during their younger years will have more difficulty during adolescence, as it feels truly alien to them to become bad. However, it's a necessary part of the process of becoming a separate individual. If your little princess is continuing to be too good, give her some room to act out.

### The Social Distinction

Now there is an important question for parents to ask themselves: "Where does our adolescent's bad side come out—at home, out in the world, or both places?" What parents should want, even though they won't like it, is for their more willful adolescent to make a very important social distinction. They want their child to let her bad side out at home where she knows she will be loved anyway rather than out in the world where adult response to that behavior can get her in serious trouble. When friends tell you what a charming and polite adolescent you have, you are shocked: "You can't be talking about our child." But friends are telling the truth. The willful adolescent is wise and controlled enough to show good social restraint when out in the world.

When early adolescents choose to show their best side at home and their worst out in the world, parents may not believe adverse information that they are given. So when a teacher reports their child's disrespect toward authority at school (which the child denies), by believing their child and disbelieving the teacher, they allow their willful child's unhealthy traits to grow.

## A Parent Is Not Just a Friend

Adjusting to early adolescent change in their child requires parents to undergo significant loss. They will never have their willful child as a little child again. If childhood was a particularly golden time where no pleasure was greater than the pleasure of each other's companionship, that time is over, and parents must grieve the loss, not act out pain from loss in anger: "You used to be such a great kid, what happened to you?"

Now, as they take more unpopular stands to safely channel the child's growth, they find that asserting authority increasingly antagonizes what used to be a harmonious relationship. The child pushes for more freedom for and freedom from than what she used to have, and parents restrain that push with loyal opposition for the child's best interests against what she urgently desires. It takes resolved parents to responsibly raise a willful adolescent.

Just because the early adolescent is pulling away from parents and is becoming more difficult to live with is no reason for parents to pull away from the adolescent. The mother who perhaps had a confiding relationship with her child is now pushed away by her adolescent who wants to talk less. Or the father who had a companionship relationship with his child is now pushed away by his adolescent who wants to spend less time together.

What should parents do? Let the willful adolescent have her or his way? No! Parents need to keep up their initiatives, the mother letting it be known that she is still as interested in talking together as ever, the father letting it be known that he is still as interested in doing things together as ever. Of course, there will be somewhat less of each kind of contact, but less should not mean none at all.

Parents must continue to show interest and be ready for times of close contact, and not treat the adolescent's separation from childhood and from them as rejection. Despite the adolescent's increased distance, disinterest, and occasional disaffection, parents still matter as much as ever, less for the company they provide than for the stability they have to give and for the love to which they are committed.

## ❓ Question

**Can't parent and adolescent be as much friends as were parent and child?**
No. During adolescence, the parent must assert unpopular authority by increasingly taking stands for the young person's best interests against what she wants, in order to direct the push for more freedom and independence in safe and responsible ways. During this time, the adolescent will not say, "Thank you for your demands and limits."

## Adjusting to Early Adolescence

Early adolescence unfolds in three identifiable stages, each troublesome to parents in its own willful way. First comes the negative attitude, with its litany of criticisms and complaints; then comes rebellion, with its active and passive resistance; and then comes early experimentation, with its testing of limits. Parents must not take any of these unwelcome changes personally.

These behavior changes do not represent actions the child is taking to purposely upset the parents. They are actions the child is doing for himself to separate from childhood and to begin the journey toward independence. Put other parents in your place, and, to varying degrees, your child would still be going through the same transformation.

### The Problem with Questions

As adolescent change begins to unfold, parents develop increased information needs: "What is going on?" As the adolescent starts spending more time away from home, parents want to know, "Where are you going, who are you going to be with, what are you going to do, and when are you going to be back?" And the adolescent does grudgingly answer these questions, but to a minimal degree: "I'm going out, I'll be with friends, we'll just be hanging out, and I'll be back later." Such answers fall somewhat short of what parents want to know, so they push to know more, at which point their adolescent gets angry: "What is this, the third degree?"

 **Fact**

At this self-conscious age, adolescents not only resist answering questions, they resist asking them as well. Why? Questions are statements of ignorance. And most early adolescents would rather stay ignorant than appear stupid. After all, it's embarrassing to have friends laugh at your question: "Come on, you don't know that?" So don't wait for questions. Give your early adolescent the information you think he needs.

The problem with your questions at this prickly age is that they represent authority and invasion of privacy, and the adolescent is resistant and protective on both counts. So you can minimize questions to get information and rely instead on nonobtrusive approaches to information gathering as much as you can. Rather than ask, try a request: "It would really ease my mind to know a little more about your plans with friends this afternoon."

Be accessible for unexpected communication at inconvenient times. Sometimes when you are busy or tired, your adolescent will feel like talking about himself. Make the time to listen at the time he wants to talk. If you say "later," you will have missed an opening, because his emotional readiness to communicate quickly comes and quickly goes. Use neutral times, like driving him somewhere, to talk. Share about yourself in order to model and encourage self-sharing by your child. If your adolescent feels that all you both ever talk about is him, he will become more reticent to share with you. And when you must ask questions, be merely factual, not evaluative. The more evaluative your questions, the more power of authority they carry and the more invasive of privacy they become.

### Helpful Questions
"What's going on?"
"How do you feel?"
"When would you like to go?"
"Why do you think it happened?"

### Evaluative Questions
"What were you thinking?"
"How could you have done that?"
"When will you ever learn?"
"Why can't you do it right?"

## When Your Adolescent Won't Talk

But suppose, in spite of all your reliance on unobtrusive information gathering and interrogatory questions, your adolescent decides that it's best to keep you in the dark and so refuses to tell you anything about what is going on. Are you doomed to parent in fearful ignorance, at the mercy of your worst imaginings?

No. Instead, you must confront him with the consequences of refusing to communicate with you. Explain the situation this way: "Of course, whether you tell me about what's happening in your life is entirely up to you. However, you do need to know that, in the absence of any information from you, I will make up my own mind about what is going on, and based on that understanding, I will decide what to do in response. The understanding I come to may be mistaken, such as concluding that you are on drugs, and the actions I take will match what I believe, such as cutting off your allowance and no overnights with friends. So, you may want to consider talking to me in order to accurately influence my understanding and to realistically affect my decisions. Of course, as I said, it's entirely up to you."

 **Alert**

Don't waste your time trying to change the early adolescent's mind ("Life is unfair!" "Work's not worth doing!" "Rules are for other people, but not for me!"). Just say what you believe and insist on what you need. He doesn't have to agree with what you think to consent to what you want.

## The Negative Attitude

The opening signal of early adolescence is the negative attitude, the birth of the "bad attitude," as parents often call it. What happened to the child who was full of positive energy all the time and a pleasure to live with? Now a turn for the worse seems to have taken place. It's like someone has pulled the plug on the young person and all her positive energy to do anything has been drained away.

Your young adolescent may start speaking in ways you don't like during this time. You have the right to say what is okay to say and what is not. You remain the authority over the household rules, and respectful speech is one of those rules.

## Developmental Lumphood

She has entered a phase of what one parent poetically described as "developmental lumphood." All the early adolescent seems to want to do is lie around and complain about having nothing to do. But when parents suggest some recreation or work around the place that needs doing, the adolescent just gets angry: "Oh, leave me alone, you don't understand, I'm too tired!" Tired of what? Of doing nothing, of being bored, of being frustrated, of not knowing what to do with herself. She knows what she doesn't want to do, but she has no clear vision of what she does want to do. When it comes to motivation and direction, she's running on empty, and she doesn't like it.

Then, as positive energy drains away, negative energy begins to build. All of a sudden, it's like having a critic in the family. She's critical of positive suggestions, of family activities, of other members of the family, and of what parents often don't see—critical of herself: "I hate being just a child!"

## Self-Rejection Is Required for Growth

She seems to be in a mood to reject everything and everyone. Why? Because she is rejecting the child she was, rejecting herself, and angry at that rejection, she turns anger at self-rejection into criticism of those around her. What particularly attracts her anger are parental demands and limits, rules and restraints, which now stand in the way of the increased freedom she wants. So a sense of grievance, a chip on the shoulder, develops: "What gives you the right to tell me what I can and cannot do? You're not the boss of the world!" But parents are the boss of her world, and now she doesn't like it. As a child, she didn't mind their authority that much, but as an early adolescent wanting more freedom to grow and room to become different, but not yet knowing how to achieve that, she resents their direction and opposition.

The birth of the bad attitude begins in early adolescence because people do not change unless they are dissatisfied with who and how they are. And the early adolescent is developmentally dissatisfied. She doesn't want to be defined and treated as a child anymore. This attitude change that provides the motivation for adolescence to begin can coincide with puberty, but it doesn't have to. When it does, the release of growth hormones only makes the process more emotionally intense and the child more willful.

# Rebellion

People do not rebel without just cause, and now the negative attitude has given the adolescent adequate grievance over undue restriction and unfair treatment by parents to justify actively and passively resisting their demands.

Rebellion is not primarily against parents. It is actually directed against the old compliant and dependent definition of being a child—in other words, the former self. To outgrow this definition, the adolescent rebels out of childhood. Early adolescent rebellion is opposition against old self-definition acted out against parents for transformation's sake.

**Alert**

Feeling down on himself doesn't justify the early adolescent's acting out this unhappiness by attacking or cutting down other members of the family. Say to the young person, "Other people in this family are not your whipping posts, to be treated badly when you feel badly. However, if you want to talk about how you feel, I would be glad to listen."

Rebellion against parents is scary, yet the adolescent rarely shares his fears, masking them with bravado instead: "I don't care what you think!" Not true. There is fear of parental disapproval: "My parents will think badly about how I have acted." There is fear of disappointment: "My parents will feel I have let them down." And there is fear of desertion: "My parents will stop loving me."

There are dangers here for an extremely willful early adolescent, who can rebel in self-defeating, even self-destructive, ways—against safety, self-interest, self-esteem, conscience, and caring relationships—getting hurt in the process. Freedom is won at too great a cost. The danger of extreme rebellion is injury to self when a self-destructive cycle can take hold. The more negatively the world reacts, the more the adolescent rebels against it, the more negative the world gets. The most powerful antidote to rebellion is challenge.

## Challenge

Although rebellion is the most common means to accomplish the transformation from childhood into early adolescence, it is not the only one. Another way is challenge. Challenge is an antidote to rebellion. Although an adolescent may swear rebellion is how independence is won, it is not. Rebellion only achieves dependence—defining oneself in opposition to what someone else wants. "I'm going to leave things on the floor because you want me to pick them up!" Undertaking a challenge, by contrast, is an independent investment of energy in oneself to grow in a direction that enhances oneself. "I've always been interested in making music, so I'm going to learn to play an instrument."

 **Fact**

> One of the best antidotes to rebellion in early adolescence is the challenge of gainful employment—having to do something one has not done before and getting paid for one's efforts. Of course, the adolescent will rebelliously resist getting a job, but if parents will keep pushing, he will grudgingly accept the challenge, soon taking pride in being able to act more grown-up. Another powerful antidote is public service—gathering self-esteem from helping others.

Of course, this is not an either/or proposition. An adolescent who commits to a lot of challenge for the sake of personal growth will still do some rebelling. However, that rebellion is likely to be less frequent and intense because he is already actively committed to some challenging avenue of personal growth. A young girl who is enamored with competitive horseback riding and a young boy who is ambitious about playing sports in college spend so much energy on the challenges they have chosen that there is less remaining energy for rebellion.

When your child enters adolescence, look for challenges that can grow your child to more independence that you can support. Look for:

- New skills to be mastered
- New responsibilities to be undertaken
- New interests to develop
- New talents to cultivate
- New service to be given
- New life experiences to open up
- New goals to pursue
- New relationships to create

## ✅ Fact

There are three Cs to a constructive adolescence: pursuing Challenge more than rebellion as a means of personal transformation, having activities to Care about more than being bored, and living Connected to family more than feeling abandoned by parents and left alone. Rebellious, bored, and disconnected youth have the most troubled adolescence.

"But," protest parents of an early adolescent, "our son doesn't want to do anything with family anymore. All he wants to do is be with friends, and if he can't do that, he'll just hole up in his room." Parents must keep asserting opportunities for involvement so the adolescent has the chance to experience ongoing membership in the family. "Why should I, when I don't want to?" demands the teenager. "Because," explain the parents, "this is forced family time." So, after protest and complaint, he reluctantly agrees to a weekend activity, ends up having fun, and is reminded that belonging to his family is just as important in its way as belonging to his group of friends.

Rebellion may take a couple of forms in early adolescence: passive and active resistance. Active resistance has to do with debate and disobedience. Passive resistance has to do with procrastination and delay. The more willful your child, the more of each type of resistance you will see. Ultimately, both kinds of resistance serve the same growth need—to help the adolescent gather the power to change. And resistance works. To some degree, on some occasions, parents will be too distracted or too tired to follow up on a demand. They will allow the adolescent's resistance to back them off for some period of time, or entirely. "More freedom" then becomes the name of adolescent power gained.

## Active Resistance

By actively resisting, the early adolescent expresses more disagreement and complaints about parental demands, questions the rightness of rules and the parental right to make rules, and endlessly argues about most anything for argument's sake. "It's like we're training a trial attorney," parents will complain, weary of the unremitting verbal challenge to their authority. It's a mismatch. Arguing takes energy for parents and is fatiguing. Arguing is energizing for the willful adolescent and is stimulating. Given that adolescents feed off arguments in a way parents generally do not, parents need to be selective about when they want to argue back. If their mind is already made up, or if they don't have the energy to argue at the moment, they need to decline the adolescent's invitation into yet another debate. And remember that, just because your opposition doesn't stop rebellion or resistance right away or completely doesn't mean it doesn't do any good. Your opposition gives a value reference, it slows rebellion down with your resistance, and it demonstrates that you care enough for his welfare to contest his refusal and earn his disfavor.

And even if they are nervously inclined or humorously tempted to laugh at some of the arguments they get into with their child at this fractious age, parents must keep a straight face. These arguments are very serious for the adolescent, who is pitting his verbal power against the more seasoned verbal power of the parents. It takes courage to pursue this confrontation. Smile and laugh at your child, and humiliation and anger will result. "I hate it when you make fun of me!" The adolescent will act injured because he has just been hurt.

## Passive Resistance

By passively resisting, the early adolescent will put off obligations and requests until it takes repeated reminders for him to do what he was supposed or told to do. "I will, in a minute!" he promises. But by now, parents know that a teenage minute can drag on for over an hour. "Now!" they command in irritation. "Well, you don't have to get upset about it!" retorts the teenager, and finally he does the dishes. But he doesn't use soap. And the parent is back to square one.

What's going on? It's a compromise called delay. It's like the adolescent is saying, "You can tell me what and I'll tell you when. When I get enough when, I'll do what you want—partly." Chores are the most common aggravation point with parents, because that's where passive resistance is most often used. Putting off work to delay work, maybe even to get out of work if the parent either gives up or decides to do the chore herself. Taking over the task is not a good idea because then the parent will really be angry at doing for the adolescent work they asked their child to perform. Supervision is the answer—using relentless parental insistence to wear down adolescent resistance.

## 🔔 Alert

For the willfully rebellious adolescent, there is no greater gift than having a parent who needs to be "right" all the time about everything. Arguments are so easy to start. And when adolescent growth has passed, behold the interesting result—a young adult who has been debate-trained to become as strong-willed as the parent.

# Early Experimentation

With new freedom gained from rebellion, the early adolescent now has room to experiment with more risk taking, to learn about the forbidden, and to test limits to see what she can get away with. Where the negative attitude had to do with gathering the motivation to change, and rebellion had to do with gathering the power to change, early experimentation has to do with gathering the experience to change, experience that lies outside the prohibitions that parents and other social authorities have prescribed.

### Getting Away with What?

"Which rules are real and which are not?" That is the question the early adolescent wants to answer. The only way to find out is to do some limit testing to see what she can get away with. Where no adverse consequence occurs, that is a place where more social freedom is apparently allowed. The more illicit freedom an early adolescent is allowed to get away with, the more willful she becomes.

This is the age when experimentation with substances can begin, particularly inhalants, tobacco, and alcohol. Following are some signs you can watch for:

- Lying
- Apathy

- Foolish decisions
- Failing grades
- Explosive temper
- Calls for your teenager where the caller hangs up without identifying himself
- Empty cans, bottles, and drug paraphernalia in your child's room, backpack, or car
- Family money and valuable items seem to have disappeared
- The child suddenly has money that is not earned or an allowance
- Decline in your own liquor supply
- Problems at school—truancy, fights, not turning in homework

This is the age when experimenting with not doing homework can begin—"I forgot it," "I did it at school," "I'll do it in the morning," "There wasn't any." And this is the age when three common kinds of social violations can occur: pranking, vandalizing, and shoplifting. Pranking involves your child playing a trick or joke that is funny to the prankster but not to the victim. Vandalizing is when your child defaces public or private property, an act that is satisfying to the person vandalizing but not to the victim. Shoplifting is when your child takes without paying, an act that is rewarding to the thief but not to the victim.

 **Fact**

Shoplifting is not about an early adolescent taking something desirable that is otherwise unaffordable. Shoplifting is about literally and figuratively seeing what one can "get away with," and it is usually done in the company of like-minded friends in a spirit of daring and risk taking.

Some parents write this early experimentation off as innocent mischief and leave it at that, but such permissiveness is not a good idea. More serious limit testing and rule breaking are likely to follow. It is better for parents to close the loop of responsibility.

## Closing the Loop of Responsibility

Once again, parents must allow the child to experience the choice/consequence connection. In the case of the prank call, which was of a threatening nature and got the elderly neighbor (who happened to have caller ID) very upset, your child has to confess to the victim, hear the victim's response, and make some restitution to the victim. In the case of vandalizing, which involved egging someone's car or tagging a neighborhood business, your child has to confess to the owner, hear the victim's response, clean up the mess, and make restitution. In the case of shoplifting, your child must be allowed to suffer arrest and detention for being caught, go back and confront the store manager, hear the manager's response, and make restitution. Parents must allow and impose social consequences to discourage the adolescent from making such out-of bounds or rule-breaking choices again.

When early experimentation with the forbidden occurs, parents must see that appropriate consequences follow. Let violations go, and parents will let willfulness grow.

Don't lose faith in the foundation of family values you have laid in childhood just because your adolescent seems to be rebelling against them now, believing and behaving differently than you have taught. These differences are more trial in nature than terminal, temporarily adopted for experimental and developmental use. During adulthood, your child will reclaim that early instruction and end up more similar to you than different. You have to trust that this will happen.

## CHAPTER 18

# Anticipating Later Adolescence

Early adolescence marks the beginning of the adolescent process, accomplishing the separation from childhood, setting the stage for later adolescent growth. Not until the early to mid-twenties will the entire process be finished. At last the young person is experienced, responsible, and resolved enough to gather the reins of young adulthood. From early adolescence on, willfulness shall grow stronger, not weaker, as your child gathers momentum of independence, intolerance for restriction, and desire for more complete freedom. This is as it should be. The parent's job is to help channel willfulness in the direction of healthy growth. This chapter describes common encounters of the willful kind that characterize the remainder of adolescence as it typically unfolds.

## Antagonism and Ambivalence

Know what to expect. Not only will there be more tension when you refuse permission or demand discussion with your willful adolescent, but there will also be more confusion as you struggle to sort out the double messages he keeps sending. Your relationship will become more antagonized, and your teenager's ambivalence will become difficult to understand.

## Adolescent Antagonism

There is a goal for the parent/adolescent relationship for which both parties need to strive when they have difficulty tolerating one another: to achieve a healthy mutual dislike. Healthy means neither party allows negative feelings to provoke harmful words or actions toward the other. Engaging in destructive behavior encourages an unhealthy mutual dislike, which can do lasting harm to the future relationship.

Parents need to expect, and they need to forewarn their child, that adolescence will put them more often at odds with each other than before, particularly around issues of freedom of action and the tolerance of differences. This is to be expected. This does not mean something is wrong with the relationship or with either party. It does mean, however, that both parties need to be mindful about keeping occasions of mutual dislike within healthy limits.

For the teenager, sometimes it can seem like parents have turned mean. "You're always on my case, in my way, against what I like, or down on how I am!" For parents, sometimes it can seem like their teenager has become exploitive. "You're either using us to get what you want or abusing us when you don't get what you want, always pushing us for more, never satisfied or appreciative of all we give."

What is behind this new antagonism? The answer is the changes wrought on the relationship between parents and teenager in consequence of early adolescence. The negative attitude, rebellion, and early experimentation all take their toll. From former closeness, distance has created estrangement. From previous harmony, disagreement has created more conflict. From previous contentment, dissatisfaction has created more criticism. From fondly remembered trust, distrust has created more questioning. From previous commonality, differences have created more intolerance. The toll that early adolescence exacts on the parent/teenager relationship is more frequent feelings of disaffection on both sides.

## Essential

Speeding up family interaction with the urgency of his demands, your teenager knows that chaos creates confusion, creating openings for freedom that would not exist if you had leisure and clarity to think. Therefore, if your teenager insists on getting an answer from you right now, yes or no, tell him the answer is no. You must insist on time to deliberate. Slow down decision making. Don't let your teenager's urgency set the pace of family life.

From leaving childhood for early adolescence at the beginning (around ages nine to thirteen) to leaving trial independence for early adulthood at the end (around twenty-three to twenty-five), the young person's conflicted response to moving on is an honest reaction to the gains and losses that come with growing up. Mixed messages just testify to how mixed the young person feels about this rewarding and costly transition.

The sometimes mutual antagonism felt at this time is normal between parents and adolescents. With a strong-willed child, it may be particularly intense. Both sides will have to alter their expectations as the previous ways of getting along no longer hold. You really and truly are in uncharted waters.

### Adolescent Ambivalence

Adolescence is also the age of ambivalence. Your teenager wants to grow up and act more independent but does not want to give up all the privileges of childhood and the supports that accompany dependency. He wants the freedom to wear what he wants but not to do laundry. The ambivalence can be confusing to parents: "Well, which way does he want it—to be treated as an adult or as a child?" The answer is "Both ways, depending on the situation." "Let me do it"/"Do it for me." "Leave me alone"/"Pay attention to me." "Don't make me go"/"You never include me." "I can handle it"/"Why won't you help?" Adolescence is an awkward dance, made more awkward by the double message parents give during this age of in-between: "We expect you to act grown up and to remember that you're still a child!" It's enough to make the sanest person a bit crazy.

## The Willful Midadolescent Push (Ages 13–15)

Midadolescence is often when your child pushes the hardest against you. In early adolescence, restriction on personal freedom was primarily a theoretical issue for the young person to argue about, establishing a grievance against the unfairness of parents to justify actively and passively resisting them. In midadolescence, by contrast, the young person really wants to be out in the world, exploring, experiencing, experimenting in the company of friends. The willful push in midadolescence is often for more freedom than is safe.

At this extremely urgent and self-centering age, when the messy room comes into full glory and the use of lying to gain illicit freedom becomes increasingly common, the midadolescent is willing to fight for more independence against parents who face more conflict than they have seen before.

During this harder-pressed stage, strong-willed parents with low tolerance for opposition must be on guard against losing control to get control, lest by overreacting they provoke their teenager into more impetuous behavior. Being firm, specific, and reasoned is the order of the day for effective parental authority during midadolescence, and understand that you will not be thanked for applying your restraining influence. Remember: strong-willed parents with no tolerance for defiance can be at high risk of abuse.

## Persuasion by Extortion

A midadolescent can be expert in pressuring parents into giving in when they have reservations about a request for freedom or might even refuse. Consider these common tactics at this age.

1.  **Time extortion.** The teenager waits until the last minute to ask permission. "I can't wait, there's no time to talk. I've got to know now!" To which effective parents reply, "If you're telling us it's now or never, then the answer is 'no.' When it comes to asking us permission, you must give us adequate time to think and to discuss with you."

2.  **Social extortion.** The teenager asks permission in front of several friends who have all been allowed to go, creating a socially awkward situation if you delay for discussion or refuse. "Come on," insists your teenager, "it's getting late and it's okay with everybody else's parents!" To which effective parents reply, "We need to discuss this matter with you by yourself in the next room. Your friends can wait while we do if they wish. We discuss family business only in private."

3.  **Emotional extortion.** The teenager makes a scene, the way a little child would throw a tantrum to get her way. "If you don't let me go you'll ruin my life, I'll hate you forever, and I'll do something terrible to myself that you'll really be sorry for!" To which effective parents reply, "When you are ready to reasonably discuss what you want to have happen, we are happy to talk with you. But threats will not get you your way."

4.  **Contractual extortion.** The teenager makes extravagant offers or unrealistic promises to buy her way from her parents. "If you let me go tonight, I won't even ask to go out for the next month!" To which effective parents reply, "Our decision is based upon evaluating your request, not on what promises you make."

## ⚠ Alert

Beware a very common manipulation at this age: overloading the opposition. Instead of starving parents for information, the teenager gives them so much data to process, they don't notice what is missing. With so much information about what doesn't matter, parents lose interest and energy to pursue what does matter.

## The Power of Prohibitions

"You can't make me and you can't stop me!" brags the mid-adolescent, to emphasize how free she really is and how power-less her parents really are to take that freedom away. Of course, the adolescent is correct. Parents are running a home, not a jail. And yet, even the most willful adolescent's freedom boast is also a statement of fear. "There's nobody to make me or to stop me or to protect me but myself! Getting hurt or getting in trouble, it's all up to me!"

It's a peculiarity of the midadolescent push that parental pro-hibitions can provide invaluable support. In early adolescence, a parental prohibition will often encourage the child to disobey for rebellion's sake; "I'll do the opposite of what I'm told!" In late ado-lescence, a parental prohibition will often be disregarded for inde-pendence's sake; "I'm too grown up to put up with being told what I cannot do." But in midadolescence, the young person is often as overwhelmed by freedom's possibilities as she is excited by them.

Imagine that your fourteen-year-old daughter gets a phone call from a high school senior inviting her to a college party. You are in the room when she receives the invitation. "Wow!" she says into the phone. "That sounds really cool. I'd love to go." Then, cupping her hand over the receiver, she silently mouths to you the word "no" several times. Taking your cue, you loudly announce, "No way! There's no way we are going to let you go to a college party with a high school senior." At which point, she flies all over you. Into the phone she lets her anger out: "Can you believe it? My parents won't let me! They never let me do anything! I wish I could go, but that's how they are!" And hanging up, she storms out of the room, slamming her bedroom door shut to emphasize her upset.

### ⚠ Alert

Midadolescents often sneak out after hours when parents are asleep. They also make "end runs"—staying overnight at friends' houses where greater latitude for social freedom is allowed, or make "double end runs"—where each teenager gets permission to sleep over at the other's home, and then both meet to enjoy an adventurous night out. So, keep your supervision up and check out all sleepover arrangements.

But what is really going on? Parents have given her the protection of their prohibition. She didn't want to go into a scary situation for which she felt socially unprepared, but she didn't want to refuse because that would make it look like she wasn't as grown up as the boy took her to be. So she relied on her parent's prohibition to get her out of a situation she didn't want to get into, blaming them for her refusal and thus saving face socially. Yes, it's complicated. During midadolescence you can consider it normal for your willful child to fight with you more, lie more often, and experiment with the pressures of peers.

## The Willful Late-Adolescent Push (Ages 15–18)

Late adolescence roughly coincides with the high school years, and the goal of that period for late adolescents is learning to act more grown up. At the beginning of high school, they find themselves at the bottom of a large heap of older students with much more worldly experience to share, more social pressure to exert, and more temptation to offer. The willful push in late adolescence is to grow up faster than may be wise.

In late adolescence, young people grow up partly within your rules and sometimes outside the rules, just as they tell you a few things, but not everything, about what is really going on in their lives. For parents, particularly strong-willed parents, these opposites can be hard to bear. But some obedience and some information have to be enough.

## Aging Out of High School Early

If your willful late adolescent is extremely physically mature for his age (fifteen looking eighteen), is academically accelerated (taking junior level classes as a freshman), or is athletically advanced (playing varsity sports during his sophomore year), that young person's peers become the older students. As a consequence, the social learning curve of his life will be steep, and that young person will grow up faster than others the same age.

In this case, you need to expect that demands for more freedoms will come earlier than you anticipated as willfulness is intensified by the influence of older peers.

There's no point in complaining that your sophomore should act like a sophomore when he is dating a senior. Instead, you must tightly contract with this fast-growing young person. You must insist on adequate communication from him about the more grown-up situations he is entering so you and he can talk about what is happening, what risks need to be understood and moderated, and what can profitably be learned from this more worldly experience.

One result of growing up very fast in late adolescence can be aging out of high school early. By the junior year, your mature, accelerated, or advanced teenager feels out of step with peers, like he has gotten everything high school has to offer socially and is ready to move on. In this case, as with academically advanced and ambitious students, early graduation from high school may be an option—taking credit by exam, courses by correspondence, courses at a local community college to prepare for a specific line of work or accumulate credits for college, even applying for early admission into college. To force a fast-maturing young person to drag out a meaningless senior year is often not a good idea. If your child is ready and wanting to move on, see what you can do to move along the process. Part of your job is to make sure that he has mastered the responsibilities of independence.

### ✔️ Fact

There are three rockets to independence during the high school years: driving a car, holding a part-time job, and social dating. Each activity increases the will for more freedom, and none should be allowed unless, in the parents' judgment, the young person is taking responsible care of business at home, at school, and out in the world.

## Reassignment of Responsibility

The more freely grown up your late adolescent wants to act, for protection's sake, the more responsibility you want to teach that young person to assume. To act adult is not just a matter of getting more freedom; it is learning to use that freedom responsibly. So to drive a car requires observing traffic laws and operating a potentially deadly machine in a safe way. This is why you hold your teenager responsible for choices made—the young person taking and getting credit for the good, owning the bad, and held responsible for the results of any unwise decisions.

During late adolescence, you are intentionally piling on more responsibilities because your goal, when he leaves your care for trial independence, is to have this step to more independence be as small as possible. More freedom without more responsibility is a recipe for trouble. You want your son empowered with as much adult responsibility as possible when he leaves your daily care.

During the high school years, you intentionally increase responsibility in two ways. You turn over more self-management responsibility, and you teach exit responsibilities. Toward the end of high school, you turn over such responsibilities as the management of school; paying some basic expenses; determining social schedule and curfew, although still keeping parents adequately informed; attending to health care by making his own doctor and dental appointments.

## Essential

> The last two years of high school are not the time for parents to get into a power struggle over doing schoolwork with their late adolescent. Parents need to turn school over to the teenager so he can see that academic performance is not an issue between him and his parents, but an issue between him and his future. Conflict with parents over grades at this late stage only prevents the teenager from making this connection and taking this responsibility.

You also list out the exit responsibilities your child will need to assume once graduated from your care, and make sure that you are using the high school years for teaching these critical skills. Money management is just one major focus; others are finding and holding a job, earning and saving money, managing a checking account or debit card, budgeting expenses, paying bills, and filing taxes.

Learning life-management skills that support a successful independence not only prepares the late adolescent for stepping out on his own, but such mastery also builds confidence and self-esteem. "When I leave home, I will know enough to take care of myself." This is the statement of willpower you want your late adolescent to be able to make when leaving your care.

It is normal for your willful older adolescent to have very intense romantic relationships and to feel grief over impending separation from you and treasured friends. Remember how this time was for you? It's a bittersweet part of life.

# The Willful Trial Independence Push (Ages 18–23)

Not only do the hardest years of parenting, adolescence, come last, but the hardest period of adolescence, trial independence, also comes last. Now the young person is living away from home for the first time, usually with roommates, working at a job, pursuing further education, or both. Although equipped with enough will for independence, the young person often does not have enough skill. The willful push in trial independence is for more responsibility than the young person can often handle—at least right away.

Independence proves challenging. There's so much freedom, and it is within the young person's choice. There's so much responsibility, and it all depends on the young person. There's so much distraction, and all around are people of a similar age out for having a good time.

Among her cohort of friends, few seem to have a clear direction in life, and when it comes to finding a firm footing in independence, many are slipping and sliding and breaking commitments. There are romantic breakups, broken job obligations, broken credit arrangements, broken leases, broken educational programs, and even broken laws. What the young person discovers, usually to some degree of cost, is that assuming responsible independence is very hard to do.

## Lifestyle Stress

In trial independence, many young people do not take good care of themselves as power of want triumphs over power of will, as impulse overrules judgment, and as temptation overcomes restraint. They stress themselves with sleep deprivation, with task procrastination, with indebtedness from credit spending, with nonstop socializing, with the mood- and mind-altering effects of substances, and with low self-esteem from feeling developmentally incompetent—unable to get their lives together at such an advanced age. In consequence, many young people go through periods, in this last adolescent passage, of despondency, confusion, uncertainty, guilt, shame, anxiety, exhaustion, and escape into substance use.

## What Parents Can Do

For parents who are committed, engaged, settled down, and practical, it is not easy to empathize with a child in her early twenties who is uncommitted, disengaged, unsettled, and unrealistic. But their impatience, criticism, and anger will only make matters worse. Better to express confidence in the child's capacity to learn from mistakes and to support the will to keep on trying.

At this last stage of adolescence, parents must change their role from being managers to becoming mentors. Barge in and try to manage the adolescent's troubled life at this late stage, when a job has been lost and bills are past due, and parents risk either rescuing their child from what responsibility has to teach or reducing communication with a child who refuses to be ordered around. Make themselves available as mentors, however, and parents offer the benefit of their experience and ideas, if they can be of service, as their last-stage adolescent tries to figure out how to choose her way out of the difficulty she got herself into.

To be an effective mentor means you are approachable. You express faith, not doubt ("You can do it"); patience, not anger ("Keep after it"); consultation, not criticism ("You might try this"); understanding, not disappointment ("It's hard to manage independence"); confidence, not worry ("You have what it takes!"). Many adolescents in this last stage before young adulthood lose their independent footing and must be encouraged to learn after the fact, from sad experience, what they did not learn before, and learning the hard way by profiting from mistakes and taking responsibility for recovery. Even the most willful children can lose their footing in trial independence. The job of parents, through mentoring, is to support the will to keep trying and to be emotionally accessible so the child can avail herself of their mature advice.

 **Question**

What about the young person who really loses her footing in life and wants to come home to recover?
That's fine, and in fact is very common. In response, parents do not rescue from unmet obligations. They simply provide a mutually agreed upon, time-limited period at home for the child to regroup—to return, to rethink, and then to reenter the world and struggle with the challenge of trying to claim independence again.

During the time of trial independence, it is natural for your child to feel anxious about her ability to take care of herself, uncertain about a life direction, and confused about the influence of peers. She may sometimes suffer from low self-esteem because she cannot manage all that is expected at this age. Make yourself available for loving counsel, when you're asked.

CHAPTER 19

# The Willful Only Child

Since the baby boom of the 1950s, families in the United States have been growing smaller. Today, somewhere between 20 and 30 percent of dual- and single-parent families have an only child. Because of family dynamics, there are tendencies that favor a high degree of willfulness developing in an only child: from the adult tendency to overparent, from the child's tendency to become demanding, from the child's tendency to become controlling or rigid, from the child's tendency to become precocious, and from the child's experience with adolescence.

## Family Dynamics

Whatever the cause or choice, only-child families are subject to a certain dynamic that multiple-child families are not. When all parental attention is concentrated on a single child, when this single child has no sibling to distract the parents' unsparing gaze, when their first child is the only chance to parent that parents are going to get, predictable pressures build. Contrary to the common assumption that single-child families are less complex and demanding to manage than multiple-child families, raising an only child is high-pressure parenting. With one offspring, the performance stakes for parents and child can feel extremely high, with both parties intensely emotionally sensitized and committed to each other's well-being.

## Pressure on the Parents

For the parents, there is pressure from knowing that this is both first and last child, the only chance at parenting they get, and so they want to make the most of their parenting, by doing it right. They want their child to turn out well. This conscientiousness makes for extremely thoughtful and labor-intensive parenting. One common outcome of this thoughtfulness is a clear and firm agenda about what they want for the child, set ideas for what they should provide and how their child should perform. Most parents of an only child do not parent by being passive and playing wait-and-see. They take initiative because parents of an only child usually have a will of their own.

 **Fact**

Two times in life when being "only" can be costly are marriage and parental end-care. When only children marry, they usually have to learn to do more sharing, adjust to more differences, and constructively resolve more conflicts than they have been accustomed to doing before. And when their parents are aging, they are the only offspring, with no sibling support available or expected to help.

## Pressure on the Child

For the child, there is no push and shove; no rough and tumble; no conflicts over dominance, differences, attention, or sharing with siblings. Nor are there child companions in the family to play with, with whom one can get additional perceptions of parents to put them into more realistic perspective. There are only adults for family company, and the child is ruled by desire to please these powers that be, to fit in to their company, to imitate their ways. When parents are one's only peers at home, peer pressure to belong can be intense. One alleviating measure is to place the child in play groups and preschool, so cooperation is learned at a young age.

## Pressure on the Relationship

As for the relationship between parents and only child, it is extremely close and knowledgeable and sensitive, often emotionally enmeshed, where unhappiness in one party stimulates unhappiness in the other, who often feels responsible for fixing the problem so everyone's well-being can be restored. They take great pleasure in each other's company, creating a mutual admiration society. Parents of only children have to be watchful against overly pressuring the child, who naturally wants to please the parents. Being sole focus of parental attention, the only child occupies a powerful position in the family, and that power is the foundation of the willfulness that many only children develop.

# The Danger of Overparenting

Most only children are very well parented. They are well attached, well loved, and well supervised; their interests and capacities are well developed; they are well self-connected; and they know what parents expect of them. But a major contributor to an only child's willfulness can be the varieties of overparenting that parents give. Wanting to do well by their one and only child can make it challenging for parents to moderate their efforts and easy to err on the side of pushing themselves too hard and pushing their child hard as a result. Overparenting is simply carrying a certain focus of concern to such an extreme degree that the child is extremely affected as a result, becoming more willful in a certain way. This interaction takes an infinite variety of forms.

## Common Types of Overparenting

Consider just a few overparenting interactions and the variety of ways an only child's willfulness can be enhanced.

- In response to oversensitive parents, an only child can become extremely vulnerable.

- In response to overdependent parents, an only child can become extremely obligated.
- In response to overambitious parents, an only child can become extremely driven.
- In response to overprotective parents, an only child can become extremely cautious.
- In response to overwatchful parents, an only child can become extremely self-conscious.
- In response to overcontrolling parents, an only child can become extremely passive.
- In response to overindulgent parents, an only child can become extremely entitled.
- In response to overpraising parents, an only child can become extremely arrogant.
- In response to overpermissive parents, an only child can become extremely selfish.
- In response to overstrict parents, an only child can become extremely rigid.
- In response to overanxious parents, an only child can become extremely fearful.

 **Alert**

Parents who become overpreoccupied with the welfare of their only child can create a tyranny of concern that they often blame on the child. "Our child monopolizes our life! She's all we think and talk about." The way to extricate themselves from this oppression is to declare more social independence of the child and begin to let the only child go.

If parents are feeling uncertain about whether to make more or less parenting effort for their only child, because of this tendency to overparent, doing less may be the better choice. As one only child put it, "I wish I wasn't all my parents had to do!" Maintaining outside interests is a good way to go. Career development or satisfying hobbies that don't involve the child provide a balancing effect for the family.

## Guarding Against Extreme Concern

Wanting to parent extremely well can drive overdedicated mothers and fathers to extreme behaviors out of concern, often provoking an overblown response in their only child, who becomes willful. Therefore, it is usually best for parents of an only child to relax their concern and moderate their efforts. In most cases, if they halved their parenting dedication, they'd probably do twice as much as many parents with larger families who have learned that turning in a mixed performance, and paying just some attention, provides enough quality of care for most children to come out okay.

The lesson is simply this: pressure translates. You can't apply a lot of pressure on your own parenting performance without putting a lot of pressure on your only child. If you demand perfection of yourself as a parent, exhibiting no tolerance for your own frailties and misjudgments, your child will learn to do the same. Why? Because with no siblings to display contrasting traits, with whom to develop contrasting relationships, and with no one in the home but parents to identify with, an only child is highly encouraged to resemble parents, who often reward acts of similarity: "Good for you, you did it just like us!"

Not only does your child unconsciously copy you, adopting your attitudes and other traits; she also consciously imitates you, out of admiration for you, identification with you, and in search of approval from you. And, of course, the child also learns to live like you by being expected to live according to the family terms you set.

# The Demanding and Controlling Only Child

From having parents who strive to please their only child, that child can learn to become demanding. From having parents who worry about their only child and want that child to turn out well, controlling parents can teach their child to value high control. Becoming highly demanding and highly controlling makes for a willful only child.

The issues of demand and control need to be separated. Demanding is a unilateral act—one person can do it unassisted. Controlling, however, requires the consent of others. With their only child, parents need to address both issues.

## ⊛ Essential

Since family forces of similarity greatly amplify pressure on the only child to believe and behave like his parents, be mindful and moderate in your treatment of yourself for the sake of your child. How willfully hard you are on yourselves is how willfully hard your only child is likely to be on himself.

## The Demanding Only Child

Being the exclusive focus of so much parental attention and support, it is hard for many only children not to grow up with a sense of entitlement:

- "If I want it, I should get it."
- "If I have something to say, people should listen to me."
- "If I feel I am right, others should agree with me."
- "If I don't like how others are treating me, they should be made to stop."
- "If I have a way of doing things, others should go along."

To the degree an only child subscribes to any of these beliefs, he can be quite demanding to live with, to play with, and to teach. Unhappily, even parents can grow weary of this tyranny of demand, finding their beloved child uncomfortably self-centered. "Me first!" "Me only!" "Me now!" What about anybody else? Indeed. So parents need to socialize their only child to understand that functional relationships need to work for two parties, not just one. Hence, they teach the principles of mutuality:

- **Reciprocity:** "Just as we do for you, we expect you to do for us."
- **Consideration:** "Just as we show sensitivity for your well-being, we expect you to show sensitivity for ours."
- **Compromise:** "Just as we sacrifice some self-interest to meet you halfway, we expect you to do the same with us."

Parents of a young only child who has not been taught to live by the principles of mutuality can pay a heavy price once the child reaches adolescence and naturally becomes more demanding in pursuit of his independence. The lesson is, start this instruction early or pay for that lack of education later on.

## The Controlling Only Child

The controlling child problem is usually the compliant parent problem. Out of the desire to please, the fear of disapproval, the discomfort with conflict, or the inability to set limits, these parents:

- Give in when they would rather refuse.
- Go along with what they don't agree with.
- Say "yes" when they wish they could say "no."
- Accept conduct they know is unacceptable.
- Adjust to treatment they know is unhealthy.
- Rescue the child from the unhappy consequences of unwise decisions.

All of these choices are in the parents' control, not the child's. So who's got the problem? Extremely indulgent parents can be guilty of extreme neglect—neglecting their parental responsibility to make healthy demands on their child. The controlling only child is being spoiled for later relationships by learning within family that others should always give that child his way and that rules for social conduct that apply to others do not apply to him.

Overly compliant parents must consider two notions. First, parenting is not a popularity contest. It is a tough process of preparation for learning the necessary skills for adult independence. And second, one responsibility parents have is to socialize their child to be nice to live with at home so he doesn't need to control relationships to get along with others later on.

## ❗ Alert

The primary influence of parents is not in what they say but in what they model. It is through how they treat themselves, other people, and the world that they instruct the child how to act. Parents who cannot tolerate admitting wrong in themselves are at risk of instilling that same intolerance in their only child.

## Intolerance for Being in the Wrong

One of the great pleasures of having an only child is the pleasure parents and child have with each other. Both want to please, both want to do right by each other. Conversely, to wrong, to do wrong, or to be in the wrong can court disappointment and disapproval that can be hard to bear. "I can't stand letting my parents down!" "We just hate having our child have to pay for our mistakes!"

This desire to please can sow the seed of perfectionism— the need to be right and do right all the time. Perfectionism sets an unrealistic expectation because "to err is human," to be ideal is not. The only way to be perfect parents is to have a perfectly behaving child, and who would want to put that kind of pressure on a beloved only child?

In the normal course of growing through their son's childhood together, both parents and only child will have misadventures, make mistakes, and commit misdeeds that put them each for the moment in the wrong. Unless this expectation is clearly communicated by parents, unless they are willing to admit their own wrongs, apologize, make amends, forgive themselves, and go forward, the only child will have a hard time tolerating being in the wrong when his time comes. Unless they can let go of hard feelings when the child has done wrong, the inevitability of her occasional wrongdoing will never feel safe.

## The Power of Being Precocious

Only children may thrive in their hothouse environment. Although the social voting age is eighteen for most young people, for an only child, the family voting age is much younger. She is often given equal say and influence in determining family activities: "What do you think we should do?" She is accustomed to being heard.

 **Alert**

There's nothing wrong in empowering the only child by including and involving her in adult decision making, but the more votes parents give their only child in determining the conduct of family affairs, the more willful that child shall become.

In cases of extremely precocious development, friends of the parents may notice how the child acts mature beyond her years, praising her for this speed of social development. "She acts so much older than other children her age!" No wonder they're impressed.

She has become more conversant with the culture and world of her parents than with the culture and world of children her own age.

When giftedness is combined with being an only child, the pressure cooker environment needs to be closely monitored for the dangers of parents living *through* their children and children becoming quite fearful of displeasing the overly dependent parents. If your only child is gifted, give her lots of opportunities to try things, mess around, and make mistakes without any vested interest in a cherished result. She needs to learn to trust her own inner compass, not *your* inner compass.

## Acting More Grown-Up

Only children are at risk of growing so verbally and socially precocious that they can have difficulty fitting in and making friends with a group of other children the same age. Such only children are more at ease with adults and with younger children they can boss around. This is why parents of an only child must arrange for adequate socializing outside of their company so the child can learn to enjoy interacting with same-age peers. Possessive parents who are reluctant to share the pleasure of their only child with anyone else only retard the social learning with peers that she needs to accomplish.

 **Fact**

To the degree that only children are lonely, it is usually not a function of being the only child at home, but rather because they feel precociously out of step with same-age peers and become socially ill at ease or even isolated on that account.

One benefit of being overly mature is that the only child is not shy about talking with adults; she is precociously skilled in expressing her needs and negotiating her way with these older people who control so many parts of her world. Assuming adultlike standing with her parents, she is not intimidated by their or other adult authority. Willful in this regard, she may consider herself the equal of any adult and therefore entitled to challenge other adult authority with which she disagrees. "When I don't agree with what you want me to do at home, I tell you and we work something out, so why shouldn't I be able to do the same with my teacher at school?"

As for the teacher, she may see the need to cut the presumptuous young student down to child size. "In this classroom, I make the rules, and your job is to obey, not to question why." Sometimes willfulness with external authority can get the only child in trouble. These are important real world lessons to learn.

## Expecting Adult Performance

When the only child puts herself on equal footing with her parents, she unwittingly puts herself under a lot of pressure. Believing that she has equal standing with her parents, she then applies equal standards of performance: "If I'm their equal, then I should be able to do what they do equally well." But this is a false assumption. She is still a child. They are adults with much more practice, education, and life experience. Then when she fails to equal their performance, losing out to them on a vocabulary game one evening, she becomes harshly critical of herself: "I don't know anything!" Not true. But because she's much younger, she knows less than her parents do, as they try to explain, which causes her to get furious at the distinction they are cruelly making to comfort her: "Don't treat me like a child!" To the only child, the term "child" feels demeaning, like she is being treated like a second-class citizen in the family.

One legacy of being an only child is exaggerated internal standards of performance that often create a lot of pressure to live up to, and can cause a self-punishing reaction when the child does not. In this case, willpower won't tolerate anything less than the high operating capacity to which the only child has become committed. If parents see their only child laboring under constant performance stress, it is their job to help the child set more realistic standards that can be reached with reasonable effort.

# The Problem with Adolescence

Most parents of an only child do not anticipate the normal changes of his adolescence. Throughout childhood, there has been so much closeness and harmony, so much mutual appreciation and cooperation, so much enjoyment of each other's company, that when the separation, differentiation, and opposition of adolescence hit, parents are really thrown for a loss. "What happened to the sweet relationship we had? Where have the good old days gone?"

### Adolescence Can Feel Twice As Hard

Actually, for parents of an only child, adolescence comes as a double whammy. First there is the loss of the old childhood comradeship, the painful falling away aspect, and then comes the surprising new abrasiveness with their adolescent. "He doesn't want to cuddle anymore. All he wants to do is criticize and argue!"

**Fact**

An only child who is used to being the center of family attention and the beneficiary of loving and indulgent parental giving can become an extremely willful adolescent who feels entitled to being given what he wants and who gets very angry when he is denied.

Parenting during childhood is poor preparation for parenting through adolescence, because parents and only child were mostly operating in agreement. What the child wanted, they usually wanted also in order to please the child. What parents wanted, the child usually wanted in order to please them. Desire to please each other prevailed. In addition, in their loving efforts to encourage their only child to speak up, assert wants, and exercise influence within the family, they unwittingly laid the groundwork for more adolescent willfulness, more argument for independence, than they are at first prepared to handle.

In many cases, parents had so little occasion to resort to discipline during childhood that they are unpracticed in providing it when it is needed in adolescence. But practice is what it takes. They just need to assert adequate guidance, supervision, and structure to help safely channel their beloved adolescent through a more difficult and challenging period of growth. In the process, what they lose in popularity they will gain in conflict, so the bargain often feels like an unhappy one.

## Delayed Adolescence

Partly because he has it so good at home, and partly because pulling away and pushing against his parents for more independence creates so much discomfort, an only child often delays the entry into adolescence. Instead of beginning to separate and differentiate from childhood between ages nine and thirteen, when most children do, he may not start the process until his midteens, even waiting until early high school to begin the transformation.

The unhappy outcome of this delay can be a collapsed adolescence, when over the period of a couple of years, early, mid-, and late adolescent changes are compressed into a very short, highly charged, and intense period of time. The grievance of early adolescence is hardly begun before the conflict over worldly freedom associated with midadolescence starts, and this midadolescent conflict is just getting under way when the late-adolescent urge to act more grown-up becomes what the teenager feels impelled to explore. So much change unfolding over so short a time makes for an extremely willful adolescence.

For parents of this adolescent only child, the disciplinary demands can be intense and the response from their angry teenager extremely painful to hear. "You just don't love me! That's why you won't let me do anything!" No, it's because parents love their only child so much that they are willing to take unpopular stands against peer pressure and impulsive wants for his best interests, during a very challenging and swiftly changing time for all concerned. Accused of not caring, their firm stands are actually hard evidence to the contrary. A collapsed adolescence can create a very willful passage with an only child. For many only children, adolescence feels like losing a lot of security with the parents.

## CHAPTER 20

# Substance Use Increases Willfulness

Like it or not, you are raising your child in a drug-filled world. From legal to illegal, mood- and mind-altering substances are everywhere. On the one hand, psychoactive drugs are nothing new. Almost every culture throughout human history has found or made some psychoactive substances that served to alter people's mental states for medicinal, religious, or recreational purposes. On the other hand, such substances exist in more variety today than ever before, with powerful legal and illegal interests ruthlessly pushing their use on people of all ages due to the enormous profits.

## Substance Use Makes Willfulness Worse

Alcohol and drugs have a chapter in this book because substance use in young people increases willfulness of a negative kind. The more serious the level of use, the more harmfully willful the child's behavior can become. A child who increasingly uses substances can become:

- More self-centered and exploitive of others
- More inclined to ignore or let go of normal responsibilities
- More unmindful of traditional rules and societal restraints
- More driven to avoid problems and escape from pain
- More inclined to abandon principle for pleasure

- More likely to engage in self-defeating and even self-destructive behavior

The more the young person surrenders to substance use, the more actively and passively willful she becomes, opposing parents who want that use to stop.

## Substance Use and Impulsive Thinking

Substance use encourages thoughts that are governed by emotion, impulse, and immediate gratification at the expense of reasoned thinking—thought governed by judgment and values. More immature decisions are the result. Parents must take a stand for reasoned thinking if willfulness, being driven by impulsive and unmindful want, is to be brought under the control of better judgment.

## Parental Denial

It does no good for parents to close their eyes and hope the threat of substance use in their child's world will just go away. It will not. By the end of high school, according to almost any survey you read, the majority of children have tried the "big three"—nicotine, alcohol, and marijuana—and many have experimented with other drugs.

### ✅ Fact

Parents often make a false assumption: "If our child knows how to get into trouble with drugs, she knows how to get out." Wrong. All she knows is that substances cause good feelings and fun times. The job of parents is to get her qualified counseling or treatment to find a sober way out and to find for themselves a support group or counseling help so they can consistently maintain healthy family demands around her.

It is in the best interests of all concerned for parents to admit the possibility of drug use and understand what helpful role they have to play. When it comes to preventing their child's substance use, parental denial is the enemy in hiding. In most cases, until parents admit and confront their child about her use of substances, the child will refuse to admit trying or using substances.

# How Parents Can Help

Although you can't actually control your child's choices when it comes to alcohol and drug use, you can inform those choices with the best information you have. You can inform your child about the nature of the problem, about the risks involved, and about keeping oneself safe should the decision to use occur. And you can keep an eye out for signs of substance using and abusing behavior.

It may help to tell your adolescent family stories about relatives who have experimented with alcohol and drugs and the results in their lives. You can tell stories about your own background and experiences. Were there any terrible losses because of drugs and alcohol? Don't gloss these over. If an uncle committed suicide because of alcoholism, the child deserves to know. If you dropped out of school because of drug-related failing grades, your child deserves to know.

## Start Education Early

Starting in your child's early adolescence, declare the topic of substances and substance use always open for family discussion. "Because you are growing up in a drug-filled world, it is important for us to talk about alcohol and drugs as they indirectly or directly affect your experience—from what you hear, from what you see, and from what you may decide to do."

In adolescence, as substance use becomes more common, encourage waiting to start until your child is older. "You need to know that the longer you can delay any use, the lower your risk of problems with substances is likely to be should you later choose to use." If, despite your wishes to the contrary, an episode of substance use occurs, let your child know that the first conse-quence will always be communication. You want to assess the child's level of use for yourself and to learn from the episode in order to inform and protect your child. "After this experience, what do you know that you didn't know before about safe substance use and the risks?" Save any sanctions until a thorough debriefing has occurred.

If either parent has had substance problems personally or any-where in his extended family, tell these cautionary stories to your child. Family examples can have enormous instructional power. And be willing to honestly answer any questions your child may have about your current use or history of use, contracting with your child to do the same with you. Honest parents can be extremely influential informers.

## Look for Warning Signs

Significant behavior changes can indicate that substance use is disorganizing your child's life. Usually he begins to exhibit some loss of normal, traditional, or characteristic responsibility. Com-mon behavior changes that can accompany significant substance use include:

- A usually smart kid makes stupid decisions
- An achieving kid starts to fail
- A truthful kid lies
- A good kid acts bad
- A mindful kid can't remember
- A conscientious kid becomes indifferent
- An even-tempered kid becomes moody
- Kids with little money suddenly have a lot to spend
- A capable kid acts stupid
- A dedicated kid loses interest
- A communicative kid is unusually quiet
- An open-natured kid becomes secretive

- A nice kid acts mean
- A responsible kid behaves irresponsibly
- A reliable kid breaks his agreements
- A motivated kid no longer cares
- A careful kid acts careless
- An obedient kid breaks the law
- An honest kid steals
- A healthy kid becomes run down

None of these changes by itself is a sure sign of substance use, but over several months, a new pattern of behavior that combines four or five of these behavior changes should be a cause for parental concern.

## Assessing Level of Use

When parents have evidence that their teenager is using substances, they need to try to estimate the level of use. What follows is a description of six categories of use for parents to consider, from least to most serious. The more serious the level of use, the more harmfully willful the child is likely to become.

 **Essential**

Informed abstinence means informing your child's understanding about substance risks and safe alcohol use in family discussions starting in early adolescence, in addition to cautioning against use and appreciating the teenager's compliance. Willful ignorance about substances only adds to the danger when substance use is tried later.

### Level One: Abstinence

How can abstinence be a substance-use problem when, by definition, no use is involved? First, there is a difference between ignorant abstinence and informed abstinence. Having your teen-ager not use alcohol or drugs in adolescence is well and good, but what happens after high school when she, off in an apartment or at college, enters the years of maximum substance use? Ignorance is no good protection should the young person now choose to use. At worst, suppose you send an ignorant, abstinent adolescent off to college to join a sorority or fraternity, organizations with well-deserved reputations for heavy social drinking? Suppose you've never done your disciplinary job of instructing the young person about strategies for safe drinking should she ever choose to use?

Second, some teenagers believe they are abstinent when they are not. When prescribed psychoactive medication for anxiety, despondency, mood swings, or impulse control, for example, they have become prescription substance users. This means that any additional use of recreational substance is not a good idea because it may adversely interact with, or reduce the helping power of, med-ication that has been prescribed. Whoever prescribes this medi-cation needs to make very clear to the adolescent what risks are associated with other substance use.

### Level Two: Experimental Use

Experimental use is about using to satisfy curiosity. If your teen-ager explains that she has been using marijuana only on weekends for the past three months and is just experimenting tell her that such frequency of use is no longer experimental, it is recreational.

Experimental use is limited to one or two times. Sometimes a teenager will experiment, find out what the drug experience is like, satisfy curiosity, and have no further desire to use that substance again. "I dropped acid once, and that was enough to convince me not to do it anymore." Of course, experimental use is not necessar-ily safe use. After all, an early adolescent can try getting drunk on antifreeze and kill herself.

You can tell your child that experimenting with a substance is really experimenting with herself. Substance use is always a gamble—the rewards of use are always accompanied by risks. She has no way of knowing how her mind and body will react. She is literally experimenting with her well-being, putting herself at risk of an unknown chemical experience and then, for good or ill, waiting to discover the outcome. Warn your child: no two people react exactly the same way to any psychoactive substance. Just because it was a great experience for a friend does not mean your child will find the same is true for her.

## Level Three: Recreational Use

If your teenager is using a substance with regularity, smoking pot or drinking alcohol when hanging out with friends on weekends, for example, then she may be a recreational user if two conditions for recreational use are met. First, the use is moderate. Moderate means that use is causing your teenager no problems in her own or in anybody else's eyes, including your own. Conditions for moderate use include knowing the contents of what you are using and being able to measure out a controlled dose. This is easier to do with alcohol than a street drug like Ecstasy, where the chemical mix is unknown because it is unregulated and the dosage is often a surprise. Second, the use is monitored. Monitored use means that sufficient sobriety is maintained so that your teenager maintains awareness of the effects of use on mind and body, thereby knowing when she has had enough.

 **Essential**

If your child is determined to recreationally use without your blessing and with sanctions for doing so, explain the principle of toxicology: the poison is in the dose. A small amount of arsenic in drinking water does you no harm, but a large amount can kill you. So, advise your child, when using any recreational substance, to be careful with the dose: start low and go slow.

Recreational drinkers are able to draw a line somewhere between a caring and a noncaring attitude that says when enough has been consumed. They want to use within the limits of maintaining contact with the values and judgments about personal behavior that normally matter to them. They don't want to cross over the "enough" line into a significantly less caring or noncaring state where words can be spoken, decisions made, and actions taken that sober reflection will cause them to later regret. Recreational using means stopping when one has had enough.

## Level Four: Excessive Use

Sometimes accidentally or intentionally, a teenager will get completely wasted. It's important for parents to determine if the excess was accidental or intentional. Accidental excess comes as a surprise, and the effects often have cautionary value. Thus, a teenager who never drank hard liquor before drinks so much so fast she bypasses feeling drunk, passes out, and is rushed to the hospital, where doctors pump out her stomach as part of their intervention to prevent alcohol poisoning. Coming to, the teenager reflects on the fact that she almost killed himself by excessive drinking and may feel afraid to drink that much again.

Intentional excess is another matter. It can be a very alluring state to adolescents because of the total freedom from normal restraint. The sense of liberation, of complete letting go, can be a state much to be desired. "Nothing matters and anything goes" as one college sorority member described it, who wore her hangover the next day like a badge of honor, accepting jokes from her sorority sisters about her drunken exploits the night before, some of which she remembered and some of which she did not. Drunken behavior is willful behavior, freely driven by want and impulse and unshackled by judgment.

# 🔔 Alert

If your child is running with a "drink to get drunk" crowd, do what you can to discourage that socializing by encouraging more sober friendships. Anytime you have a teenager who likes to drink to get drunk, you have a problem drinker on your hands. Advise your child, drunken freedom is never free. There are always consequences.

## Level Five: Abuse

Once a teenager descends into substance abuse, discipline problems get more frequent and serious. The first sign of substance abuse is a significant loss of caring about performance, values, reputation, and relationships that previously mattered. Now freedom from not caring has taken hold. And now the second sign of substance abuse appears. Increasingly she begins to make bad decisions—educational, familial, and social. For example, she may skip school, tell lies more frequently to parents, and break laws.

Unfortunately, a dependency between the two signs of abuse can now occur. Lack of caring encourages bad decisions, bad decisions are dismissed by lack of caring, and lack of caring encourages more bad decisions. At this time, you may want to consider getting an assessment by a certified drug abuse counselor.

Most teenagers who reach this level of abuse do not self-correct without some outside help. You cannot effectively play a role in this situation without getting some outside help for yourself as well. A healthy, functioning family is more likely to be able to help a child to recover from substance abuse.

## Level Six: Addiction

The most serious level of substance use is addiction, at which point the teenager has become compulsively dependent on a self-destructive substance to survive. The number one priority for the young person at this point is doing whatever it takes to maintain the destructive habit that feels life-sustaining. Two kinds of dependencies have now become established. There is psychological dependence, some signs of which are denial, compulsion, and escape. And there is physical dependence, some signs of which are tolerance, craving, and withdrawal.

Sometimes parents misunderstand the power of addiction. "If you could start using, why can't you just stop?" The answer is because the decision to start using in the first place was mostly under the teenager's control, but by the time she has descended into addiction, the power of dependency has taken the decision to stop on her own mostly out of her self-control. Now she needs help to stop.

##  Essential

With addiction, inpatient or outpatient treatment is advisable. This is when self-help, twelve-step groups like Alcoholics Anonymous and Narcotics Anonymous usually have a role in supporting sobriety and guiding recovery into a healthier, drug-free life. This is when support for parents from another twelve-step group, Al-Anon (for those living with an addicted member of the family), can be invaluable, helping them maintain emotional sobriety so they can support their child in constructive, and not enabling, ways.

The bad news is that by the end of adolescence, most young people have had experimental, recreational, and some excessive experience with alcohol or drugs. The good news is that most young people who use do not abuse alcohol or drugs or become addicted.

Remember, the best way to have drug-free kids is to have drug-free parents—parents who either don't use, or if they do, do so in a moderate and responsible fashion. The worst enablers of substance-abusing children are substance-abusing parents who don't want to take any stand against their child's use for fear of exposing and endangering their own.

# Willpower to the Rescue

Earlier in this book, willfulness was discussed in a positive way. It is appropriate to end this book with that emphasis now. To safeguard your child from substance problems, parenting to encourage a certain kind of willfulness is an extremely powerful preventative, the will to engage with normal challenges of growing up. If you will train your child to develop this willfulness, you reduce his susceptibility to substance use and abuse.

## The Nine Wills for Engagement

Growing up poses many challenges. It takes a strong will to engage these challenges and to acquire the life skills each has to teach. When these skills are learned, healthy growth is enhanced. When these skills are not learned, as with a substance-using child, disengagement from challenge retards healthy growth.

Compare two seventeen-year-olds from comparable backgrounds and experiences who are different in this regard. First Child has remained substance-free. Second Child has been using substances since age thirteen:

- When it comes to meeting the challenge of commitment, First Child has developed the will to keep promises to self and others, but Second Child has disengaged and routinely breaks promises to self and others.
- When it comes to meeting the challenge of completion, First Child has developed the will to finish what is started, but Second Child has disengaged and routinely doesn't finish what is started.
- When it comes to meeting the challenge of consistency, First Child has developed the will to maintain continuity of effort, but Second Child has disengaged and routinely doesn't maintain ongoing effort.

- When it comes to meeting the challenge of confrontation, First Child has developed the will to encounter painful situations, but Second Child has disengaged and routinely avoids dealing with painful situations.
- When it comes to meeting the challenge of control, First Child has developed the will to let judgment rule over impulse, but Second Child has disengaged and routinely lets impulse rule over judgment.
- When it comes to meeting the challenge of consequences, First Child has developed the will to own the results of actions taken, but Second Child has disengaged and routinely disowns results of actions taken.
- When it comes to meeting the challenge of closure, First Child has developed the will to decide by a challenging choice when deciding gets difficult, but Second Child has disengaged and routinely decides by default, letting circumstance decide when choice gets hard.
- When it comes to meeting the challenge of communication, First Child has developed the will to speak up about and talk out hard feelings, but Second Child has disengaged and routinely shuts up about or acts out hard feelings.
- When it comes to meeting the challenge of caring, First Child has developed the will to hold on to what he deeply believes and what has traditionally mattered, but Second Child has disengaged and routinely betrays deep beliefs and what has traditionally mattered.

Without benefit of a strong will, notice what attributes substance-using child Second Child sacrifices. By breaking promises to self and others, the child has lost some faith in his capacity for self-reliance. By repeatedly starting much but finishing little, the child has lost some confidence in his capacity to follow through and meet personal goals. By repeatedly being unable to keep up a healthy daily regimen, the child has lost some capacity for self-care.

By repeatedly choosing to escape personal pain, the child has lost some capacity to tolerate and talk out emotional hurt. By repeatedly giving in to the lure of immediate gratification, the child has lost some capacity to resist temptation. By repeatedly denying the connection between bad choice and bad consequence, the child has lost some capacity for assuming personal responsibility. By repeatedly letting circumstance determine difficult decisions, the child has lost some capacity for mental toughness. By repeatedly refusing to express hard feelings directly, the child has lost some capacity for open and honest communication. By repeatedly betraying deep beliefs and what has traditionally mattered, the child has lost some capacity to maintain personal integrity. These enormous losses are the tragedy of willfulness completely run amok.

## Encouraging Willfulness for Engagement

What can parents say to encourage their child to develop will in a positive way? You can offer an alternative focus for a strong will that will serve him well. You can suggest that he use his will to keep promises and agreements, finish what he starts, put effort into actions that support his well-being, face hurt feelings openly and honestly, and exert his will to resist temptation.

You can encourage him to use his willfulness to learn from his mistakes, make a choice when all the alternatives seem difficult, talk about problems instead of acting out, and direct his willfulness to keep his actions moving in the direction of his strongest beliefs.

The art of parenting a strong-willed child is learning how to moderate the bad side, enhance the good side, and not act to make a challenging situation worse. One way to enhance the good side is to nurture and encourage the will, but in positive directions. Without a strong will, children cannot effectively engage with the challenges of life and develop the best in themselves as they grow. Congratulate yourself for the courage to shape those traits in a beneficial manner, and to help create a strong human being who successfully launches into adult life!

# APPENDIX A

# Helpful Websites

*www.aap.org*
Articles to support healthy parenting from the American Academy of Pediatrics

*www.carlpickhardt.com*
Monthly articles about parenting by author/psychologist Carl Pickhardt, PhD.

*www.challengingbehavior.org*
A resource that promotes a strategy called positive behavior support

*www.drugstrategies.com*
Guidance on effective drug treatment programs

*www.familyeducation.com*
Information about a wide range of parenting topics

*www.got-2-b-kidding.com*
A blog about teaching and rearing children, including tips on disciplining strong-willed children

*www.onlychild.com*
Information about parenting an only child

*www.npin.org*
Research-based information about parenting

*www.parenting-ed.org*
Information about effective parenting

*www.parents-talk.com*
Information from dialoguing with other parents

*www.parentswithoutpartners.com*
Information about single parenting

*www.pocketparent.com*
Information about positive discipline up to age twelve

*www.tnpc.com*
Information from a variety of parenting experts

*www.thesuccessfulparent.com*
Information about parenting adolescents

# APPENDIX B

# Helpful Books

Bowers, Ellen, PhD. *The Everything® Parent's Guide to Positive Discipline, 2nd Edition* (Avon, MA: Adams Media, 2011).

Dobson, James C. PhD. *The Strong-Willed Child* (Carol Stream, IL: Tyndale House Publishers, 1997).

Fisher, Erik, PhD. *The Art of Empowered Parenting: The Manual You Wish Your Kids Came With* (Austin, Texas: Ovation Books, 2007).

Forehand, Rex L. *Parenting the Strong-Willed Child* (Lincolnwood, IL: NTC Publishing Group, 1996).

Furedi, Frank. *Paranoid Parenting: Why Ignoring the Experts May Be the Best for Your Child* (Chicago: Chicago Review Press, 2002).

Henner, Marilu. *I Refuse to Raise a Brat* (New York: HarperCollins Publishers, Inc., 1999).

Kindlon, Dan, PhD. *Too Much of a Good Thing: Raising Children of Character in an Indulgent Age* (New York: Hyperion, 2001).

MacKenzie, Robert J. *Setting Limits with Your Strong-Willed Child* (New York: Crown Publishing, 2001).

Pickhardt, Carl, PhD. *Keys to Successful Step-Fathering* (New York: Barron's, 1997).

Pickhardt, C. E. *The Case of the Scary Divorce—A Jackson Skye Mystery* (Washington, DC: Magination Press, The American Psychological Association, 1997).

Reynolds, Randy. *Good News About Your Strong-Willed Child* (Grand Rapids, MI: Zondervan, 1995).

Runkel, Hal Edward. *Scream Free Parenting: The Revolutionary Approach to Raising Your Kids by Keeping Your Cool* (New York: Broadway Books, 2007).

Skenazy, Lenore. *Free-Range Kids: How to Raise Safe, Self-Reliant Children (Without Going Nuts with Worry)* (San Francisco: Jossey Bass, 2010).

Smiley, Kendra. *Aaron's Way: The Journey of a Strong-Willed Child* (Chicago: Moody Press, 2004).

# Helpful Support Groups

## Al-Anon Family Groups
*www.al-anonfamilygroups.org*
757-563-1600
For helping families recover from a family member's problem drinking.

## Circle of Parents
*www.circleofparents.org*
773-257-0111
For providing mutual-support groups in which parents can help each other.

## Parents Anonymous
*www.parentsanonymous.org*
909-621-6184
For strengthening families, breaking the cycle of abuse, and helping parents create safe homes for their children.

# Index